Radical Faith

An Alternative History
of the Christian Church

Radical Faith

An Alternative History of the Christian Church

by

John Driver

edited by

Carrie Snyder

Canadian Cataloguing in Publication Data

Driver, John, 1924-
    Radical Faith : an alternative history of the Christian church

Translation of: La fe en la periferia de la historia.
Includes bibliographical references.
ISBN 0-9683462-8-6

1. Christian sects – History. I. Snyder, Carrie. II. Title.

BR 157.D7413 1999   280.09   C99-931212-X

RADICAL FAITH:
AN ALTERNATIVE HISTORY OF THE CHRISTIAN CHURCH

Copyright © 1999 by Pandora Press
        51 Pandora Avenue N.
        Kitchener, Ontario, N2H 3C1
        All rights reserved
Co-published with Herald Press,
        Scottdale, Pennsylvania/Waterloo, Ontario
International Standard Book Number: **0-9683462-8-6**
Printed in Canada on acid-free paper
Book design, layout, and editing of the English text by Carrie Snyder
Cover design by Clifford Snyder

This book is a translation, by the author, of
        Juan Driver, *La fe en la periferia de la histora. Una historia del pueblo cristiano
        desde la perspectiva de los movimientos de restauracion y reforma radical*
        (Guatemala: Ediciones Clara-Semilla, 1997).
        ISBN: 84-89389-08-X

07 06 05 04 03 02 01 00 99 10 9 8 7 6 5 4 3 2 1

Table of Contents

Author's Preface

Blessed are you who are poor, for yours is the kingdom of God. Blessed are you who are hungry now, for you will be filled. Blessed are you who weep now, for you will laugh. (Luke 6:20-21)

Some twenty years ago in Buenos Aires, I listened to Enrique Dussel outline his vision for a history of the church. Dussel, an Argentine professor, argued that church history should tell the story of the common people of God. As an heir to the radical tradition, I was convinced that this focus provided the best perspective from which to relate the history of the Christian church. The seeds for this alternative history of the Christian people are found in Dussel's vision.

This is the story of the church as perceived by the outsiders: the "little ones," as Jesus called them in the Gospels; the "heretics," as they have been called since the time of Constantine; and the minority movements, those who follow the models patterned by the Abrahamic and Messianic minorities of biblical history. This is the story of the poor and the oppressed, surprised by the grace of God and by His merciful initiative in their behalf: those who, by human standards, have stood outside the institutions of salvation. This is the story of those called to prophetic mission and martyrdom. It is the story of a people who, powerless, are called by God to participate in His mission in the world.

This history of God's people will not tell of the Ecumenical Councils, nor relate the theological debates and dogmatism which arose from these deliberations. This is not a history of the efforts employed by Princes and Popes to resolve the conflicts between Empire and Church. It will not reflect on the crusades and conquests carried out in the name of God.

To tell this story, I look to the version of history found in the Bible, with its vision of the Kingdom of God and His righteousness. Here, the presence of God's people is asserted: a people who have always confessed

---

(1) Luke 1:46-47; 49-54

My soul magnifies the Lord, and my spirit rejoices in God my Savior ... for the Mighty One has done great things for me, and holy is His name. His mercy is for those who fear Him from generation to generation. He has shown strength with His arm; He has scattered the proud in the thoughts of their hearts. He has brought down the powerful from their thrones, and lifted up the lowly; He has filled the hungry with good things, and sent the rich away empty. He has helped His servant Israel, in remembrance of His mercy.

---

that God is king, and who live in certainty that He will reign forever. With the Psalmist, they celebrate God's righteous rule, praising the One who brings justice to the oppressed, feeds the hungry, sets free the prisoner, and watches over the stranger, the widow, the orphan. (Psalm 146: 1, 7-9).

In this alternate history of the Christian church, I wish to build on the story of the Messianic people who lived in expectation of the radical restoration of God's kingdom, in all its vigor and splendor. The Gospel of Luke articulated one of the earliest visions for the restorationist movement, describing God's kingdom in eloquent terms: those who have faith in God's promise will be richly rewarded, and the most humble will be lifted by grace. (1) The history of the church should reflect this promise, and tell the story of those most humble and unassuming, who will inherit the earth.

It is my sincere hope that this book offers a vision of church history aligned with the biblical vision of God's people.

Chapter 1

The Story of the Christian People

Twenty-two years ago, in 1961 in Nazareth of Galilee, while I was working in an Arab settlement with Paul Gauthier and recounting to him the history of Latin America, I became emotional about the fact that Pizarro, with a small handful of Spanish soldiers, had conquered the Inca Empire. At that, the French worker priest asked me: "Are you moved by the exploits of the conqueror? Is this a Christian interpretation? Was not the Indian the poor one?" With shame I recognized that all of the history that I had learned was actually an anti-Christian inversion, and I later wrote a letter to a historian friend: "Some day we should write a history in reverse, from the perspective of the poor, from the viewpoint of the oppressed!" Each Sabbath, in the synagogue of Nazareth, we would read and re-read Isaiah 61:1 and Luke 4:18: "The Spirit of the Lord is upon me, because he has anointed me to bring good news to the poor ...." What was for me a conversion experience twenty-two years ago, a dream, has today begun to become a reality, after considerable patience and much resistance in order to overcome the misunderstandings. Enrique Dussel [1]

Introduction

How should we recount the story of the Christian people? It is a story which begins in Palestine during the middle of the first century and continues until our own times in the late twentieth century. We must recognize that our review of this story will not be objective; absolute historical objectivity is impossible. From the very moment of its inception, an historical event is being experienced, observed, interpreted, evaluated, and has already become a subjective artefact. With this in mind, we will explore the traditional ways of recounting the history of Christianity, and offer alternative perspectives for retelling the story.

Traditional Ways of Understanding the History of Christianity

The Church as an Institution

A common approach to the history of the church is to view it as an established institution, and to enumerate and evaluate the off-shoot organizations produced by the church. This approach has been commonly taken by the official church, be it Catholic or Protestant. Viewed from the perspective of the powerful and influential, this version of history is generally positive in its evaluation and conservative in its interpretation. In simple terms, this is history written by the winners.

Like all interpretations, particular criteria are employed to determine which events are of historical significance. This approach grants importance to the empirical institution. For example, traditional Catholicism identifies the twelfth and thirteenth centuries as being high points in church history. Special emphasis is given to the rule of Innocent III, 1198-1216, when papal power was at its height and St. Augustine's "City of God" was thought to have been realized most fully.

Official Protestant interpretations use similar criteria to determine which events are of historical value. Moments during which the church exercised great social and political influence are generally identified as being high points in Protestant history. The Protestant Revolution of the sixteenth century is considered an important period for the development of the church, as is the spread of Protestant influence world-wide which took place during the nineteenth century.

The Development of Church Doctrine

A different approach to church history focuses on the development of the doctrine and dogma which define Christian faith. The development of doctrine arose out of the need for Christians to distinguish themselves from non-Christians by a tangible statement of belief, rather than by the values reflected in everyday activity. Traditional Catholic analysis places historical emphasis on the development of doctrinal definitions: the Apostles' Creed of the second century; the clarification of Trinitarian doctrine at the Councils of Nicea, in 325, and Constantinople, in 381; the Christological doctrine, at the Council of Chalcedon, in 451.

Concern for church unity led to the creation of static doctrinal parameters which determined Christian orthodoxy. Eventually, good Catholic doctrine came to be defined as that "which has been believed everywhere, always, and by all."[2] Christians whose beliefs agreed with the bishops and their congregations were considered to be orthodox, literally meaning *right thinking.* Dissidents to these ideological formulations were considered to be heterodox, literally meaning *other thinking,* or heretics.[3]

Protestants share this approach to church history. Classic Protestantism has long been concerned with establishing right doctrine. Indeed, the Lutheran Reformation was essentially about doctrinal reform.[4] This view of the church's development was emphasized by later Protestant scholars, and the sixteenth and seventeenth centuries were identified as high points in the church's history because of the doctrinal reform which occured during that period.[5]

Geographic Expansion of Influence

Another approach to the history of Christianity looks especially at the geographic expansion of the church: its demographic and institutional growth, and extension of influence. Using these criteria, the great epochs of missionary expansion are determined to have particular historical validity. In the fourth century, the church became a dominant force in the Empire with the victory of Constantine over his rivals. Eusebius, the early church historian, saw in this event cause for great celebration among Christians.[6]

The sixteenth and seventeenth centuries, during which the Spanish and Portuguese were expanding their empires, are of great importance to Catholic history, due to the so-called "Christianization" of a large part of the world, including the western hemisphere. We were reminded of this interpretation of Christian history during the recent celebration of the five hundredth anniversary of the "discovery" of the Americas, by the papal call to a "new evangelization."[7]

Protestant historians also emphasize the church's expanding influence. The distinguished North American historian, Kenneth Scott Latourette, for example, believed that one could discern Christianity's "major epochs ... as pulsations in the life of Christianity as reflected in its vigour and its influence upon the ongoing history of the race."[8] Latourette identified three main factors which may be used to discern these pulsations: first, the expansion or recession of geographic territory where Christians are found; second, new movements arising out of Christian belief; and finally, the effect of Christianity as judged by humankind as a whole.

Many Protestants view the nineteenth century as a high point in Christian history due to the enormous extension of Protestant influence in

---

*(1) Kenneth Scott Latourette, **A History of Christianity***
The century from A.D. 1815 to A.D. 1914 presented striking contrasts. Western civilization was again moving into a new age. Many of the forces which were moulding that civilization were either openly or tacitly hostile to Christianity. The faith was threatened in its chief strongholds. But new life in Christianity swelled to a flood. This was especially marked in the form of Christianity, Protestantism, which had come into being as recently as the sixteenth century. ... Christianity spread over the surface of the globe. ... Especially through its share in shaping the United States of America, Christianity gained in the total world scene. ... [F]or the first time Christianity is becoming really world-wide. ... Christianity is more potent than in any earlier era. [10]

---

the world. Latourette adheres to this historical perspective, referring to the period between 1815 and 1914 as "the great century" due to the "abounding vitality and unprecedented expansion" of Protestant influence.[9] (1)

We cannot ignore the fact that Christian extension of influence has always been accompanied by extraordinary imperial expansion. During the fourth and fifth centuries, or Eusebius' "golden age," the Roman Empire was extending and consolidating its powerful presence in the world. Spanish and Portuguese conquests of the sixteenth and seventeenth centuries were carried out under the altruistic guise of bringing Christian truth to the peoples of the New World. Conquistadores were accompanied by friars of recently organized missionary orders. These same countries were becoming world powers due to their "altruistic" expansion.

The nineteenth century, during which Christianity, according to Latourette, spread world-wide, also marked the culmination of empire-building enterprises for Great Britain and the United States. The great Christian influence exercised during that century was accompanied by political, military and commercial activities of the great Protestant imperial powers. These examples offer a different perspective on the validity of using the Church's expanding geographic influence as an historical measuring stick: what is really being measured?

The Biographies of Church Leaders

Church history may also be approached through the life stories of leading protagonists and outstanding church leaders. Undoubtedly, our modern emphasis on individualism has contributed to this method's popularity; however, a series of biographies fails to do justice to the fundamentally corporate nature of the Christian movement. The biblical story, in both the Old and New Testaments, is remarkable for the importance it assigns to peoplehood, and although individual participation has been important to the development of the church, limiting church history to these individuals' stories is an inadequate representation thereof.

The Development of Worship

Finally, one may approach church history by tracing the development of worship, both corporate and personal.[11] There is a widespread conviction among Christians that humanity's Divine purpose is to know and worship God. This conviction logically extends to the desire to interpret the development of Christian spirituality and worship as the key to church history. However, it is impossible to separate the life of the worshipper from the liturgical forms which give expression to worship. Spirituality and meaningful liturgy are essential to the life of God's people, but in and of itself worship is not an adequate lens through which to view church history.

Toward a Biblical Vision of History

Professor Dussel's statement, with which this chapter began, anticipates the thesis of this book: the Bible contains a vision for salvation which modern Christians should incorporate into our historical account of the church.

The Abrahamic Community

Israel and the Christian church each look back to the story of Abraham, and identify it as a key moment in their collective histories (Gen. 12:1-3; Heb. 11:8-19). The Exodus is often viewed as the moment when Israel recognized that it was God's people, but according to biblical testimony, God's covenant with Abraham laid the foundation for the liberation of Israel (Exod. 2:24-25; 6:2-8). In confessions of faith, ancient Israelites recognized that they owed their existence as a people to the vocation of Abraham, despite a different tale of origination which claimed Israel's father to be "a wandering Aramean ... [who] went down to Egypt and lived there as an alien, few in number, and there he became a great nation, mighty and populous" (Deut. 26:5). Israel owed its collective existence to God's merciful initiative toward the patriarchs, Abraham and his descendants.

In biblical context, the call of Abraham was God's response to humanity's failure at Babel (Gen. 11:1-2:13). Human society had attempted to build a fortress tower to secure its future influence, but had failed in utter confusion. The Abrahamic community of faith was the divine alternative to these coercive human enterprises.

Weakness characterized this faith community and was emphasized in one of its earliest confessions of faith (Deut. 26:5-10). The Abrahamic people were insignificant among the secular powers of the period, but political and religious institutions were not ultimately instrumental in Israel's survival as a nation. The true meaning of Israel's history was found in minority movements which prophesied restoration. The secret to Israel's survival was found in the suffering servant of Yahweh: a faithful remnant, rather than a monarchy or priestly hierarchy (Is. 41-53).

The Messianic Movement

Israel's Messianic movement believed in and awaited the radical restoration of God's redeeming promise as expressed in ancient covenants. Significantly, the authentic prophets, the Messiah, and the Messianic community all suffered persecution at the hands of established political and religious powers. Non-conformity in the world was the fundamental stance of the Messianic community. In the New Testament, the Christian community was described as the alternative to all other human societies. (Matt. 5-7). This is what the apostolic witness meant when he wrote: "there is no other name under heaven ... by which we must be saved" (Acts 4: 12).

The creation of a Messianic community was fundamental to Jesus' mission. Juan Mateos, an eminent Spanish Bible scholar, argued that Jesus was interested not in promoting ideology, but in provoking thought and action. Jesus wanted his vision to be lived out in communities of believers, who freely chose to follow his message. (2)

---

*(2) Juan Mateos, **Nuevo Testamento***
Jesus did not propose ideologies; for that reason he did not share his message with everybody. He spoke to the people in parables, in order to awaken their interest and make them think. What he set himself to do was to form a community in which his vision was lived out. As long as there are no communities like this, there is no salvation; Jesus' purposes are thwarted and his teaching and example are turned into just another ideology. Of course, violence cannot be used in the formation of these communities. If being a free person is essential to this group, then membership must be based on free choice. ... For that reason, all those who believe in Jesus are called to form communities which fully live out his message.[12]

The New Testament church, in its worship and doctrine, confessed that God's true purposes would flow through the community of the slain Lamb (Phil. 2:5-11; Rev. 5:9-10). The sealed scroll in Revelation 5 hints that history's nature is mysterious: only the slain Lamb is worthy to take the scroll and to open its seals. That God will form and redeem a new community of believers, through the Messiah, is a declaration of history's true meaning.

Israel begged to have a king "like other nations" (I Sam. 8:5). Israel's subsequent trajectory was largely determined by its succession of monarchs. Nevertheless, a current of protest persisted in Israel, calling them back to faithfulness, to their true reason for being, that they might become a blessing for all the peoples of the earth (Gen. 12:3). Although there were kings in Israel, they were to be guided by God's law (Deut. 17:14-20).

Within the New Testament, and even in the Messianic community, we find traces of this other vision of history. Some of Jesus' closest followers requested positions of power and influence in a kingdom they imagine would resemble contemporary secular kingdoms (Matt. 20: 20-28). This vision was only a temptation, not an actuality, among those gathered around Jesus. However, within several centuries the secular power of the Roman empire would establish the Christian church, and many Christian historians and apologists would defend that which clearly contradicted ancient biblical and Messianic visions of the true history of the people of God.

Toward a Non-Constantinian Story of the Christian People

Church historians have generally accepted Constantinian presuppositions. In the fourth century, the Christian church ceased to be a persectued minority movement and became an established institution, protected by secular powers. This turn of events is called Constantinianism. First reflected in the writings of Eusebius of Caesarea, "the father of church history," Constantinianism has exercised a vast influence over our perception of the Christian story.[13]

Constantine, Roman Emperor from 306 to 337, was the principal protagonist in the events which changed the nature of the Christian church. Although Constantine did not accept Christian baptism until he was on his deathbed in 337, Eusebius' view of the church "was characterized by a passionate enthusiasm for Constantine as its 'leader'."[14] In order to better understand the importance of these events, we will explore the process of Constantinianization which implacably altered the course of the Christian church.

The Constantinianization of the Church

An imperial edict signed in 311 by Galerius, Licinius, and Constantine granted official immunity to the Christian movement, which had been persecuted until this point. The edict granted protection to Christians, provided they pray for the welfare of the state. (3)

> *(3) excerpted from an edict signed in 311*
> *We ... are pleased to grant indulgence to these men, allowing Christians the right to exist again and to set up their places of worship; provided always that they do not offend against the public order ... It will be the duty of Christians to pray to God for our recovery, for the public weal and for their own; that the state may be preserved from danger on every side, and that they themselves may dwell safely in their homes.* [15]

Another imperial edict, signed in 313, granted religious liberty to Christians, and the return of property confiscated during recent persecutions. This edict encouraged the free practice of religion in order to maintain peace throughout the Empire. (4)

Other imperial edicts issued in 313 granted economic subsidies to fund publicly the Christian clergy, and exempted them from civic duties so that they could dedicate themselves to religious activities, and contribute to the common good. [17]

> *(4) excerpted from an edict signed in 313*
> *Christians ... who choose that religion are to be permitted to continue therein, without any let or hindrance, and are not to be in any way troubled or molested ... it accords with good order to the realm and the peacefulness of our times that each should have freedom to worship God after his own choice ...* [16]

In 321, the Christian church was granted legal status which permitted it to receive and hold properties bequeathed to it. During the same year, "the venerable day of the Sun" was officially declared a holiday in the city of Rome, although exemption was granted in the countryside to allow farmers to harvest their crops. [18]

In 380, Theodosius' edict established Christianity as the official religion of the Empire. This once illegal and persecuted movement was transformed into a legitimate power, itself capable of persecution. The rhetoric of the Empire no longer encouraged the free practice of all

> **(5) Excerpted from an edict signed in 380**
> *It is our desire that all the various nations which are subject to our clemency and moderation, should continue in the profession of that religion which was delivered to the Romans by the divine Apostle Peter ... We authorize the followers of this law to assume the title of Catholic Christians ... but ... the others ... shall be branded with the ignominious name of heretics ...* [19]

religions but branded any non-Catholic Christian a heretic, to be punished according to God's will. (5)

In 438, only four centuries after the death of Christ, non-Christians were forbidden to serve in the Empire's armed forces. From this moment on, the Roman legions would be exclusively Christian. The power of the state had been placed at the service of the church; but the church had also placed itself at the service of the state. In the words of English historian, Lord Acton: "All power corrupts, but absolute power corrupts absolutely."[20]

Conclusion: An Upside-Down History of the Church

Due to the Constantinian changes, the history of the Christian church became what Professor Dussel termed an "anti-Christian inversion."[21] The church's memory was twisted to serve the purposes of established powers and their institutions, rather than the needs of the Christian people. We intend to outline an alternative story, an upside-down history of God's people. We will read the Bible anew, and move through the centuries searching for stories of radical restoration, movements which surface time after time in the annals of church history. The biblical story will determine what is significant to our collective memory. In order to recapture a truly radical vision, we will root our exploration in the stories of the Abrahamic minority and the Messianic community.

We use the term "radical" not in its popular sense, which refers to that which is extreme, spectacular, or violent, but in its literal one, which derives from *radix*, and means root. The most radical restoration restores the church to its essence, and roots it in the message of the Messiah. The stories we will recount are of movements which attempt this radical restoration.

[1] Enrique D. Dussel, *Historia General de la Iglesia en América Latina* (Salamanca: CEHILA, Ediciones Sígueme, 1983), 12. My translation.

[2] Justo L.González, *A History of Christian Thought,* vol. 1 (Nashville: Abingdon Press, 1970), 21. This definition was articulated in its classic form by Vincent of Lerins in the fifth century.

[3] Concern for sound doctrine led Irenaeus, bishop in the Church in Lyon during the late second century, to write his principal work, "Against the Heretics." In the nineteenth century, Marcelino Menéndez y Pelayo wrote a massive work of two volumes entitled *Historia de los Heterodoxos Españoles.* Another example, from a positive perspective, is found in Enrique Denzinger's classic text, *El Magisterio de la Iglesia, Manual de los Símbolos, Definiciones y Declaraciones de la Iglesia en Materia de Fe y Costumbres* (Barcelona: Editorial Herder, 1955).

[4] George Huntston Williams, *La Reforma Radical* (México: Fondo de Cultura Económica, 1983), 939.

[5] Examples found in the following sources: Reinhold Seeberg, *Text-Book of the History of Christian Doctrines,* 2 vols. (Grand Rapids: Baker Book House, 1952); Justo L. González, *A History of Christian Thought,* 3 vols (Nashville: Abingdon Press, 1970); Jaroslav Pellikan, *The Christian Tradition: A History of the Development of Doctrine,* 5 vols. (Chicago: The University of Chicago Press, 1971).

[6] "Ecclesiastical History," X.ix.5-9, in *Eusebius. The Ecclesiastical History,* II (Cambridge, Mass.: Harvard University Press, 1957), 479-80.

[7] Leonardo Boff, *New Evangelization: Good News to the Poor* (Maryknoll: Orbis Press, 1991), xii.

[8] Kenneth Scott Latourette, *A History of Christianity* (New York: Harper and Brothers, 1953), xxii.

[9] Latourette, 1061.

[10] Latourette, xxiv-xxv.

[11] Horton Davies, *Worship and Theology in England* (Princeton: Princeton University Press, 1962). Davies approaches church history through the development of worship.

[12] Juan Mateos, *Nuevo Testamento* (Madrid: Ediciones Cristiandad, 1975), 28, 44. My translation.

[13] Eduardo Hoornaert writes: "Eusebius' project departs altogether from what a history of the church at the service of the memory of the Christian people ought to be. He departs from ancient Israel's historiographical motif, replacing it with a dynastic one. He abandons the tradition of the Law, the prophets, and the liberation of the lowly and marginalized, and replaces it with the tools of recollection precisely of an imperial church that sees in the emperor the successor of Moses and David, an individual chosen by God to prepare the way of the Lord and to liberate his people. For Eusebius, the enemies are the Montanists, the Donatists, and the followers of Novatian, or the Jews or the 'gentiles' (the nations), and not the structures of the empire, not the power of the rich who exploit the peasantry through heavy tribute and the urban slave population through forced labor. The church is identified with one of its parts, merely: its organizers. We hear nothing of the 'organized' (except in the martyrdom accounts). Eusebius' book was to prove an excellent text for a course intended to prepare future organizers of church structure. But it is a complete failure as an ecclesial exercise in 'striking root.' It is useless as a tool for the recollection of the covenant God has struck with us in Abraham and transmitted to us through Moses, the prophets, Jesus, the Apostles, and the saints. The memory of the hopes and struggles of a Christian people striving to resolve urgent problems of survival, health, or basic human rights finds no room in the *Ecclesiastical History* of Eusebius of Caesarea. ... Eusebius' project prevailed simply because it confirmed in writing, and with a thesis, a practical route that an influential sector of church leadership ... had begun to travel: the path of an alliance between the ecclesiastical estate and political society. This new model of church, based on an alliance of church and state, finds in Eusebius' *History* a theoretical confirmation of its practice." Eduardo Hoornaert, *The Memory of the Christian People* (Maryknoll, New York: Orbis, 1988), 15-16.

[14] Hoornaert, 13.

[15] Henry Bettenson, *Documents of the Christian Church* (New York: Oxford University Press, 1967) 15.

[16] Bettenson, 16.

[17] Bettenson, 17-18.

[18] Bettenson, 18-19.

[19] Bettenson, 22.

[20] Quoted in Hoornaert, 22.

[21] Dussel, 11 n. 1.

Chapter Two

A Biblical Vision of the People of God

For Christ did not send me to baptize but to proclaim the gospel, and not with eloquent wisdom, so that the cross of Christ might not be emptied of its power. For the message about the cross is foolishness to those who are perishing, but to us who are being saved it is the power of God. ... Where is the one who is wise? Where is the scribe? Where is the debater of this age? Has not God made foolish the wisdom of the world? For since, in the wisdom of God, the world did not know God through wisdom, God decided, through the foolishness of our proclamation, to save those who believe. ... For God's foolishness is wiser than human wisdom, and God's weakness is stronger than human strength. Consider your own call, brothers and sisters: not many of you were wise by human standards, not many were powerful, not many were of noble birth. But God chose what is foolish in the world to shame the wise; God chose what is weak in the world to shame the strong; God chose what is low and despised in the world, things that are not, to reduce to nothing things that are, so that no one might boast in the presence of God. (1 Cor. 1:17-18, 20-21, 25-29)

Introduction

In the preceding text, Paul observed that the Messianic community of the first century was made up largely of outsiders and outcasts. Indeed, the people of God have often been outsiders and exiles, not only during Paul's time, but also during that described in the Old Testament. The people of God are those who work for the Kingdom of God, even though they may live on the margins of society.

The People of God in the Old Testament

Israel as Outsider

According to an ancient confession of faith, God's people were always to remember that they owed their existence to His merciful initiative, and to Abraham's vocation (Josh. 24:2-18). The Abrahamic minority was chosen as the divine alternative to the failed human enterprises at Babel (Gen. 11:1-9). In contrast to those at Babel, Israel confessed its fragility as a society: Israel had been an oppressed and enslaved people, aliens in a foreign land, when God mercifully delivered them. (1)

---

(1) Deut. 26:6-8
When the Egyptians treated us harshly and afflicted us, by imposing hard labor on us, we cried to the Lord, the God of our ancestors; the Lord heard our voice and saw our affliction, our toil and our oppression. The Lord brought us out of Egypt with a mighty hand and an outstretched arm, with a terrifying display of power, and with signs and wonders.

In Israel, God was remembered as the One who had chosen to redeem a miserable band of slaves. This rescue spoke of the wonderful and unlikely grace of their God. Israel's experience being an exiled and enslaved people gave it reason to treat outsiders with particular respect. Generous provisions protected the rights of the poor, widows, orphans, indentured servants, and strangers. (2) One provision commanded that the gleanings of Israel's harvest be left on the fields for the poor and the stranger (Lev. 19:9-10).

(2) Deut. 23:7
You shall not abhor any of the Edomites, for they are your kin. You shall not abhor any of the Egyptians, because you were an alien residing in their land.

Such provisions were very different from the codes which regulated internal relationships among Israel's neighbors. In these nations, slaves were treated as property. The Sinaitic covenant dictated that slaves must be protected from mistreatment, and any slave fleeing a cruel master should not be returned to him (Exod. 21:26-27; Deut. 23:15-16).

There were other reminders of Israel's former status as an outsider, and of its debt to God's mercy. Observing the Sabbath day of rest was a privilege which reminded the people of their years of slavery (Deut. 5:14-15). Likewise, the land in Israel was not to be sold, for it belonged to God, and His people must remember that they lived there as "strangers and sojourners" (Lev. 25:23). However, as Israel became permanent inhabitants and property owners in Canaan, it was easy to forget God's promises of protection (Deut. 8:11-18).

Monarchic versus Charismatic Leadership

The ability to lead God's people was a charismatic gift from God; that is, leaders were chosen by God, not man. This is illustrated in Exodus by the story of Moses, a man who first attempted, unsuccessfully, to free his people of his own volition, and later answered God's call to try again. Angered by the oppression suffered by his people, Moses killed and buried in the sand an Egyptian who had struck an Israelite. Nothing good came of this violence, and Moses fled to a neighboring land (Exod. 2:11-15). Years later, God appeared to Moses in the burning bush, and called on him to lead the Israelites out of Egypt. Only with God's guidance and grace was Moses able to lead his people out of slavery (Exod. 3:2-12).

Israel's leaders were traditionally chosen by God, not man, and there was resistance to establishing a monarchy in Israel. After it had been established, a prophetic attempt was made to limit regal abuses of power. A series of provisions guided the monarchy toward more charismatic leadership (Deut. 17:14-20). Prophets confronted the monarchs and the priestly hierarchy, continuing to defend outsiders. Israel survived exile because of these prophets, who preached a message of hope. (3) Redemption could be found even in the bitterness of exile, and the suffering of an innocent people was not absurd, but potentially redemptive (Isa. 42-53).

---

(3) Isa. 61:1-2
The spirit of the Lord God is upon me, because the Lord has anointed me; he has sent me to bring good news to the oppressed, to bind up the brokenhearted, to proclaim liberty to the captives, and release to the prisoners; to proclaim the year of the Lord's favor, ... to comfort all who mourn.

The Messianic People in the New Testament: Jesus

Tax Collectors and Prostitutes

The God of Israel protected the outsider. Himself an outsider, Jesus also understood and sympathized with the disadvantaged and estranged. Jesus believed that his Messianic mission in the world was to embrace the poor, the blind, the enslaved, and to show them the Kingdom of God. (4) His vision was fundamentally counter-cultural. Jesus knew that the Messianic movement would be a community of outcasts. He anticipated Paul's message with which we began this chapter. Rejected by his own people, Jesus recognized that God was calling the outsiders, and rooted his message and practices in this belief.

> **(4) Luke 4:18-19**
> *"The spirit of the Lord is upon me, because he anointed me to preach the gospel to the poor. He has sent me to proclaim release to the captives, and recovery of sight to the blind, to set free those who are downtrodden, to proclaim the favorable year of the Lord."*

From the outset, his concern for outcasts in Palestine caused conflict between Jesus and Jewish religious authorities. Jesus' enemies accused him of fraternizing with despicable people: "Look, a glutton and a drunkard, a friend of tax collectors and sinners" (Luke 7:34; Matt. 11:19)! Indeed, Jesus did share his table with many people from many walks of life. But in doing so, he fulfilled Isaiah's prophetic vision and gave sight to the blind, taught the lame to walk, cured the sick, and brought hope to the poor. (5)

> **(5) Luke 7:22; Matt. 11:5**
> *The blind receive their sight, the lame walk, the lepers are cleansed, the deaf hear, the dead are raised, the poor have the good news brought to them.*

The Pharisees were scandalized by the meals which Jesus and his disciples shared with many outcasts, but Jesus insisted on sharing communion with people who were outside the favor of the religious majority. He did not call the righteous, but those in need of mercy: the poor, children, women, the sick, tax collectors, the ritually impure, strangers, and Samaritans. (6)

Jesus' parables guided and comforted the sinners in his audience. The parables of the lost sheep, the lost coin, and the lost son carried similar messages of mercy and forgiveness. Perhaps the parable of the vineyard laborers best illustrates Jesus' compassion for the outsider. The laborers hired at the eleventh hour received the same wages as those who had worked all day. At the end of this parable, Jesus proclaimed: "'So the last will be the first and the first will be last'" (Matt. 20:16). Indeed, the Messianic movement was embraced first by gentile outsiders, along with "the tax collectors and the prostitutes," and only later by those who claimed Abrahamic heritage (Matt. 21:31).

> *(6) Matt. 9:11-13; Mark 2:16-17; Luke 5:30-32*
> *"Why does your teacher eat with tax collectors and sinners?" But when he heard this he said, "Those who are well have no need of a physician, but those who are sick. Go learn what this means, 'I desire mercy, not sacrifice.' For I have come to call not the righteous but sinners."*

The Messianic movement described in the New Testament was a minority movement which emerged on the edges of Judaism. The community was socially, economically, religiously, and geographically marginalized.

Many unexpected sources bore witness to the Messianic gospel. A Samaritan woman proclaimed that "'Jesus is the Messiah'" and "'God is truth'" (John 4:29, 42). Mary Magdalene told the disciples that "'Jesus has risen from the dead'" (John 20:18). A Roman centurion, a despised agent of the foreign occupation, confessed that "'Jesus is the Son of God'" (Mark 15:39). This appears exceptional only if we read the Bible from a traditional Constantinian perspective. Read from an upside-down perspective it makes perfect sense.

Humble Beginnings

Jesus was born into a humble condition. He was poor. His family had been political refugees. The women in his genealogy were social outcasts.[1] Jesus was an outsider (John 1:11). Yet through Jesus' unorthodox message, "grace and truth" were realized (John 1:17).

Jesus came from "Galilee of the nations," situated on the geographic, social, economic, and religious periphery of Judaism. The Gospels emphasized the Galilean origins of the Messianic movement, which is surprising given that the early church must have felt great pressure to acquire social and religious acceptance.[2] When official Judaism wished to insult those who dissented from religious orthodoxy, they would ask, "'Are you, too, from Galilee'" (John 7:52)? Respectable Jews found it unthinkable that the Messiah could come from Galilee, for no prophet in all scripture had come from there before (John 7:41; 7:52). Given the official tendency to discredit anything Galilean, one might have expected the Messianic movement to play down its humble beginnings. That it chose not to, speaks to the radical power of Jesus' message.[3]

The humble origins of the Messianic movement is not an unprecedented anomaly, but one among many reminders that the kingdom of God often emerges from below. The Gospels of Luke and John placed a positive emphasis on the Samaritans, despite Jewish prejudice against them. Israel's outcasts were not only the recipients of God's grace, but were also agents of God's saving purpose. Such examples point toward a subversive economy of salvation. We have often ignored the implications of a Gospel mediated by outsiders. Jesus, the outsider of Nazareth, came as prophet, priest, and king, and was the definitive model for Christian witness and ministry, and for the exercise of kingly power.[4]

The earliest names given to, or assumed by, the primitive Messianic community arose out of Jesus' message: "foreigners and sojourners," "exiles," "pilgrims," "the meek," "the little ones," and "the poor." The values reflected in these names were unlike those which were predominant in Judaism, and in Rome. The primitive church embraced images which emphasized its status as humble, needy, and outside of orthodox belief, images which reflected the community's identity and mission.

The Messianic People in the New Testament: Paul

Paul understood and bore witness to Jesus' message. In fact, Paul articulated Jesus' compassion for the outsider as a theology of election, in which the outcasts would be chosen to enter the kingdom of God. According to Paul, the doctrine of divine election, which has inspired much theological debate throughout church history, expresses God's favor toward the outcasts: those who "once were not a people ... now are God's people ... [and] have received mercy" (1 Pet. 2:10).

At the Jerusalem council, and again at Antioch, Paul defended the rights of the despised and outcast. For example, Paul sought to convert the

Gentiles but did not force them to partake in the rite of circumcision. Paul's convictions put him in opposition to many fellow believers, including Peter, and he suffered persecution at the hands of Jewish believers who were "enemies of the cross" (Phil. 3:18).

Reporting on Paul's mission, Luke frequently used the term "the way."[5] The early Messianic community often referred to itself using this name, the source of which is found the Gospels. Israel's exilic prophets had foreseen the first Exodus, in which God's people would be returned to their land. These same prophets prophesied a new Exodus, in which God's people would be led out of Babylonian captivity, and back to Jerusalem: "a voice cries out in the wilderness: Prepare the way of the Lord" (Isa. 40:3). While Israel's prophets identified Yahweh as being "the way," the evangelists applied the scripture to Jesus, and saw him as "the way" toward a new Exodus, and new covenant of salvation (John. 14:6). Thus, the Christian people identified themselves as sojourners on a path to the promised land.

The Messianic People in the New Testament: Peter

The first book of Peter provides us with an understanding of the nature and identity of Christian communities scattered throughout the Roman Empire in the latter decades of the first century, and of their relationship to the surrounding society.[6]

Peter addressed his letter to those living as exiles in the Roman Empire because they had chosen "to be obedient to Jesus Christ" (1 Pet. 1:2). Peter wrote to them from "Babylon," an obvious reference to Rome, which was intolerant to the Christian communities (1 Pet. 5:13). Using the metaphor of "the way," Peter proclaimed that God's people would be freed through the leadership of a new Moses, Jesus the Messiah. The letter encouraged these communities to live honorably for the glory of God, despite their exile. (7) Deeds were more effective than words.

> **(7) 1 Pet. 2:12**
> *Keep your behaviour excellent among the Gentiles, so that, though they malign you as evildoers, they may see your honorable deeds and glorify God when he comes to judge.*

In order to place Peter's letters in their context, we must consider the social factors which affected these Christian communities. The Roman Empire was a place of great social displacement. Many people were on the move, including those who had been disinherited, slaves, invading barbarians, and foreigners. None of these outsiders had any legal rights, because they were not recognized as being citizens. In a very tangible way, the Christian communities fulfilled the exiled's social and spiritual need for security and belonging. (8)

> **(8) Eph. 2:19**
> *You are no longer strangers and aliens, but you are citizens with the saints and also members of the household of God.*

A key word for Peter was *oikos* which is translated as "house." Social outsiders found community within the household or family of God. The church became an alternative to, and protest against, the social fragmentation that characterized urban life in the Roman Empire. The followers of Jesus built a new kind of communal life within households of extended Christian families. These household communities offered intimations of the kingdom of God yet to come, "where righteousness is at home" (2 Pet. 3:13). Exiled in the Roman Empire, these communities proclaimed heavenly citizenship (Phil. 3:20).

House churches evinced the emergence of a new order, where social, racial, economic, and religious barriers might be overcome. The creation of a new kind of family offered the possibility that barriers separating Jews and Gentiles, free and enslaved, men and women, cultured and illiterate might be broken down. The outcasts of the Empire were welcomed into the house of God.

The term *paroikia* is translated as "exile," and implies living without citizenship in a foreign land, deprived of one's civil rights. By the end of the first century, the word *paroikos*, which is rooted in *paroikia* and is translated as "sojourner," no longer applied to social outsiders, but to the local Christian assembly. (9) By the middle of the second century, the term was frequently used in this context, and the meaning of *paroikos* irrevocably evolved away from its root. (10) This is how the Latin word *parochia*, and the English word "parish" which is rooted in it, came to refer to the local church. After the Constantinian shift, the root meaning of *paroikos* was entirely lost.

> **(9) First Letter of Clement to the Corinthians**
> *The Church of God which sojourns* [paroikos] *at Rome, to the Church of God sojourning* [paroikos] *at Corinth.*[7]

The word "parishioner" refers not to a stranger or sojourner, but to a person who belongs, socially and ecclesiastically.[9]

---

(10) Example of **"paroikos"** *referring to Christian assemblies,* **The Martyrdom of Polycarp**
The Church of God which sojourns [paroikos] *in Smyrna, to the Church of God sojourning* [paroikos] *in Philomelium, and to all the congregations* [paroikia] *... in every place: Mercy, peace, and love from God the Father, and our Lord Jesus Christ, be multiplied.*[8]

Conclusion

Early Christians were marginalized not only because their values were based on Jesus' life and teachings, but because of contemporary economic and political factors. In Italy, Alexandria, and Egypt, the creation of large landholdings led to the displacement of small farmers, who drifted to the cities where large slums began to form. Fugitive slaves and other outcasts came to the cities seeking anonymity and survival. At the beginning of the Christian era, the population of Rome is estimated to have swollen to more than a million inhabitants.

At first, authorities sought to relieve the most urgent socio-economic problems using "bread and circus" techniques, and provided the needy with wheat, oil, salt, wine, and clothing. However, to avoid draining the imperial treasury, Augustus Caesar limited the number of dole recipients to 200,000. The limitation was in effect until the reign of Diocletian, toward the end of the third century.

The Roman population was divided between the citizens and the popular masses, who were not seen as politically valuable. The Roman citizenry was a privileged minority, living in the midst of impoverished masses. The vast majority of Roman Christians was to be found within this latter sector of society, which included slaves, poor freedmen and their families, dancers and singers, prostitutes, unattached women, and children.[10]

By forming synagogues, Jews created an effective exilic social system. The Jews were scattered throughout the Roman Empire in these communities. Considered by secular authorities to be outsiders, they were able to preserve their religious and national identity.

Likewise, Christians were able to strengthen and preserve their essential identity in house churches, which could be found in cities throughout the Empire. In these communities, exiles could find belonging. The biblical story of God's people is about a people serving God's kingdom, a kingdom which embraces the outsider.

Notes

[1] In the genealogy found in Matthew's Gospel, all the women mentioned (Tamar, Rahab, Ruth, the wife of Uriah the Hittite, and Mary) would have been considered outcasts according to social norms of the day.

[2] Matt. 21:11; 26:32; 27:55; 28:7,11,16; Mark 1:9,14; 14:28; 15:41; 16:7; Luke 23:5,49,55; 24:6; John 7:41,52; Acts 10:36-38.

[3] Sean Freyne, *Galilee, Jesus and the Gospels: Literary Approaches and Investigations* (Philadelphia: Fortress Press, 1988), 268. "The narratives of Jesus the Galilean that have been left to us in the gospel portraits of his career there are an eloquent testimony of just how radical and transforming that experience had, after all, proved to be."

[4] John Howard Yoder, Douglas Gwyn, Eugene F. Roop, and George Hunsinger, *A Declaration on Peace* (Scottdale, PA: Herald Press, 1991).

[5] Acts 9:2; 18:25-26; 19:9,23; 22:4; 24:14,22.

[6] The following section relies largely on the following source. Eduardo Hoornaert, *The Memory of the Christian People* (Maryknoll, New York: Orbis Press, 1988), 31-36.

[7] Alexander Roberts and James Donaldson, eds., *Ante-Nicene Fathers*, vol. 1, (New York: Charles Scribner's Sons, 1925), 5.

[8] Roberts and Donaldson, 39.

[9] K. L. M. A. Schmidt, et al., "Paroikos," in Gerhard Kittel, *Theological Dictionary of the New Testament*, vol. 5 (Grand Rapids: Eerdmans), 853.

[10] Hoornaert, 39-40.

Chapter 3

Christianity in the Second and Third Centuries

For the Christians are distinguished from other men neither by country, nor language, nor the customs which they observe. ... They dwell in their own countries, but simply as sojourners. ... They marry as do all; they beget children; but they do not destroy their offspring. They have a common table, but not a common bed. They are in the flesh, but they do not live after the flesh. They pass their days on earth, but they are citizens of heaven. They obey the prescribed laws, and at the same time surpass the laws by their lives. They love all men, and are persecuted by all. They are unknown and condemned; they are put to death, and restored to life. They are poor, yet they make many rich; they are in lack of all things, and yet abound in all ... The soul dwells in the body, yet is not the body; and Christians dwell in the world, yet are not of the world. ... The soul is imprisoned in the body, yet preserves that very body; and Christians are confined in the world as in a prison, and yet they are preservers of the world.
(*The Epistle to Diognetus,* V, 1-VI, 7)[1]

Introduction

Despite the obvious similarities which linked Christians of the first three centuries to their Jewish and pagan neighbors, the Christian church was a community of contrast. When Christian apologists, like the author of "The Epistle to Diognetus," compared Christians to their contemporaries, they expressed wonderment at the Christians' unusual way of life. However, the "invisibility" of the Christian way, to which this apologist alluded, was not merely a spiritualized expression of faith. The early church had not yet created formal institutions, easily identifiable to outside observers. They met in their own houses rather than in specially designated places of worship. The social structures of this new movement continued to be dominated by the spirit of Jesus' message, and outsiders were welcomed. The community's mission was to bear witness, in their everyday lives, to Jesus' life and message. They saw themselves as the "soul within the body" and "preservers of the world."

Social Composition of the Early Church

All Walks of Life

The Gospels tell us that the early church was made up primarily of outcasts. However, participation in the early church was not limited to those of humble origin. People from all social classes were faithful to the Messianic mission. Among those named in the New Testament were Pharisee insiders – including Saul, who was later called Paul – municipal officials, merchants, and centurions. This trend continued after the apostolic period.

According to Pliny, Roman governor of Bithynia during the second decade of the second century, there were "many persons of all ages and classes and of both sexes" already in the movement.[2] Pliny made an official investigation into the Christian movement, and detained and tortured "two maid-servants, who were called deaconesses."[3] Pliny may not have been the observer best qualified to discuss the social make-up of the early Christian movement, but other evidence suggests that outsiders figured prominently among the ranks of the early church. (1)

In the late second century, Tertullian of North Africa wrote about the growing popularity of the Christian movement. (2) People from many

---

(1) Athenagoras, **A Plea for the Christians,** *circa AD 180, XI*
But among us you will find uneducated persons, and artisans, and old women, who, if they are unable in words to prove the benefit of our doctrine, yet by their deeds exhibit the benefit arising from their persuasion of its truth: they do not rehearse speeches, but exhibit good works; when struck they do not strike again; when robbed they do not go to law; they give to those that ask of them, and love their neighbors as themselves.[4]

walks of life were professing their faith, including those of high social standing. However, Tertullian's statement implies that Christians of high rank were still unusual within the movement. Although some wealthy people were joining the movement, the bulk of these newcomers were outcasts who found a new identity within the Christian community. In his investigation of

> *(2) Tertullian,* **Apology I**
> *People of both sexes, every age and condition, even high rank, are passing over to the profession of the Christian faith.*[5]

Christian communities in Rome, Peter Lampe reported that until the end of the second century these were made up largely of slaves and other marginalized people.[6]

Idealization of Poverty

Hermas's writings, produced during the middle of the second century in Rome, reflected the Christian movement's idealization of poverty. Jesus had asked his followers to dispose of their earthly riches, and in keeping with this message, Hermas urged catechumens to revoke their wealth before proceeding with baptism. (3)

In his apology, Aristides wrote about the mutual aid practiced by the Christian community around the middle of the second century. He testified to the generous and familial spirit of the community, which opened its doors to anyone in need. (4)

> *(3) Hermas,* **Similitude,** *IX, xxx, xxxi*
> *When the Lord, therefore, saw the mind of these persons ... he ordered their riches to be cut down, not to be taken away for ever, that they might be able to do some good with what was left them. ... Now this age must cut down in these things, and in the vanities of their riches, and then they will meet in the Kingdom of God ....*[7]

Writing in Alexandria at the close of the first century, the author of the Epistle of Barnabas warned the church against the dangers of the "Black One." Those who followed the "Black One" were vain and selfish, and neglected to consider the hardships of those in need. The Christian ethic demanded consideration of all people, particularly the marginalized. (5)

> *(4) Aristides,* **Apology According to the Greek Fragments,** *XV, 7*
> *They do not despise the widow, nor the orphan; he who has gives abundantly to him who has not. If they spot a stranger, they receive him under their roof and rejoice with him as a true brother. They do not regard one another as brothers in the flesh, but in the spirit.*[8]

> *(5)* **The Epistle of Barnabas,** *XX*
> Those who follow the way of the "Black One" are *those who attend not with just judgment to the widow and orphan, ... who love vanity, follow after reward, pity not the needy, labour not in aid of him who is overcome with toil, ... who turn away him that is in want, who oppress the afflicted, who are advocates of the rich, who are unjust judges of the poor, and who are in every respect transgressors.*[9]

Worship in the Early Church

One of the earliest descriptions of the life of the primitive church was written by Pliny, a non-Christian contemporary. Pliny undertook an official investigation of Christians, who were suspected of illegal activities. His report to the Roman Emperor, Trajan, was written around A.D. 112. (6)

The secular observer was impressed by the close relationship between the Christians' simple liturgy and their upright and transparent way of living. The commitments, or sacraments, assumed by the Christians seemed dangerously like conspiracy to Pliny because they symbolized a radical social commitment. According to Pliny, the Christians would worship at daybreak on a chosen morning. During this simple ceremony they would take a communal oath to abstain from any wrongdoing. Later in the day they would share a meal together. This common meal was the *agape* which Christians continued to observe each Sunday evening, in good Pauline tradition.

> *(6)* *Pliny,* **Epistle to Trajan,** *X, XCVI*
> *On an appointed day they had been accustomed to meet before day-break, and recite a hymn antiphonally to Christ, as to a god, and to bind themselves by an oath, not for the commission of any crime, but to abstain from theft, robbery, adultery and breach of faith, and not to deny a deposit when it was claimed. After the conclusion of this ceremony it was their custom to depart and meet again to take food; but it was ordinary and harmless food.*[10]

"The Teaching of the Twelve Apostles," the *Didache*, is one of the oldest post-canonical documents of the Christian church, written near the end of the first century. Again, the author underscored the close relationship between the liturgy of the Lord's Supper and the quality of social relationships within the community. The act of eating together restored and maintained relationships within the community. (7)

Other documents confirm the practices and concerns of the early church. The first Apology of Justin Martyr, written in Rome around A.D. 150, recorded the Sunday rituals of his church community. He described how the community gathered to read

> *(7)* **The Didache, *XIV, 1-2***
> *On the Lord's own day, gather together and break bread and give thanks, after confessing your transgressions, so that your sacrifice may be pure. Let no one who has a quarrel with his comrade meet with you until they are reconciled, so that your sacrifice may not be defiled.*[11]

the writings of the apostles and prophets, after which their leader would address and instruct the group. At the end of the service, they would pray together. Then the leader would distribute bread and wine and water, and give thanks over it. A portion of bread and wine would be put aside and taken by the deacons to those who were absent. Finally, the wealthier members of the community would make offerings which would be used to assist orphans and widows, the sick and needy, prisoners, and strangers. Sunday was a day of communal celebration and worship. (8) The day's activities focussed on sharing material goods, breaking bread together, and caring for those in need.[12]

The Eucharistic liturgy found in the *Didache*, written toward the end of the first century, demonstrated an equilibrium of liturgical forms with charismatic freedom of expression in worship. The liturgy included formulaic prayers as well as free participation by charismatic prophets. In this community, the memory was still fresh of experiences like those that inspired the Pauline texts in Romans 12 and I Corinthians 12.[14]

> *(8) Justin Martyr,* **Apology, I, 67**
> *But Sunday is the day on which we all hold our common assembly, because it is the first day on which God, having wrought a change in the darkness and matter, made the world; and Jesus Christ our Saviour on the same day rose from the dead.*[13]

Economic Lifestyles in the Early Church

The writings of Greek apologist, Aristides, described the life and thought of Christian communities in Greece and Asia Minor around A.D. 125. Addressed to Emperor Hadrian, Aristides's writings defended the Christians

> **(9) Aristides, Apology according to the Syriac Version, *XV, 4-8***
> *And if there is among them a man that is poor and needy, and they have not an abundance of necessaries, they fast two or three days that they may supply the needy with their necessary food. They diligently keep the precepts of Christ; they live justly and humbly, as the Lord God has commanded. Every morning and, at all hours, they praise and glorify God for his benefits, giving thanks for their food and drink.*[16]

against rumors circulating in the Empire. He noted the Christians' generous treatment of outsiders and the disadvantaged. They treated their servants and children as brothers and sisters, and distributed their wealth to the less fortunate. Aristides observed that the ritual of fasting was more than an exercise in spiritual discipline or a technique for overcoming the body's carnal desires. One fasted in order to share with the needy. The Christians lived according to Jesus' message.[15] (9)

The writings of Hermas described the Christian communities in Rome around A.D. 150. He noted that economic inequalities contributed to the suffering and sickness not only of the poor, but also of the wealthy. An abundance of food was just as harmful as a lack of food. Christian generosity offered a remedy for the ills of both groups. This simple observation remains valid in our own world. (10)

> **(10) The Pastor of Hermas, Vision *III, 9, 3-4***
> *... [D]o not partake of God's creatures alone, but give abundantly of them to the needy. For some through the abundance of their food produce weakness in their flesh, and thus corrupt their flesh; while the flesh of others who have no food is corrupted because they have not sufficient nourishment. And on this account their bodies waste away.*[17]

Attitudes Toward Violence and Warfare in the Early Church

The church fathers who wrote during the period following the New Testament era were unanimous in their opposition to all violence against humans, including warfare. Writing around A.D. 180, Athenagoras argued against all forms of murder. He opposed abortion and infanticide. He objected to the violence of the spectacles in which gladiators fought wild beasts in the arena. He also vehemently opposed the killing of human beings in warfare. Athenagoras argued against a double-standard which viewed one kind of murder as wrong, and another as right. One could not logically condemn a woman for killing her child, if, when that child is grown, one sends it to its death in war or in sport. (11)

---

(11) Athenagoras, **A Plea for the Christians,** *35*
But we, deeming that to see a man put to death is much the same as killing him, have abjured such spectacles [the contests of gladiators and wild beasts]. How, then, when we do not even look on, lest we should contract guilt and pollution, can we put people to death? And when we say that those women who use drugs to bring on an abortion commit murder, and will have to give an account to God for the abortion, on what principle should we commit murder? For it does not belong to the same person to regard the very fetus in the womb as a created being, and therefore an object of God's care, and when it has passed into life, to kill it; and not to expose an infant, because those who expose them are chargeable with child-murder, and on the other hand, when it has been reared to destroy it.[18]

Swords to Ploughshares

During this period, Christians and Jews were debating whether or not the Messiah had actually come. According to the Jewish perspective, there had been no change in the condition of the world, and therefore the Messiah could not have appeared. During these discussions, the Messianic prophesies of Isaiah 2 and Micah 4 were invoked to support the argument against the Christian claim. These texts prophesied nations united in their belief, and swords hammered into plowshares.

Justin Martyr, writing on behalf of the Christians, recognized that the Jewish argument rang true: the world would experience change with the coming of the Messiah. He argued that such changes were occurring, and not merely in the inner spiritual lives of individuals. Transformations were already happening in the midst of Christian communities. (12)

---

(12) Justin Martyr, **Dialogue with Trypho,** *110*
We who were filled with war, and mutual slaughter, and every wickedness, have each through the whole earth changed our warlike weapons – our swords into ploughshares, and our spears into implements of tillage – and we cultivate piety, righteousness, philanthropy, faith and hope, which we have from the Father Himself through Him who was crucified.[19]

Justin Martyr was the first of many early church fathers who shared this vision. Later in the second century, Theophilus was named bishop of Antioch. He became the first Christian writer with formal ecclesiastical authority to express the conviction that the vision of peace prophesied in Isaiah 2 and Micah 4 was already being fulfilled in the Christian community (*Theophilus to Autolycus*, III, 14).[20]

Irenaeus became bishop of the church in Lyon toward the end of the second century. He also argued that the Christian church was fulfilling the prophetic vision articulated in Isaiah 2 and Micah 4 (*Against Heresies*, IV, 34, 4).[21] At about the same time, Tertullian, the great Christian thinker of North Africa, was making a similar argument. Both writers observed that the Christian community followed a new, pacific law, which urged non-violent practices in all situations.[22] At the beginning of the third century, Origen, who lived in Egypt and Palestine, expressed his conviction that the Christian community lived according to Jesus' message of peace. (13)

These five Christian writers were representative of the common vision of the early apostolic church. They wrote between A.D. 150 and 250, and came from throughout the Roman Empire: from Rome, from Palestine-Egypt, from Lyon in southern France, and from North Africa. Despite their diverse situations, all reflect a similar sense of identity in similar communities of peace.

---

(13) Origen, **Against Celsus,** *33*
We no longer take up "sword against nation," nor do we "learn war any more," having become children of peace, for the sake of Jesus, who is our leader, instead of those whom our fathers followed.[23]

Military Service

Early Christians were not only opposed to the violence of warfare, but also refused to participate in ceremonies performed by the Roman Legions. Ceremonies for swearing patriotic allegiance were celebrated regularly in conjunction with the religious rites of the Roman army. Christians considered these ceremonies idolatrous, and many suffered martyrdom for their refusal to participate.

Tertullian described this situation in his tract, *De Corona*, written in 211. *De Corona* was the first Christian tract dedicated entirely to the discussion of Christian participation in the army. A soldier had refused to participate fully in a military ceremony. In order to receive a bonus offered by the Emperor, the soldiers had to present themselves dressed in official military uniform, which included a laurel wreath. This man, whose name is unrecorded, refused to wear the wreath on his head, out of Christian conviction. Instead, he carried it in his hand. He was arrested and presumably executed for disobeying military protocol.[24]

In *De Corona*, Tertullian indirectly recognized the presence of other Christians in the Roman army when he accused them of attempting "to serve two lords," and bemoaned the fact that some contemporary Christians would view this incident as a "merely formal matter."[25] Tertullian concluded that many Christians were compromising their convictions to avoid persecution.

However, Tertullian was not only concerned about the potentially idolatrous practices involved in military ceremonies. He was most troubled by the question of whether or not Christians should be involved in any aspect of warfare. How could a Christian avenge the wrongs of the Empire when he did not believe it right to avenge his own? (14)

> *(14) Tertullian, De Corona, XI*
> *Shall it be lawful to make an occupation of the sword, when the Lord proclaims that he who uses the sword shall perish by the sword? And shall the son of peace take part in the battle when it does not become him even to sue at law? And shall he apply the chain, and the prison, and the torture, and the punishment, who is not the avenger even of his own wrongs?[26]*

Tertullian was convinced that Christians must act consistently, even if this meant suffering martyrdom. He made careful consideration of potentially compromising situations, including that of a soldier already in the Roman army wanting to become a Christian. He cited examples of soldiers who approached John the Baptist, and centurions who were mentioned in the New Testament, but Tertullian remained firm in his conviction that a Christian must always strive to follow Jesus' message. (15)

Tertullian simplified the controversy by identifying the military as an essentially unchristian institution. He placed the problem of idolatry within the larger context of militarism. The act of idolatry was not located in the

> *(15) Tertullian, De Corona, XI*
> *Neither does military service hold out escape from punishment of sins, or exemption from martyrdom. Nowhere does the Christian change his character.[27]*

ceremonies themselves, which were secondary, but in all military life, in which the Emperor usurped the place of Jesus. When one recognized that military service was not acceptable to Christians, then secondary matters such as the military wreath and idolatrous ceremonies ceased to distract one from the issue at hand: Christians could not, in good faith, serve in the military.

Evangelization in the Early Church

The Spread of Christianity

During the second and third centuries, Christianity was gradually spreading throughout the Roman Empire. When Constantine assumed power at the beginning of the fourth century, estimates suggest that Christians made up about five percent of the entire population. However, there remain few eyewitness accounts of how the church grew during this time.

The oldest archaeological evidence of an early Christian meeting-house dates from around 240. At that time, the congregation in Europos, located on the banks of the Euphrates river in Asia, knocked down a wall in their meeting-house to accommodate a larger group of people: sixty instead of thirty. In 251, Eusebius reported that there were 154 ministers in the church in Rome, and more than 1,500 widows (*Ecclesiastical History*, XLIII, 43).[28] By 300, estimates suggest that approximately one out of every twenty Roman inhabitants was a Christian.

The growth of the church was not due to organized missionary activity. There is no historical evidence of any mission directed by church authorities during this time, and any Christian missionary active between the times of Paul and Constantine remained anonymous, with the exception of Pantenus in India.[29]

Very few prayers for conversion survive from the early centuries. According to Alan Kreider, most of these were prayers obeying Jesus' command to pray for enemies and persecutors.[30] There is no evidence of public evangelistic preaching during this period, nor was much theological reflection given to the evangelizing mission of the Christian church. The charismatic ministry of itinerant apostles, referred to in the New Testament (Eph. 4:11), soon waned and eventually disappeared.

Converting to Christianity was not an easy choice during this time. We do not find the distinction, later popularized by modern promoters of church growth, between the tasks of evangelism and discipleship. The catechumenate – the period of teaching and training for people who wished to become Christians – could last for years. The lifestyle and the commitment of catechumens were valued more than their doctrinal confessions. New Christians were expected to share their goods, to love their enemies, and to maintain absolute fidelity within their marriages. The Christian communities lived according to a radically different ethical code than Roman society in general, and perhaps for this reason alone they continued to grow.

Martyrdom

Martyrdom was the most public form of evangelistic witness among early Christians. The Christian apologist Quadratus observed in A.D. 125 that although Christians risked torture and death for proclaiming their faith, the movement was growing. He argued that this was proof of God's power. (16)

In Rome around A.D. 150, Justin Martyr wrote about his conversion to the Christian faith, and credited the powerful witness of Christian martyrs. According to his account, Christians had been accused of sensual excesses, and even cannibalism. Justin Martyr realized that they were being slandered with outrageous falsehoods: such accusations didn't make sense given the fearlessness with which they faced death. He was proud to name himself a convert to the faith.[32]

> *(16) Quadratus,* **The Epistle to Diognetus, *VI, 9; VII, 7-9***
> *Christians, though subjected day by day to punishment, increase the more in number. ... Do you not see them exposed to wild beasts, that they may be persuaded to deny the Lord, and yet not overcome? Do you not see that the more of them are punished, the greater becomes the number of the rest? This does not seem to be the work of man: this is the power of God; these are the evidences of His manifestation.*[31]

It is impossible to ascertain whether or not the writings of Christian apologists contributed substantially to the growth of the church. Compared to the literary production of the period, the apologists produced a considerable volume of work, the tone of which was characterized by deep personal conviction. The apologists suffered death, as the name Justin *Martyr* testifies. They were active participants in a witnessing community, and sought to defend the Christian movement.

Conclusion: A Living Witness

The living reality of the Christian people was probably the most important factor in the growth of the early church. The Christian people were different than their neighbors. Their worship, which went hand in hand with their counter-cultural lifestyle, was vital and dynamic. They were willing to talk about their faith and life anywhere and everywhere to anyone who would listen. Yet they are largely anonymous to us.

Humble and philosophical Christian writers alike radiated a message of hope, for the present as well as the future. The community of social outsiders offered an other-worldly vision of justice, equality, fraternal love, and compassion in the midst of corrupt social structures. They offered an alternative to a disintegrating society overwhelmed by divisive problems. Above all, they offered a place where the oppressed and outcast were treated as equals. In 303, the father of a reader in the Egyptian church was named Copreus, which means "off the dung heap."[33] Hermas, whose writings were almost included in the New Testament, had been a slave. Further, women formed a clear majority in Christian communities in the third century. The women's house, the courtyard of the traditional household, was probably a primary location for evangelization during this period.

The lifestyle of the Christian community sent a clearer message to pagans than did the public and private articulation of its doctrines. The evangelistic invitation of the early church called for more than intellectual adherence to doctrinal propositions. It called for a new social and spiritual reality, in which communion was both local and universal. Years of apprenticeship were sometimes required to truly understand the spirit of this new world of Messianic salvation. The process of the catechumenate could take years before reaching the stage of baptismal commitment.

There are many possible reasons which explain the growth of the early church: miracles, healings, fear of coming judgement, and the witness of martyrs. However, Origen identified the primary reason for the spread of Christianity in his reply to the pagan critic, Celsus. Origen argued that the proof of Jesus' divinity was to be found in the existence of communities which owed their lives to his saving initiative (*Origen Against Celsus*, III, 33).[34] In the midst of a chaotic society, these communities offered a new and different order, evidence that God was making all things new.

Notes

[1] Alexander Roberts and James Donaldson, eds., *Ante-Nicene Fathers*, vol. 1 (New York: Charles Scribner's Sons, 1925), 26-27.

[2] Henry Bettenson, ed., *Documents of the Christian Church* (New York: Oxford University Press, 1967), 4.

[3] Bettenson, 4.

[4] Alexander Roberts and James Donaldson, eds., *Ante-Nicene Fathers*, vol. 2 (New York: Charles Scribner's Sons, 1925), 134.

[5] Roberts and Donaldson, vol. 3, 17.

[6] Robert Jewett, "A Social Profile of the Early Christians at Rome," *Interpretation* 43.3 (1989): 297-298.

[7] Alexander Roberts and James Donaldson, eds., *Ante-Nicene Fathers*, vol. 2 (New York: Charles Scribner's Sons, 1925), 53.

[8] Daniel Ruiz Bueno, ed., *Padres Apologistas Griegos* (Madrid: La Editorial Catolica, 1954), 131.

[9] Alexander Roberts and James Donaldson, eds., *Ante-Nicene Fathers*, vol. 1 (New York: Charles Scribner's Sons, 1925), 149.

[10] Henry Bettenson, ed., *Documents of the Christian Church* (New York: Oxford University Press, 1967), 3-4.

[11] Edgar J. Goodspeed, *The Apostolic Fathers* (New York: Harper and Brothers Publishers, 1950), 17.

[12] Alexander Roberts and James Donaldson, eds., *Ante-Nicene Fathers*, vol. 1 (New York: Charles Scribner's Sons, 1925), 186.

[13] Roberts and Donaldson, vol. 1, 186.

[14] Edgar J. Goodspeed, *The Apostolic Fathers* (New York: Harper and Brothers Publishers, 1950), 15-16. "Now about the Thanksgiving (Eucharist), give thanks thus: First about the cup, 'We thank you, our Father, for the holy vine of your servant David, which you have made known to us through your Servant Jesus. Glory to you forever.' And about the piece of bread, 'We thank you, our Father, for the life and knowledge you have made known to us through Jesus your servant. Glory be yours forever. Just as this piece of bread was scattered over the mountains, and then gathered together and became one, so let your church be gathered together from the ends of the earth into your kingdom. For

the glory and the power are yours through Jesus Christ forever.' ... After you are satisfied, give thanks thus: 'We give you thanks holy Father, for your holy name, which you have made dwell in our hearts, and for knowledge and faith and immortality, which you have made known to us through Jesus your servant ... Remember, Lord, your church, to save it from all evil and to make it perfect in your love, and gather it together in its holiness from the four winds, into your kingdom which you have prepared for it. For the power and the glory are yours forever. ... Lord, come quickly! Amen.' *But permit the prophets to give thanks as much as they please.*" (The Teaching of the Twelve Apostles, IX,1-X,7; emphasis mine).

[15] Daniel Ruiz Bueno, ed., *Padres Apologistas Griegros* (Madrid: La Editorial Catolica, 1954), 145.

[16] Ruiz Bueno, 145. My translation. We find here echoes of the prophetic vision: "Is not this the fast that I choose: to loose the bonds of injustice, to undo the thongs of the yoke, to let the oppressed go free, and to break every yoke? Is it not to share your bread with the hungry, and bring the homeless poor into your house; when you see the naked, to cover them, and not to hide yourself from your own kin?" (Isa. 58:6-7).

[17] Alexander Roberts and James Donaldson, eds., *Ante-Nicene Fathers*, vol. 2 (New York: Charles Scribner's Sons, 1925), 16. Note also Justin Martyr's observations: "We who also valued above all things the acquisition of wealth and possessions, now bring what we have into a common stock, and communicate to every one in need. ... And the wealthy among us help the needy; and we always keep together; and for all things wherewith we are supplied, we bless the Maker of all through his Son Jesus Christ." (Justin Martyr, *Apology I*, 14,2; 67,1). Roberts and Donaldson, vol. 1, 167, 185-186.

[18] Roberts and Donaldson, vol. 2, 147.

[19] Roberts and Donaldson, vol. 1, 254.

[20] Roberts and Donaldson, vol. 2, 115. Theophilus based his conviction on Isaiah 66:5.

[21] Roberts and Donaldson, vol. 1, 512.

[22] Roberts and Donaldson, vol. 4, 154. "For the wont of the old law was to avenge itself by the vengeance of the glaive, and to pluck out 'eye for eye,' and to inflict retaliatory revenge for injury. But the new law's wont was to point to clemency, and to convert to tranquility the pristine ferocity of 'glaives' and 'lances', and to remodel the pristine execution of 'war' upon the rivals and foes

of the law into the pacific actions of 'ploughing' and 'tilling' the land." (Tertullian, *An Answer to the Jews*, III).

[23] Roberts and Donaldson, vol. 4, 558.

[24] Roberts and Donaldson, vol. 3, 93.

[25] Roberts and Donaldson, vol. 3, 93.

[26] Roberts and Donaldson, vol. 3, 99-100.

[27] Roberts and Donaldson, vol. 3, 100.

[28] Christian Frederick Cruse, trans., *The Ecclesiastical History of Eusebius Pamphilus* (Grand Rapids, MI: Baker Book House, 1958), 265.

[29] Robin Lane Fox, *Pagans and Christians* (New York: Alfred A. Knopf, 1987), 282.

[30] Alan Kreider, "Worship and Evangelism in Pre-Christendom," *Vox Evangelica* 24 (1994): 8, 31 n. 13.

[31] Alexander Roberts and James Donaldson, eds., *Ante-Nicene Fathers*, vol. 1 (New York: Charles Scribner's Sons, 1925), 27-28.

[32] Roberts and Donaldson, vol. 1, 192-193. "For I myself, too, when I was delighting in the doctrines of Plato, and heard the Christians slandered, and saw them fearless in death, and of all other things which are counted fearful, perceived that it was impossible that they could be living in wickedness and pleasure. For what sensual or intemperate man, or who that counts it good to feast on human flesh, could welcome death that he might be deprived of his enjoyments, and would not rather continue always the present life, and attempt to escape the observation of the rulers; and much less would he denounce himself when the consequence would be death? ... and I confess that I both boast and with all my strength strive to be found a Christian." (Justin Martyr, *Apology II*, 12:1-2; 13:1-2).

[33] Robin Lane Fox, Pagans and Christians (New York: Alfred A. Knopf, 1987), 282.

[34] Alexander Roberts and James Donaldson, eds., Ante-Nicene Fathers, vol. 4 (New York: Charles Scribner's Sons, 1925), 477.

Chapter 4

Ancient Movements: The Montanists

One of those who was but a recent convert, Montanus by name, ... was carried away in spirit, and wrought up into a certain kind of frenzy and irregular ecstasy, raving, and speaking, and uttering strange things, and proclaiming what was contrary to the institutions that had prevailed in the church, as handed down and preserved in succession from the earliest times.

He excited two others, females, and filled them with the spirit of delusion, so that they also spake like the former, in a kind of ecstatic frenzy, out of all season, and in a manner strange and novel. ...

[Who] is this new teacher? His works and his doctrines sufficiently show it. This is he that taught the dissolutions of marriage, he that imposed laws of fasting, that called ... little places in Phrygia a Jerusalem in order to collect men from every quarter thither; who established exactors of money, and under the name of offerings, devised the artifice to procure presents; who provided salaries for those that preached his doctrine ...

(Eusebius, *Ecclesiastical History*, V, 14-18) [1]

Introduction: Historical Sources

To reconstruct the story of the Montanists, we must make use of Eusebius's *Ecclesiastical History*, which was hostile to the "heretical" movement. Polemical church writings are the only surviving historical records which afford us an understanding of the movement. The church did not carefully conserve the testimonies of "heretics," so although official documentation may be biased in its interpretation, few other sources are available.

Eusebius consulted four principal sources when reporting on the Montanist movement: Apollonaris of Hierapolis, the historian; Miltiades;

and Apollonius and Serapion, bishops of the church in Antioch. Apollonaris of Hierapolis wrote his account more than forty years after the events had taken place, and it reflected prejudices accumulated during the long struggle between ecclesiastical authorities and the Montanists. Eusebius's account was written almost two centuries after the events took place.

One source offers a fresher perspective. Tertullian participated in the Montanist movement during the last thirteen years of his life, and his writings during this period tell of the general orientation of the movement, and provide some of the story's concrete details.

The Montanist Movement

The Montanist movement arose in Asia Minor, in the Phrygian Christian church at a time when it was suffering great persecution. The names of several people have been associated with the prophetic movement: Montanus, Alcibiades, Theodotus, and later Priscilla and Maximilla. The Montanists were distinctive because of their clear conviction that they were a "new prophecy movement," a charismatic revival which contrasted with the traditional institutional structures of ecclesiastical authority (*Ecclesiastical History*, V, 3).[2]

Phrygia was located about fifteen miles from Philadelphia, in Asia Minor. Christians from the rural villages of Phrygia had come into the church from pagan backgrounds. They were of humble origin and many were slaves. They lived under difficult conditions and were subjected to persecution, first by the imperial authorities, and later by mainstream Christians. The Phrygian Christians began to interpret their miseries as eschatological, even apocalyptic, signs.

The church in the rest of the Empire began to take notice of the Phrygian movement around A.D. 172. At this time, debate about the movement was going on in Rome. Irenaeus, the highly respected bishop of the congregation in Lyon, in southern France, interceded with Roman ecclesiastical authorities on behalf of the movement.

Eusebius's account offered a frankly negative interpretation of the Montanist movement, and it is sometimes difficult to distinguish between fact and exaggeration. Nevertheless, his account highlighted a series of elements which characterized the Montanists in their early days.

The severe persecution to which Christian communities in Phrygia and Asia Minor were subjected considerably affected their attitudes toward secular society, and the established church, both of which opposed them. Not all Christian churches suffered from such persecution. For example, the church in Syria suffered official persecution only briefly, in A.D. 112, when Ignatius of Antioch was martyred in Rome. The church in North Africa was not persecuted until after A.D. 180.

However, Christians in Asia Minor suffered four major persecutions during the second century: under Trajan in A.D. 112, under Antoninus Pio is A.D. 155, and under Marcus Aurelius in A.D. 165 and 185. The Montanist movement is generally thought to have arisen during the second persecution, around A.D. 156, when Polycarp, the beloved bishop of the church in nearby Smyrna, suffered martyrdom.

Christians were not only persecuted by imperial authorities. Their pagan neighbors sometimes betrayed them as if they were common criminals, and cried out for their deaths during judicial procedures. "The Martyrdom of Polycarp," a Christian document written in the following century, described the fury of the gathered crowd toward Polycarp, who had confessed to being a Christian. (1)

---

(1) **The Martyrdom of Polycarp,** *XII*
The proconsul was astonished and sent his herald to proclaim in the midst of the stadium thrice, "Polycarp has confessed that he is a Christian." This proclamation having been made by the herald, the whole multitude both of heathen and Jews, who dwelt at Smyrna, cried out with uncontrollable fury, and in a loud voice, "This is the teacher of Asia, the father of the Christians, and the overthrower of our gods, he who has been teaching many not to sacrifice, or to worship the gods." Speaking thus, they cried out, and besought Philip the Asiarch to let loose a lion upon Polycarp. But Philip answered that it was not lawful. ... Then it deemed good to them to cry out with one consent, that Polycarp should be burnt alive.[3]

> **(2) Tertullian, De Fuga in Persecutione, 9**
> *Accordingly, John also teaches that we must lay down our lives for the brethren; much more, then, we must do it for the Lord. ... Seek not to die on ... beds ... nor in soft fevers, but to die the martyr's death, that He may be glorified who has suffered for you.*[4]

Tertullian was attracted to the Montanist movement around 207, some thirteen years before his death. In his later writings, he reflected on the heroic attitudes of the Montanists who faced suffering and death. Indeed, Tertullian thought them to be examples of true Christians, glorified by their suffering. He considered a martyr's death to be the most honorable, even desirable, for a Christian. (2)

Suspicious of Civil Authorities

Persecuted as they were by imperial authorities, the Christians of Phrygia tended to be suspicious of civil government. In order to protect the interests of their parishioners and ensure the tranquillity and growth of their communities, bishops of churches throughout the Empire had begun seeking alliances, or at least truces, with secular powers. The Montanists, as portrayed in Tertullian's writings, refused to participate in this alliance-building. Tertullian was convinced that the Montanists were acting in the true spirit of Christianity.

Tertullian opposed all symbols of Roman oppression. In his tract, "On the Pallium," he explained why he chose to wear the "pallium," the dress of commoners, rather than the traditional Roman toga. Tertullian argued that the toga symbolized Roman conquest, while the pallium was ancient and practical and had once been worn by people of all ranks. (3)

> **(3) summary of Tertullian, On the Pallium**
> *[The toga] was introduced by the Romans after their victory over Carthage and became a symbol of violent conquest and oppression, while the pallium had been used in ancient times by persons of every rank and condition. ... It is to be recommended for its simplicity and usefulness.*[5]

In his tract, "De Corona," Tertullian opposed service in the Roman army and questioned the value of patriotism. Military service required allegiance to a power other than Christ's, and this was not acceptable to those of the Christian faith. (4)

Insofar as Tertullian can be considered a faithful interpreter of the Montanist movement, he provides an example of its

---

(4) summary of Tertullian, De Corona
The military wreath is forbidden for the simple reason that war and military service are irreconcilable with the Christian faith. The Christian pledges allegiance to one alone: in the baptismal promise; he knows only one service: that which he renders to Christ the King.[6]

---

opposition to any compromise with civil authorities. His writings, directed primarily against the Roman imperial ideology, also opposed the bishops who were willing to make concessions in their dealings with Rome. At the beginning of the third century the church suffered persecution under Septimus Severus, and the Montanist movement proved to be the church of martyrs. It seemed that imperial authorities considered the "heretics," the Marcionites and the Montanists, to be more dangerous and subversive than the rest of the Christian church.

A Crisis of Spiritual Authority

The Montanist movement emphasized the role of the Holy Spirit in the life of the church. Eusebius considered this to be the movement's most offensive characteristic. The Montanists were reacting against the increasing institutionalization of ecclesiastical authority. They wanted to restore the tradition of charismatic leadership to the church.

Charismatic and prophetic leadership had held a prominent position in the early church. Prophets had a place in the Pauline communities, as described in the New Testament. Written around A.D. 100, *The Didache* discussed the participation of prophets in community assemblies, and even commented on how to interpret their messages.[7] Justin Martyr, debating with Jews around A.D. 150, wrote that the ongoing presence of charismatic prophecy among Christian communities, and its disappearance from Jewish communities, indicated that the Christian church was displacing Judaism.(5)

Over the course of several centuries, spiritual authority in the church became institutionalized, taking the form of canon, creed, and monarchical episcopate. Struggling against heterodoxy, and particularly against the ideas

(5) Justin Martyr, Dialogue With Trypho, 82:1

For the prophetical gifts remain with us, even to the present time. And hence you ought to understand that [the gifts] formerly among your nations have been transferred to us. And just as there were false prophets contemporaneous with your holy prophets, so are there now many false teachers amongst us, of whom our Lord forewarned us to beware.[8]

of Marcion in Rome, the church began to form a canonical list of scriptures. These scriptures were recognized by the church as its spiritual authority, and became the canon against which all other related writings were measured.

The Apostles' Creed probably originated as a confession of faith used by catechumens in the Christian congregation in Rome. By A.D. 150, the Apostles' Creed was being used to identify followers of the bishop of Rome. Those who did not subscribe to this confession of faith were considered heretical.

Beginning early in the second century, the presence of the bishop was seen to guarantee the unity of the church. In A.D. 112, Ignatius of Antioch wrote one of the first endorsements of a hierarchical system of church administration. He told Christians to follow the bishop's commands as Jesus followed God's commands. He suggested that the bishop must guide the church in the proper direction, overseeing all religious ceremonies. Further, Ignatius argued that any ceremony not overseen by the bishop should not be considered valid. In short, Ignatius endorsed a homogenous standard of worship in the growing church. (6)

(6) Epistle of Ignatius to the Smyrnaeans, VIII

See that ye all follow the bishop, even as Jesus Christ does the Father. ... Let no man do anything connected with the church without the bishop. Let that be deemed a proper Eucharist, which is [administered] either by the bishop or by one to whom he has entrusted it. ... It is not lawful without the bishop either to baptize or to celebrate a love-feast; but whatever he shall approve of, that is also pleasing to God, so that everything that is done may be secure and valid.[9]

Ignatius proposed that a bishop would serve his local congregation. However, Ignatius's proposal was soon broadened, and the bishops of large urban congregations began to dictate orthodoxy to the bishops of smaller churches. Christian orthodoxy was determined by the agreement of these principal bishops. Eventually, the bishop of Rome came to be recognized as *primus inter pares* of all the bishops in the Empire. This led to the institutionalization of church authority, and the formation of a monarchical episcopate.

During the second and third centuries, the Christian church stopped focussing on the future, or on the present, and looked increasingly to the past to validate its purpose. The imminent Parousia of the future, and the charismatic prophecies of the present were no longer defining characteristics of the church's identity. The church found its purpose in the past, and Christian orthodoxy arose out of the composition of the apostolic canon, the creation of the Apostles' Creed, and the establishment of an apostolic episcopate. In this process, "right living," or orthopraxy, became less and less useful for identifying Christians.

The Montanist movement was essentially a protest against the institutionalization of authority in the church. Montanists advocated the formation of communities in which Christians could hear the living voice of the Holy Spirit. The Montanist movement was not interested in creating new dogmas. Even enemies of the movement conceded that the Montanists adhered to doctrinal orthodoxy. However, the movement did not depend on the guidance of bishops and theological dogmas, but focussed instead on continuing an apostolic practice.

A Rigorous Christian Ethic

The church was becoming less disciplined than it had been in the past. The Montanist movement called on Christians to renew their commitments to a rigorous ethic. Traditionally, the sexual practices of Christians had been noticeably different than those of their pagan neighbors, who lived in a relatively libertine society. In this regard, Montanists went even further than other Christians. The movement lived in a highly charged eschatological atmosphere, and limited their members to one marriage relationship only. If a partner died, a second marriage was seen as successive bigamy.

Virginity was idealized by all Christians. Sexual abstinence was considered superior to sexual relations, even within marriage. However, the Montanists went even further, and considered married life incompatible with the highest fulfillment of Christian experience. This belief was out of character with the Judeo-Christian tradition, and probably was brought to the church through pagan converts. Some of the Phyrgian pagan religions held similar beliefs. Ironically, although the church in Rome condemned this belief toward the end of the second century, the practice nevertheless lived on in the form of clerical celibacy.

In his tract, "On Exhortation to Chastity," Tertullian praised the virtues of virginity and sexual continence. His argument was bolstered by quotations from the Montanist prophetess, Priscilla, who preached against indulging the carnal nature. Visions came through purity, which was dulled even by a first marriage. (7)

---

*(7) **Tertullian,** On Exhortation to Chastity*
Again, through the holy prophetess, Priscilla, the Gospel is thus preached: that "the holy minister knows how to minister sanctity. For purity," says she, "is harmonious, and they see visions; and, turning their face downward, they even hear manifest voices, as salutary as they are withal secret." If this dulling [of the spiritual faculties], even when the carnal nature is allowed room for exercise in first marriage, averts the Holy Spirit; how much more when it is brought into play in second marriage. [10]

The Montanists took other spiritual disciplines more seriously than did the rest of the church. For example, in order to exercise personal spiritual discipline, they fasted for several days each week, and for extended periods during the year. Congregational discipline was also practiced more rigorously among the Montanists. They believed that the church's holiness was located in the concrete lives of its members, not in its institutional vocation, as the mainstream church believed.

The Montanists had a different attitude toward women than did the mainstream church, which had little interest in exploring the role of women in ministry. The New Testament church had followed Jesus' lead and recognized that women had a place in ministration, but gradually the forces of ecclesiastical law and order limited women's ministry in the church. Before she died, in about A.D. 179, Maximilla, Montanus's follower, and a prophetess, complained of being "driven as a wolf from the sheep. I am not a wolf. I am word, spirit and power." [11]

As in biblical tradition, the Montanist movement believed that women as well as men could receive charismatic gifts of the Holy Spirit. This must have been an exhilarating experience of liberation for these rural women, accustomed to the servility of traditional social structures.

An Eschatological Vision

The hope of a restored millennial kingdom was attractive to the persecuted communities of Phrygia and Asia Minor around the middle of the second century. Writing several centuries later, Eusebius, the church historian, believed that the kingdom had already arrived in the Constantinian golden age, and he was not interested in imagining another. However, the security of a living hope provides those who are suffering with the strength to carry on in their daily struggles. The Book of Revelation had been addressed to Christian communities in Asia Minor. Fifty years later, in precisely the same geographical region, the Montanist movement lived in hope of an imminent change.

The Montanist movement was a popular expression of Christianity. Their beliefs bore similarities to those of the Christian communities for whom John's Revelation was intended. The Montanists lived out their faith with great sincerity, and apocalyptic enthusiasm. They believed that within the city of Rome – indeed, within the entire imperial structure – the kingdom of darkness was engaged in mortal combat with the kingdom of light.

Like John before him, Montanus was an apocalyptic prophet who called on the church to repent before the imminent appearance of the kingdom of God. He called for renewed eschatological hope, recognition of charismatic authority, and ethical sincerity. Eusebius labelled the movement heretical because of its apocalyptic nature, but this belief was widely shared among early Christians. (8) Justin Martyr, writing around A.D. 150,

> *(8) Justin Martyr,* **Dialogue with Trypho,** *80*
> *Do you really admit that this place, Jerusalem, shall be rebuilt; and do you expect your people to be gathered together, and made joyful with Christ and the patriarchs ...? Or have you given way? ... I and others, who are right-minded Christians on all points, are assured that there will be a resurrection of the dead, and a thousand years in Jerusalem, which will then be built, adorned, and enlarged, [as] the prophets Ezekiel and Isaiah and others declare.*[12]

argued that after the resurrection of the dead, Jerusalem would be the site of the kingdom of God. He stated firmly that all "right-minded Christians" agreed that this would be so.

The Montanist movement revived many of the themes contained in John's vision. The Montanists took their term for the Spirit, *Paraclete*, from John. The movement and the Book of Revelation both showed antipathy toward the oppressive system embodied by Rome. Eschatology and millennialism, martyrdom, conflict between Rome and Jerusalem, and the exaltation of virginity were themes central to the Book of Revelation, and reappeared with renewed vigor in the Montanist movement.

Conclusion

These ideas and practices may appear to us to be strange and exaggerated, but they reflected and answered the needs of an oppressed and persecuted people who resisted subjugation to the authorities. Montanism was a radical response by the rural poor to the imperial powers and to the bishops of powerful urban congregations. This response was not limited geographically to Asia Minor, but was present throughout the Empire. It was a popular reaction against the church's institutionalization of spiritual authority.

Unfortunately, the larger church suffered the consequences of this struggle. Rather than dedicating its energies to becoming a living witness to the Kingdom of God, the church spent its strength combating these dissident groups. The first meetings of the bishops were organized to combat the influences of Montanism and to neutralize its effects among the poor and oppressed classes.

The Montanist movement gained sympathizers throughout the Empire. Irenaeus, the highly respected bishop in Lyon, wrote to the bishop in Rome, begging him not to quench the Spirit by coercive and repressive measures against the Montanists. Tertullian, the great Christian leader in North Africa, found himself in the middle of the controversy between the church bishops and the Montanists. He chose to cast his lot with the latter, convinced that they represented the true church. Tertullian insisted that the

Paraclete had been given to the church to bring a new quality of life, rather than a new doctrine. He did not hesitate to say that the Montanists were men of the Spirit.

Rejected by the mainstream church, the Montanists organized themselves into congregations. Instead of including the title of "bishop" among their ministries, they recognized "patriarchs" and "companions (*koinonos*) of the Lord."[13] This informal honorific was used among the Christians of Asia Minor, and was endowed especially upon the confessors and martyrs in their midst, such as Polycarp.

In the cities, the mainstream church gradually imposed its will. However, vestiges of the movement persisted, particularly in rural areas of the Empire, until the fifth century. Even after the Montanist movement disappeared, radical movements with similar agendas for renewal continued to appear on the stage of church history. Among these were the following movements: Novatianism, monasticism, Donatism, Waldensianism, and Anabaptism.

Notes

[1] Christian Frederick Cruse, trans., *The Ecclesiastical History of Eusebius Pamphilus* (Grand Rapids, MI: Baker Book House, 1958), 194-200.

[2] Cruse, 182-183.

[3] Alexander Roberts and James Donaldson, eds., *The Ante-Nicene Fathers*, vol. 1 (New York: Charles Scribner's Sons, 1925), 41.

[4] Roberts and Donaldson, eds., vol. 4, 121.

[5] Johannes Quasten, *Patrologia*, vol. 1 (Madrid: La Editorial Catolica, 1968), 612.

[6] Quasten, 605.

[7] Edgar J. Goodspeed, *The Apolstolic Fathers* (New York: Harper and Brothers Publishers, 1950), 16.

[8] Alexander Roberts and James Donaldson, eds., *The Ante-Nicene Fathers*, vol. 1 (New York: Charles Scribner's Sons, 1925), 240, 243.

[9] Roberts and Donaldson, vol. 1, 89-90.

[10] Roberts and Donaldson, vol. 4, 56.

[11] W. H. C. Frend, *The Rise of Christianity* (Philadelphia: Fortress Press, 1985), 256.

[12] Alexander Roberts and James Donaldson, eds., *The Ante-Nicene Fathers*, vol.1 (New York: Charles Scribner's Sons, 1925), 239.

[13] Roberts and Donaldson, vol. 1, 40.

Chapter 5

Ancient Movements: Monasticism

Abba Antony was baffled as he meditated upon the depths of God's judgements, and prayed thus: "Lord, how is it that some die young and others grow old and infirm? Why are there some poor and some wealthy?" [1]

Someone asked Abba Antony: "What rules shall I keep to please God?" The old man replied: "Keep my instructions, and they are these: Wherever you go, recollect God in your mind's eye. Whatever you do, do it after the example of Holy Scripture. And wherever you stay, be in no hurry to move." [2]

Abba Antony said: "Fish die if they are long out of the water. So monks who dally long outside their cell or with men of the world, lose their will to solitude. ... Perhaps, if we dallied outside, we might lose our inner guard." [3]

Pachomius proceeded to gather around him those who after their conversion, desired through him to come to God. ... He forbade them to concern themselves for the things of this world .... Above all things, he admonished them to renounce the world, their families, and even, in accordance with the Gospel, themselves, so that they might take up their cross and follow the Saviour. [4]

When a monk told him of a vision he had experienced, Pachomius made this reply: "The most beautiful vision is a pious man, and the best revelation is this, when you see the invisible God in that visible man." [5]

Introduction: The Egyptian Monastic Movement

In order to contextualize the early monastic movement, we must explore the political and socio-economic environment in Egypt near the end of the second century. Evangelistic testimony of early apostolic and post-apostolic communities had led to the growth of the Christian church, particularly in urban centers of the Roman Empire. During the first century of its existence, the Christian movement was largely limited to the cities. However, this began to change as a result of intense persecution during the second century. As we explored in the previous chapter, the Montanist movement arose in a rural area in Phrygia, a province of Asia Minor, in the wake of a severe imperial persecutions aimed at the Christians.

The Roman emperor Decius launched the first systematic persecution of universal scope, beginning with the execution of Roman bishop Fabian in January 250. Thousands of Christians were martyred. Some Christians yielded to the pressure, and saved themselves through bribes or other means. This led to a crisis in the church over how to deal with lapsed Christians. In the next chapter, we will explore how this crisis led to the emergence of the Donatist movement at the expense of the church's unity in North Africa. A second wave of persecution was launched about seven years later, under emperor Valerian. Among those martyred in that persecution were Sixtus, bishop of Rome, and the venerated pastor and theologian of the North African church, Cyprian of Carthage.

However, the most unexpected consequences of these persecutions occurred in Egypt. The persecution combined with economic pressures forced many to abandon the cities and villages situated along the Nile in lower Egypt. They fled to the desert seeking safety and survival. The fleeing Christians were joined by peasant farmers from the area who were barely subsisting and were forced to migrate in search of resources. From 250 onward, there was a growing emigration of displaced and persecuted Christians to the semi-desert and desert areas of Egypt.

Antony and Anchorite Monasticism

Historical Sources

The writings of Athanasius, 296-373, bishop of Alexandria, provide the principal description of Antony's life and work. Enigmatic in his attitudes and actions, Athanasius was something of a celebrity in the church of his time. He ardently defended orthodox doctrine against those with dissenting opinions, such as Arius and Melitus. Rather than yielding to the Empire's pressures, Athanasius was willing to live in exile. Although he was comfortable circulating in the official worlds of both the Empire and the church, he was friend and defender of the monks, Antony, Pachomius, and Serapion. Egyptian monasticism became well known throughout the Roman Empire due to the efforts of Athanasius. He authored a biography of Antony, probably written shortly after Antony's death in 356.

Antony's Early Life

Antony, 251-356, was born into a Christian family in lower Egypt. His parents were peasant farmers who enjoyed relative economic independence. Antony, around the age of eighteen, assumed responsibility for the household and his younger sister following the untimely death of his parents.

Several months later, Antony was on his way to a church meeting when it occurred to him that the apostles had given up everything to follow Jesus. Some sold their possessions and shared the money with those in need. At the assembly, he listened carefully to the reading from the Gospel and heard the Lord say to the rich man: "If you wish to be perfect, go, sell your possessions, and give the money to the poor, and you will have treasure in heaven" (Matt. 19:21).

Upon leaving the meeting, Antony gave away his inheritance, some 207 acres of fertile land, so that it would no longer be a burden to him or his sister. Later, he sold his other possessions and gave the money to the poor, saving a few things for his sister.

When visiting the assembly again, Antony heard the voice of the Lord, through the Gospel, say to him: "Do not worry about tomorrow." Antony could not resist the calling. He gave all his remaining possessions to the poor. He placed his sister into the care of a nearby convent. Freed from the cares of the household, Antony dedicated himself to the cultivation of spiritual disciplines.

In a nearby village, Antony met a hermit who had committed himself to a life of solitude, and he sought to emulate the hermit's example. Antony lived in solitude for the next fifteen years on a small plot of land at the desert's edge. He prayed constantly and read the Bible until he had completely memorized large portions of it. He cultivated the arid soil to support himself and to share with those in need.[6]

After fifteen years, Antony left his hermit companions and his humble shelter. He travelled to a mountain in the desert east of the Nile. There, near Pispir, he lived in an abandoned fortification and dedicated himself to a life of solitude as an *anchorite*, which literally means one who retires, or lives as a recluse, in the desert. He remained there until the great persecution of 303, under the emperor Diocletian.

Antony's Struggle with Demons

Christendom has been fascinated by Antony's titanic struggle with demons. It has been a favorite theme in western Christian art. Antony's struggle with the powers of darkness, described with terrifying realism, has also been emphasized in some currents of spirituality within the western Christian tradition. Antony experienced vivid visions of beasts and reptiles breaking through the walls and raging at him. His only protection against these demons was prayer, and prayer was effective. The Lord staved off the demons, and they could not harm Antony. (1)

Antony was convinced that prayer and the ascetic life were the only useful weapons against such demons: "We need not fear their apparitions, for they are nothing and they disappear quickly – especially if one fortifies himself with faith and the sign of the cross."[7] Antony understood the demonic dimensions of both personal and social evil, and this ever-deepening

---

*(1) Athanasius, **The Life of Antony***
The demons, as if breaking through the building's four walls, and seeming to enter through them, were changed into the forms of beasts and reptiles. The place immediately filled with the appearances of lions, bears, leopards, bulls, and serpents, asps, scorpions and wolves. ... The lion roared, wanting to spring at him; the bull seemed intent on goring; the creeping snake did not quite reach him; the onrushing wolf made straight for him .... "Faith in our Lord is for us a seal and a wall of protection." So after trying many strategies, they gnashed their teeth because of him, for they made fools not of him, but of themselves. In this circumstance also the Lord did not forget the wrestling of Antony, but came to his aid.[8]

understanding led him to become an anchorite. In his innermost being, Antony struggled against the demons that attacked him, and with God's grace he prevailed over them.

Antony also struggled against the demons present in Egypt's unjust institutions. Convinced that these were responsible for the economic and social evils that afflicted the people, he fought against them from his secluded retreat deep in the Egyptian desert. He prevailed against these social demons by creating an alternative community, outside the official structures of the time.

Socio-economic Considerations

In his biography, Athanasius emphasized the religious motivations that led Antony to make decisions which determined the extraordinary direction of his life. Athanasius would have the reader think that Antony made all major decisions on his way to church, or on his way back home, inspired by the liturgical services and the union with his congregational brothers and sisters. Antony was, without doubt, motivated by religious considerations. However, he was surely also motivated by fundamental socio-economic considerations.

In his reflections, Antony asked himself: "And why are the rich unrighteous and grind the faces of the righteous poor?"[9] Antony had been a failure in his early life, and had come to question the values of secular society. He was not alone. Ascetic people like himself continued to arrive at Antony's hut in the desert, until they made up a large population of like-minded sojourners. The pressures put upon them by tax collectors were among their reasons for fleeing to the desert.

The community, as described by Athanasius, was made up of tents in the hills. People prayed, sang, fasted, and studied. They maintained peaceful relationships within their community. They lived as equals, neither victims nor perpetrators, but in a social structure all their own, and emptied of traditional hierarchies. (2)

> *(2) Athanasius,* **The Life of Antony**
> *Their cells in the hills were like tents filled with divine choirs – people chanting, studying, fasting, praying, rejoicing in the hope of future boons, working for the distribution of alms, and maintaining both love and harmony among themselves. It was as if one truly looked on a land all its own – a land of devotion and righteousness. For neither the perpetrator nor the victim of injustice were there, nor complaint of a tax collector.*[10]

Athanasius made specific mention of the absence of tax collectors in the anchorite community. There is an interesting etymological connection between anchorite, whose meaning we've already discussed, and the term used by Egyptian tax collectors to refer to the problem of tax evasion. Those who were fleeing to the desert, and escaping the tax collectors, were called *anacoresan*. The flight to the desert had become a form of popular protest against the oppressive conditions imposed by the Ptolemies of Egypt. Now, during the Roman imperial period, the same form of protest was being taken. People fled to the desert to escape forced labor and economic taxation by secular authorities.[11]

Eventually, the term anchorite was applied exclusively to people who had fled to the desert for religious reasons and there practiced an ascetic life. However, religious motivations alone did not lead to the unprecedented growth of both the anchorite movement, and later, under the leadership of Pachomius, the cenobitic movement. In both cases, individuals fleeing from oppression organized alternative monastic communities in the desert, radically different than the conditions and institutions of secular society. The social dimensions of anchorite Christianity were rooted in the teachings of John the Baptist and Jesus himself.

Letters from Emperors

An interesting relationship developed between the desert monks and the emperor Constantine, and his sons who succeeded him, Constantius, and Constans. The socio-political importance of the anchorite movement did not go unnoticed. Although it may seem strange to us, the emperors wrote letters to Antony, addressing him as a father and pleading for a response. Antony was unimpressed by the emperors' advances, for he understood that although they were powerful, they were only men. God's law, as given through Jesus, not the emperors, was the true law. (3)

---

(3) Athanasius, The Life of Antony
[Antony] did not, however, make a great deal of the writings, nor did he rejoice over the letters. ... He called the monks and said, "Do not consider it marvelous if a ruler writes to us, for he is a man. Marvel, instead, that God wrote the law for mankind, and has spoken to us through his own Son."[12]

Antony did not wish to receive letters from the emperors; however, at the insistence of others, he eventually responded. He wrote about salvation and the coming judgement, and advised the emperors that Jesus was the eternal ruler. Antony also asked them to consider the needs of the poor, and to show them justice. (4)

> *(4) Athanasius,* **The Life of Antony**
> *He offered counsel on things pertaining to salvation – that is, not to count present realities as great, but rather to consider the coming judgment, and to recognize that Christ alone is the true and eternal ruler. He implored them to be men of human concern, and to give attention to justice and to the poor.*[13]

Unlike the North African Donatists, whom we will discuss in the next chapter, Antony did not openly express his antipathy toward imperial authority. His attitude reflected a New Testament radicalism which his bishop and biographer, Athanasius, seemed never fully able to understand or appreciate. From his cell in the desert, Antony warned against behaving toward others with cruelty, and tirelessly supported victims of injustice. He advised those who came to him to withdraw from worldly life, and many did. Even some of those in the military service, or in prosperous positions, were swayed by Antony's admonishments, and chose to become monks.[14]

Pachomius and the Cenobite Movement

Pachomius's Early Experiences

Pachomius, 286-346, was born into a pagan family living near Esneh in upper Egypt. His parents were poor peasants and as a child Pachomius was deprived of a formal education. His mother tongue was Coptic, and his social roots were in the lower classes, among the rural outsiders of Egyptian society.

When Pachomius was twenty years old, Constantine became involved in a life and death struggle with pretenders to the imperial throne, and ordered a military mobilization. The young pagan from upper Egypt found himself, along with other young Christian men, conscripted into Roman military service. For reasons unclear, the entire group was imprisoned in Thebes where members of the local Christian congregation compassionately provided for their needs. The group was still incarcerated in Antinoae when Constantine prevailed over his adversaries and issued an imperial edict granting freedom to all conscripts.

Traditionally, church historians have placed great import on Pachomius's apparent military service. Some historians suggest that his military experience impelled the regimented organizational structure which he imposed onto cenobitic monasticism. They have even theorized that Pachomius was the son of a Roman military family, and a soldier. In reality, he was no more than a recruited peasant, conscripted against his wishes, who soon deserted.[15]

These experiences made a tremendous impression on Pachomius. As soon as he was freed, he applied for Christian baptism and dedicated himself to the life of an ascetic. At first, he assumed the solitude of a hermit, becoming the disciple of an elderly anchorite, Palaemon. The two hermits spent their time in prayer and manual labor. They sold their produce and shared with the poor. Pachomius continued this life of semi-solitude for a number of years.

Building a Community

Pachomius was not ultimately looking for solitude. He believed that spiritual fulfillment could be better achieved within a community. Around 330, Pachomius dedicated himself to forming an ascetic community.

An angel appeared to him in a vision and called him by name. The angel directed him to found a monastery in the desert. (5) In response, Pachomius sought to establish a community for those who came to him in the desert in Tabenna. Pachomius's asceticism took a cenobite, or communitarian, form. The term comes from two Greek words, *koinos*, meaning common, and *bios*, meaning life. The major difference between the eremitic life of Antony and the cenobitic practice of Pachomius was the social dimension of the latter movement.

> *(5)* **Leben des Heiligen Pachomius**
> *He was praying alone in the desert of Tabenna when he heard a voice call him by name, and a supernatural radiance flooded his soul. Then an angelic figure spoke to him: "Remain here, Pachomius, and found a monastery, for many will come to you who want to be saved. Direct them according to the rule that I shall give you."*[16]

At the turn of the fourth century, a peasant class of farmers lived in lower Egypt. Many were forced to abandon their lands and villages due to their growing fiscal burden, exacerbated by the extortion and violence employed by law enforcement agents. Some sought the protection of patrons, but risked losing their independence and falling into servitude. Others fled to the desert. The exodus was so great that state-run enterprises complained about losing their sources of cheap labor. Clearly, the Egyptian ascetic movement, in both its anchorite and cenobite forms, offered a palatable alternative to the adverse conditions suffered by the outcast.

Life in these communities was austere and regimented. Day-to-day life consisted of penitential exercises, prayer, and manual labor. According to Jerome's description, brothers shared a household under the direction of a superior. They sought to avoid excesses by fasting, and limited themselves to one meal a day. A rule governing their spiritual discipline prescribed prayer twelve times each day and twelve times during the night. The Eucharist was celebrated twice a week, administered by a clergyman in their midst. The communities were largely made up of laymen. Pachomius tenaciously resisted all pressures to be ordained. Only toward the end of his life did he apparently give in to these pressures.[17]

Discipline was strict. The monks dressed alike. They wore a brown habit with a *capuche*, or large, cape-like hood, a sleeveless tunic, a leather mantle with a belt around the waist, and carried a cane. Household superiors served under the direction of the father, or *abba*, of the monastery, who was responsible to Pachomius until his death in 346, and then to his successor, Theodore.

Like Antony's anchorite movement, Pachomius's cenobite movement was enormously popular. By the year of his death, he had established nine monasteries for hundreds of brothers and two households for sisters. All the communities came together in Tabenna twice a year to celebrate Easter, and the anniversary of the movement's beginning, on August thirteenth. During Jerome's time, around 390, almost 50,000 people gathered in the desert for the celebration of Easter.[18]

The monastic movement represented the most important social change to occur in the Empire during the period following Constantine's rule. Egyptian anchorites and cenobites offered a new approach to Christian spirituality, accompanied by a radically different lifestyle. Pachomius's monasteries were new forms of the rural village. From this time forward, the Christian movement had a solid base in rural, as well as in urban, communities. In the eastern part of the Empire, the continued presence of cenobitic and anchorite men and women changed the shape of Christian communities.[19] However, two centuries would pass before Benedict of Nursia would arrive in Rome with a vision for a monastic community, and a rule under which to order the life of western monasticism.

Conclusion

The Egyptian monastic movement contributed much to western Christianity. Many Christian religious orders have emerged since the Italian hermit, Benedict, *c*.480-*c*.550, formed a small monastic community and prepared an elemental rule to order their common life. All of these groups bear the strong influence of the eastern monastic tradition.

The Order of Cluny, in France, was established in the tenth century. The Cistercians, established late in the eleventh century, were the order from which the Trappists emerged in 1664, with a new program for reform. The Franciscans, organized in 1209, produced a number of reform movements, including the Spirituals, the Observants, and the Capuchins, as well as a second order for women, and a third order for lay persons of both sexes. This opened the order to a wider level of participation than was possible within the traditional structures of Roman Catholicism. In the twelfth century, lay communities for women, Beguines, and men, Beghards, were founded in the Low Countries. The Dominican order began in 1220, and the Society of Jesus, the Jesuits, in 1540.

Monasticism influenced the creation of committed Christian communities, with values and lifestyles which differed from those of society in general. The walls around monasteries fulfilled a symbolic function, as well as a practical one. Monasteries have been communities of contrast, and their non-conformist lifestyles have sent a powerful prophetic message to all Christians.[20]

Monasticism has traditionally derived its lifestyle and values from the Gospels. Those who enter monastic orders have always committed themselves to the "evangelical counsels" or "counsels of perfection," that is, poverty, chastity, and obedience. Their economic practices, personal as well as collective, are communitarian. Chastity has been interpreted as celibacy in all monastic orders in western Christianity, with the exception of the tertiary orders. Obedience to superiors in everything except that which would be a sin is seen as obedience to Christ.

Monastic communities have acted as prophetic minorities in the midst of Christendom, set apart by their different lifestyle. Traditionally, they sought the church's official recognition to justify their existence. By granting them recognition, the established church admitted the need for a counter-cultural and prophetic presence within the church.

However, by seeking the church's official approval, the western monastic movement tacitly recognized the existence of two levels of Christianity, and two means of salvation. One could choose the way of obedient discipleship, summed up in the evangelical counsels, or the way of sacramental salvation, summed up in the sacramental means of grace.

Despite these ambiguities, the mere existence of Christian prophetic minorities has served to denounce materialism, economic injustices, libertine immorality, sexism, and other forms of violence. Insofar as it remained faithful to its ancient desert roots, the monastic movement has been a voice crying in the wilderness, calling all Christians to authentic repentance and salvation.

The presence of this ancient monastic tradition points to the essential sojourning nature of God's people, an incalculably valuable reminder to a church which has made peace with secular powers. The voices of Antony and Pachomius remind us that as God's people we are always sojourners and pilgrims in this world.

Notes

[1] Owen Chadwick, trans., "The Sayings of the Fathers," *Western Asceticism* (Philadelphia: The Westminster Press, 1958), 156.

[2] Chadwick, 37.

[3] Chadwick, 40.

[4] From "Leben des Heiligen Pachomius," quoted in Walter Nigg, *Warriors of God – The Great Religious Orders and Their Founders* (London: Secker and Warburg, 1959), 59.

[5] "Leben des Heiligen Pachomius," 53.

[6] Robert C. Gregg, trans., *Athanasius, The Life of Antony and the Letter to Marcellinus* (New York: Paulist Press, 1980), 30-32.

[7] Gregg, 48.

[8] Gregg, 38-39.

[9] Owen Chadwick, trans. "The Sayings of the Fathers," *Western Asceticism* (Philadelphia: The Westminster Press, 1958), 156.

[10] Robert C. Gregg, trans., *Athanasius, The Life of Antony and the Letter to Marcellinus* (New York: Paulist Press, 1980), 64.

[11] Gregg, n. 95, 138-139.

[12] Gregg, 89.

[13] Gregg, 90.

[14] Gregg, 94.

[15] Jean-Michel Hornus, *It is not Lawful for Me to Fight* (Scottdale, PA: Herald Press, 1980), 142.

[16] From "Leben des Heiligen Pachomius," quoted in Walter Nigg, *Warriors of God – The Great Religious Orders and Their Founders* (London: Secker and Warburg, 1959), 53.

[17] W. C. H. Frend, *The Rise of Christianity* (Philadelphia: Fortress Press, 1985), 577.

[18] Frend, 577.

[19] Frend, 579.

[20] Gerhard Lohfink, *Jesus and Community* (Philadelphia: Fortress Press, 1984), 157.

Chapter 6

Ancient Movements: The Donatists

Constantine Augustus writing to Militiades, bishop of Rome: *Caecilianus, the bishop of Carthage, was accused ... by his colleagues in Africa; ... the multitude are found inclining to deteriorate, and in a manner divided into two parties, and among others, that the bishops were at variance; I have resolved that the same Caecilianus, together with ten bishops, who appear to accuse him, and ten others, whom he himself may consider necessary for his cause, shall sail to Rome. ... Since it neither escapes your diligence, that I show such regard for the holy catholic church, that I wish you ... to leave no room for schism or division.*

Constantine Augustus writing to Caecilianus, bishop of Carthage: As I ascertained that some men, who are of no settled mind, wish to divert the people from the most holy catholic church, by a certain pernicious adulteration, I wish thee to understand that I have given ... the following injunctions; that, among all the rest, they should particularly pay the necessary attention to this .... Wherefore, if thou seest any of these men persevering in this madness, thou shalt, without any hesitancy, proceed to the aforesaid judges, and report it to them, that they may animadvert upon them, as I commanded ....

(Eusebius, *Ecclesiastical History*, X, 5-6) [1]

Introduction: An Overview of the Donatist Movement [2]

Our understanding of the schismatic North African movement, which came to be known as Donatism, relies on the undoubtedly biased records of the established church. Even the Donatists' direct testimony was mediated through the polemical writings of their adversaries.

Donatism, named for the movement's most prominent leader, was one of the most interesting developments in the early church's history. The explosive popular movement spread rapidly across the northern part of the African continent. In 392, Jerome wrote that Donatism had overtaken virtually all of Africa.[3] Even Roman emperors were powerless against the Donatists during the latter half of the fourth century. Throughout North Africa, Roman Catholicism was reduced to a dissident minority.

Challenging the Ecclesiastical Hierarchy

The seeds of the Donatist schism were planted during imperial persecutions under Diocletian in 304-305. Severe persecution induced some church leaders to yield to secular authorities, and they turned over copies of the scriptures with which their congregations had entrusted them. Many North African Christians condemned the cowardly actions of these traitors, or *traditores*, as they were called.

In 311, immediately following the death of Mensurius, bishop of Carthage, the archdeacon Caecilianus was consecrated as bishop of Carthage and primate of the church in North Africa. This sudden move led to further division in the church. Caecilianus was seen by many as an opportunist and an imperialist, of questionable faith, and intransigent in his dealings. Despite popular suspicion otherwise, Caecilianus had not lapsed under persecution, although one of the bishops who consecrated him had. Nevertheless, he lacked the full confidence of the church, and was accused of partiality.

The actions of the *traditores* were popularly condemned by many North African Christians. A group of Christians was detained by imperial authorities in the rural area of Numidia and taken to Carthage for trial. Incarcerated and interrogated, they refused to deny the faith, and declared that anyone who held communion with Christian traitors would not receive the rewards of paradise. These confessors were following the leadership of Cyprian and Tertullian, who believed that the power to bind and to loose resided within the Christian community. Their declaration challenged the ecclesiastical hierarchy, particularly those clergy who had vacillated under persecution, turning over the scriptures to imperial authorities.

Donatism was a popular movement made up of a large group of Christians in Carthage who rejected Caecilianus's leadership. They were joined by many pastors of the rural congregations scattered throughout the province of Numidia. Several factors lent cohesion and solidarity to the movement, including the memory of the recent witness of North African martyrs and confessors, and faithfulness to the theology and example of Cyprian.

Capable and cultured urban leaders showed great sensitivity toward their rural brothers and sisters, who were sincere but often fanatical in their expressions of faith. Among these urban leaders were Macrobius, the adversary of Augustine, Parmesian, the Carthagian who led the movement for thirty years, and Donatus himself. Social differences within the Donatist movement mattered less than the common faith commitment uniting them.

The Church's Imperialist Ties

Political and economic differences contributed to the Donatist schism. Christianity in North Africa had always been decidedly Roman. Latin was the official language of the church, and despite seven centuries of a Christian presence in North Africa, the Bible had not been translated into any indigenous North African language. The Roman imperialist mentality was reflected in the church to the extent that the bishop of Rome was the arbiter of ecclesiastical matters in North Africa. The dissidents recognized the church's imperialistic ties, and referred mockingly to the Catholic church in Africa as "ultramarine," because its bishops were at the service of a distant power.

The indigenous population, living far from Carthage in rural provinces such as Numidia, tended to be poor. The Catholic elite, living in the capital city of Carthage, had strong socio-economic ties to Rome. Many indigenous peoples, such as the Berbers of the Numidian plateau, found that Donatism gave them hope in their struggle for survival, and a forum from which to protest the injustices inherent in the socio-economic order. The alliance between North African lower classes and leaders of rural Numidian churches fundamentally contributed to the emergence and growth of the Donatist movement.

In the interest of maintaining the political unity of the Empire, Constantine convoked the parties involved in the North African conflict to an imperial audience in Rome, in the presence of the Roman bishop. The result of this meeting was that Constantine arbitrarily decreed Caecilianus innocent. In North Africa, there was strong resistance to the imperial decree. The most serious and committed sector of the North African church responded to the outcry by electing their own bishop, Mayorinus, who was consecrated by Numidian bishops. The schism was now a concrete reality.

In 317, Constantine ordered that Donatist properties be confiscated and their church leaders exiled. However, Constantine's attempts to impose a solution onto the crisis simply served to confirm the convictions of many African Christians that there existed a fundamental enmity between civil powers and the church. Finally, in 321, Constantine grudgingly accepted the Donatist movement. By this time, Mayorinus had died and the schismatic group had consecrated Donatus as their new bishop.

Consecrated in 316, Donatus was a gifted leader. He was an eloquent orator, and his adversaries sometimes accused him of arrogance. Intelligent, cultured, and charismatic, he inspired confidence and loyalty among his followers, who soon called him "Donatus the great," a decidedly uncommon sobriquet for an ecclesiastical leader. He was "the pride of the church of Carthage and a man clothed with the glory of a martyr."[4] According to popular opinion, Donatus possessed the power to work miracles. Even Augustine, his strongest adversary, called Donatus "a precious stone" because of his writings, none of which survived.[5]

The Decline of the Movement

Donatus led the movement until 350. During this time, the church loyal to Rome had become a minority in Christian North Africa. Of course, there were deficiencies in the Donatist movement which became increasingly evident during its long period of absolute ascendency. Despite its beginnings as a dissident movement of outsiders, Donatism became, *de facto*, an established church.

Donatists began to show an unbecoming spiritual arrogance and elitism, evident in some of their actions and declarations. (1) The Donatist church enjoyed enormous popularity in Africa, and people joined in ever-increasing numbers, including those who lacked the ardent conviction which had first led to the emergence of the movement. By turn of the fifth century, the Donatists' adversaries found themselves struggling against a movement that was already in decline.

> *(1) Ascribed to Donatists*
> *It is not fitting that the sons of the martyrs and the spawn of* traditores *should assemble together.*[6]

Around the turn of the fifth century, the relationship between Catholics and Donatists was largely characterized by polemics. Augustine of Hippo was the principal spokesman for the Catholics in these debates. In 405, the imperial authorities again intervened in the conflict. An imperial edict, celebrated in Carthage, was issued proscribing the Donatist movement. However, despite being declared heretical by imperial authorities, and despite its weakened internal condition, the Donatist movement survived until the beginning of the eighth century. At that time, what was left of Christianity in North Africa was swept away by the forces of Islam, initiating the long period of Islamic dominance in the region.

A Community of the Spirit

The doctrine of the Holy Spirit was important to the Donatist movement, as it had been to the North African church during the time of Tertullian. Donatists saw the church as a community of those chosen by God, who awaited their destiny in the eschatological harvest. Using the same imagery as had their predecessors, Cyprian and Tertullian, the Donatists envisioned the church as the garden of God and the ark of salvation.

The Spirit of God informed the life of the church, and its source was found in the Bible. The presence of the spirit could be seen in the actions and virtues of the people: the martyrs, the confessors, the believers. (2) For the Donatists, to be a Christian was to be like the bishop and martyr, Marculus, who spoke always from the Bible, and carried the possibility of martyrdom in his heart.[8]

> *(2)* **The Acts of Saturninus, XX:**
> *In our church, the virtues of the people are multiplied by the presence of the Spirit. The joy of the Spirit is to conquer in the martyrs and triumph in the confessors.*[7]

A Disciplined and Holy Community

The vision of Donatus, and of the movement that bore his name, was simple. Just as God was one, His church was also one, and its primary characteristic was holiness. The Donatists believed that the integrity of the church was rooted in the integrity of its members, who committed themselves to faith through baptism, and lived in unity with their pastors.

They demonstrated their faith through repentance, and through their suffering witness under persecution. A Donatist's ultimate goal was to suffer a martyr's death. They believed that only those within the chosen community would find salvation. The Donatists were not interested in seeking imperial favor, global influence, or even in claiming universality. In fact, the Donatist movement was closer in character to the North African Christian communities of the previous century than were their contemporary adversaries, Caecilianus and the Catholic church.

"Where is the church?" This question was hotly debated by Donatists and Catholics. The Donatists' response was very simple. They believed that the church was in Africa, in the Donatist community. They defended their separation from Caecilianus and his followers by arguing that the blessed must walk their own path, not the path of the impious. (3)

(3) Bishop Petilian, quoted in Augustine, **The Letters of Petilian, the Donatist,** *II, 46-107*
In the first Psalm David separates the blessed from the impious, not indeed making them into parties, but excluding all the impious from holiness. "Blessed is the man that walketh not in the counsel of the ungodly, nor standeth in the way of sinners."[9]

Augustine was confronted by sincere groups of Donatist pastors and laymen who were convinced that Augustine and his group were the "sons of the *traditores*."[10] Donatus, like Montanus before him, believed that the church's holiness was manifested in the life of its members, rather than through the invisible spiritual presence of Christ. Augustine, the representative voice of the Catholics, believed that the church's holiness depended on its sacred institutions.

The problem of how to treat Christians who yielded under the pressure of persecution had been present in the North African church since the days of Cyprian. Both Donatists and Catholics were willing to restore lapsed Christians to the church's fellowship, provided that they first sincerely repented. However, the Donatists went further than the Catholics and demanded purity of the clergy. They believed that the sacraments lost their validity if they were administered by clergy guilty of mortal sin. In AD 400, the Donatist bishop Petilian argued that the clergy's conscience must itself be clean in order to cleanse the consciences of those baptized by him. (4)

> *(4) Petilian*
> *What we look for, is the conscience of the giver [of baptism] giving in holiness to cleanse that of the recipient. For he who knowingly receives faith from the faithless receives not faith but guilt.*[11]

At the turn of the fifth century, Augustine dedicated a dozen years to combating the Donatist movement. A result of this polemic was that the Catholic church clarified and defined its position on a number of points under question. Augustine defended the Catholic position on the church's universality against the Donatists. Augustine insisted that only in a truly universal church can God's promises to Abraham be fulfilled. Therefore, the church's authenticity depended on continued fellowship with the apostolic community throughout the entire world.

Augustine believed that the church on earth was a "mixed body," made up of the pure and the impure, and that separation of the two would not occur until the last judgement.[12] (5) Augustine's explanation did not clarify the difference between the world and the church – both seemed to fall into the same metaphor of the field, where wheat and weeds were left to grow together – and his answer didn't satisfy his Donatist adversaries.

In Augustine's rendering, the church was the true people of God, made universal through its sacraments, and whose head and root were not individual ministers but Christ alone. Thus, the validity of the sacraments was guaranteed, no matter who administered them, and the means to grace were objective.

> *(5) Augustine,* **The Letters of Petilian, the Donatist,** *III, 2-3*
> *[T]he field is the world – not only Africa; and the harvest is the end of the world – not the era of Donatus.*[13]

A Community of Martyrs

Members of the Donatist movement suffered great persecution at the hands of imperial authorities. However, persecution did not incite the Donatists to armed revolution, but prepared them to expect martyrdom. In 411, in a consultation with Catholics in Carthage, the Donatists made a confession of faith, identifying themselves as a people who "suffer[ed] persecution, but d[id] not persecute."[14]

Persecution was instigated by other Christians – the Catholic church in alliance with imperial authorities – and was the lot of the faithful. Like Tertullian a century and a half earlier, Donatus taught that persecution was the divine medium which distinguished the just from the unjust. To both leaders, salvation and suffering were intimately related.

Rural churches on the Numidian plateau were passionately devoted to the memory of their martyrs. Urns containing the ashes of martyrs were placed beneath the altars of their modest chapels, which had been built, by the congregations, according to the design of ancient basilicas. The martyrdom of Christians was a constant theme in their worship.

These highland chapels in rural Numidia reflected the essence of the Donatist movement. Each chapel was dedicated to the memory of a group of martyrs whose lives of witness unto death provided the focus for the religious life of the community. Every Christian hoped to be buried someday within the walls of his or her chapel. Their faithfulness to their beliefs was probably without equal in the Greek and Roman world of the period.[15]

Social Protest and the Donatist Movement

During the rule of Constantine's successors, the olive plantations of North Africa were expanded and the industry grew. A large imperial bureaucracy emerged to support the commercialization of the product, which led to higher taxes. Much of the rural population was subjected to extortion by cruel, abusive officials. People struggled against debt and the possibility of falling into servitude.

By the middle of the fourth century, rural North Africa had become predominantly Christian. Rural Christian communities were increasingly alienated from the urban Catholic hierarchy, divided by social and economic differences. The Donatist movement provided a forum from which to protest these socio-economic injustices.

The Circumcellions emerged out of this socio-religious context around 340. The movement began as a social protest in the tradition of the martyrs, and of Maccabean inspiration. They claimed to be Donatists, but were unwilling to submit to their pastors' authority. The Circumcellions formed roving armed bands and sought to vindicate the rights of the oppressed. Their tactics included seizing and destroying the records of rich creditors. They made threats and committed acts of violence which carried both symbolic and concrete weight.[16]

The Circumcellions, the extremist wing within the Donatist movement, actively opposed not only the religiously oppressive imperial authorities, but social and economic oppressors as well: large landholders, rich creditors, and the upper classes in general. These social revolutionaries claimed that their actions were justified by biblical authority. Devoted to the memory of the martyrs, they lived in expectation of a martyr's death. Some fanatical militants even sought out martyrdom, hurling themselves from cliffs in the mountains. They lived on provisions ransacked from Christian chapels in rural Numidian villages. The Circumcellions were probably the first Christian group to confront, openly and violently, the existing social order. In many ways, they anticipated the agro-biblical movements of Europe in the late Middle Ages.[17]

The Circumcellions and the Donatists shared an open animosity toward imperial power. The former used violence to defend the poor and the outcast against economic and social oppression. The latter limited themselves to non-violent forms of protest, although this often resulted in persecution, exile, and even death. Both groups were not merely opposed to the Roman Empire, as a political institution, but to the "world," which they saw as being under Satanic domination. The Empire was simply the concrete and visible agent of demonic power.[18]

The Relationship Between Church and State

Constantine

The Donatist protest was primarily concerned with the constitution of the church, not dogmatic matters. Donatists insisted on choosing pastors recognized for their moral integrity and untarnished reputations. They believed that church discipline should be exercised by Christians in congregations or regional assemblies, not by secular authorities.

Constantine acted as a political authority interested in forging harmonious relationships between groups of Christians in the Empire. In order to maintain unity, Constantine stood behind Caecilianus, the bishop of Carthage whose appointment had caused much controversy. Constantine hoped that his own Christian example would positively influence the dissenters. (6) He effectively appointed himself a vicar of God. Donatus' question, directed to adversaries in the Catholic church, aptly and eloquently summed up the Donatist protest: "What has the Emperor to do with the church?"[20]

> *(6) Constantine,* Letter to Domitius Celsus
> *With the favor of the divine piety I shall come to Africa and shall most fully demonstrate with an unequivocal verdict as much to Caecilianus as to those who seem to be against him just how the Supreme Deity should be worshipped.*[19]

The Donatists' antipathy toward the state only increased when imperial authorities violently repressed some of their practices, such as the rebaptism of lapsed clergy. Instead of healing the schism, these coercive actions simply increased the number of martyrs venerated by the Donatist movement.

Augustine: Christians Persecuting Christians

In its polemic against the Donatists, Augustine of Hippo became the principal spokesman for established Christianity. At first, Augustine insisted that heretics be treated with tenderness. However, in the heat of debate, he was moved to justify violence against schismatic Christians in order to "compel people to come in."[21] Augustine effectively laid the theological foundation for the imperial policies of Theodosius, for whom heterodoxy would be a crime punishable by the state. Augustine did not believe there was room in the church for minority opinions or practices. (7) In vain Cresonius, his Donatist adversary, argued that truth had often emerged among minorities.

> *(7) Augustine,* **Of True Religion**, *IV, 6*
> *[The church is] the true mother of all Christians.*[22]

The persecution of Christians at the hands of other Christians was the last step in the process begun when Constantine granted special privileges to the orthodox clergy associated with Caecilianus, and denied it to the Donatists. In letters and debates between 399 and 412, Augustine justified the state's intervention in the religious life of its subjects, and thereby legitimized religious persecution.

Augustine traced the origin of the state to the fall of Adam. The state was the divine medium for maintaining law and order on the earth. With Constantine's conversion to Christianity, the emperor was divinely commissioned to protect the security of the church so that it could dedicate itself to its mission of universal salvation. However, the Donatists, steeped in the biblical tradition of the Old and New Testaments, believed that there was fundamental opposition between the state and the church, vividly signified by the state's repression of heretics and schismatics.

Augustine ignored the protests of Donatists. He believed that the relationship between church and state could be envisioned in terms of "the two swords," a theory based on the dubious exegesis of Luke 22:38.[23] The theory suggested that two divinely commissioned agents, the church and the state, would exercise spiritual and temporal authority over society.

Confident in his theory, Augustine did not hesitate to request help from secular authorities in the church's struggle against heretics and schismatics. Augustine made this request not only out of concern for the eternal salvation of his adversaries, the Donatists, but also because he feared a social revolution. The principles and ideals of Donatism might encourage the indigenous population of North of Africa to rise up against their absentee landlords. Augustine believed that relationships between the classes were determined by divine order, and therefore a Roman Africa was the will of God.[24]

The Intervention of Imperial Authorities

In 396, Augustine appealed to the imperial authorities in Hippo to intervene in the activities of the Donatists. Augustine believed that the Donatists were not merely schismatics, but dangerous heretics whose activities were illegal. He invoked repressive official action because he thought it would be the most effective means of quelling the Donatist menace.

In a letter, Augustine explained that he first believed that no one could be forced to love Christ. His opinion was changed when he saw that coercion had unified his own town, once swayed by the Donatist teachings, and now safely under the wing of the Catholic church. (8)

---

(8) Augustine, **Letters,** *XCIII*

Originally my opinion was, that no one should be coerced into the unity of Christ, that we must act only by words, fight only by arguments, and prevail by force of reason. ... But this opinion of mine was overcome, not by the words of those who controverted it, but by the conclusive instances to which they could point. ... My own town, which although it was once wholly on the side of Donatus was brought over to the Catholic unity by the fear of imperial edicts.[25]

In the same letter, Augustine invoked the parable told in Luke 14:23, in which the rich man "compel[led] people to come in" to his house to share in a feast. Augustine used the text to justify the violent persecution of the Donatists and to compel them to follow orthodoxy. This was not a common interpretation of this text, yet Augustine's questionable exegesis would come to characterize certain strains of western Christendom.

Augustine, once a sensitive, thoughtful young man, became in his old age one of the fathers of the Inquisition. The leaders of the Inquisition in the Middle Ages claimed Augustinian authority for their actions. Likewise, the edict of Theodosius, which authorized the use of the death penalty against Donatists who rebaptized lapsed Christians, was invoked in the sixteenth century by imperial authorities who were seeking to repress the Anabaptists.

Despite the severe restrictions placed on the Donatist church by the imperial decree of 412, Augustine remained intransigent to the end. In 417, Boniface was sent to Africa to serve as governor and military commander of Roman Africa, and Augustine became deeply attached to him. While Boniface was guarding the southern border of Numidia, his wife died. Deeply affected by the death of his wife, Boniface considered abandoning his military career for the monastic life. Upon learning of this, Augustine wrote to Boniface, persuading him to continue serving God as a soldier. He urged him to consider that active military service was a gift to God, and that peace could be obtained only through the waging of war. (9)

> *(9)* **Letters of St. Augustine,** *189, 4, 6*
> *Do not think that it is impossible for any one to please God while engaged in active military service. ... Think, then, of this first of all, when you are arming yourself for battle, that even your bodily strength is a gift of God. ... For peace is not sought in order to the kindling of war, but war is waged in order that peace may be obtained.*[26]

Augustine's struggle against Donatism led him to abandon the biblical vision of *shalom* and accept that of the *pax romana*. He eventually formulated an apology for military service as a Christian vocation. Augustine argued that warfare was only evil when it arose out of human cruelty or savagery or the lust for domination. War that promoted peace, and was waged on God's behalf, was good and Christian. (10)

> *(10) Augustine,* **Reply to Faustus the Manichaean,** *XXI, 74-75*
> *What, indeed, is wrong with war? ... No one should ever question the rightness of a war which is waged on God's command. ... God commands war to drive out, to crush or to subjugate the pride of mortals.*[27]

Conclusion

In 430, the year of Augustine's death, Roman Africa fell into the hands of Vandals, who dismantled the structures of the Catholic Church. Christianity continued to exist precariously in North Africa for another century, thanks to the ongoing commitment of the outsiders, the poor, and the oppressed, who had been the dynamic force behind the Donatist movement. In this ironic manner, the values held by the Donatist movement of an earlier period were vindicated.

Notes

[1] Christian Frederick Cruse, trans., *Ecclesiastical History of Eusebius Pamphilus* (Grand Rapids, MI: Baker Book House, 1958), 429-432. Both introductory quotes are drawn from this source.

[2] This section relies largely on the following source. W. H. C. Frend, *The Rise of Christianity* (Philadelphia: Fortress Press, 1985), 653-683.

[3] Frend, *The Rise of Christianity*, 653.

[4] Walter Nigg, *The Heretics* (New York: Alfred A. Knopf, 1962), 112-113.

[5] Nigg, 112-113.

[6] Nigg, 113. Originally quoted in F. Ribbeck, *Donatus and Augustine* (1857), 441.

[7] W. H. C. Frend, *The Rise of Christianity* (Philadelphia: Fortress Press, 1985), 654.

[8] Frend, *The Rise of Christianity*, 654.

[9] Philip Schaff, ed., *Nicene and Post-Nicene Fathers*, vol. 4 (New York: Charles Scribner's Sons, 1901), 558.

[10] W. H. C. Frend, *The Rise of Christianity* (Philadelphia: Fortress Press, 1985), 655.

[11] Frend, *The Rise of Christianity*, 654.

[12] Philip Schaff, ed., *Nicene and Post-Nicene Fathers*, vol. 4 (New York: Charles Scribner's Sons, 1901), 598.

[13] W. H. C. Frend, *The Rise of Christianity* (Philadelphia: Fortress Press, 1985), 669.

[14] Frend, *The Rise of Christianity*, 655.

[15] Frend, *The Rise of Christianity*, 656.

[16] Frend, *The Rise of Christianity*, 572-573.

[17] Frend, *The Rise of Christianity*, 573.

[18] Frend, *The Rise of Christianity*, 573-574.

[19] W. H. C. Frend, *The Early Church* (Philadelphia: Fortress Press, 1982), 131-132.

[20] Walter Nigg, *The Heretics* (New York: Alfred A. Knopf, 1962), 114.

[21] W. H. C. Frend, *The Rise of Christianity* (Philadelphia: Fortress Press, 1985), 672.

[22] Frend, *The Rise of Christianity*, 670.

[23] Frend, *The Rise of Christianity*, 671.

[24] Frend, *The Rise of Christianity*, 671.

[25] Frend, *The Rise of Christianity*, 671.

[26] Philip Schaff, ed., *Nicene and Post-Nicene Fathers*, vol. 1 (New York: Charles Scribner's Sons, 1901), 553-554.

[27] John Helgeland, Robert J. Daly, and J. Patout Burns, *Christians and the Military: The Early Experience* (Philadelphia: Fortress Press, 1985), 81-82.

Chapter 7

Medieval Movements: Peter Waldo and the Waldensians

In the Roman Council celebrated under Alexander III, we saw Waldensians, simple and uncultured people, so named for Waldo, their head, who lived in Lyon, on the Rhone. They presented to the Pope a book, written in Gallic, that contained the text and explanation of the Psalms, and many other writings from the Old and New Testaments. They asked that they be authorized to preach – thinking that they were prepared for this – when, in reality, they were not capable of anything more than the very simplest rudiments. ... They go about two by two, barefoot, without baggage, holding everything in common, like the apostles. Nakedly, they follow a naked Christ. If we were to grant to them a place along side ourselves, we would be the ones to be cast out.
(Walter Map, *De nugis curialum*). [1]

Realizing that the activity of the clergy was impregnated by avarice, simony, pride, anxiety, concupiscence, false glory, concubinage, and other evils ... so has he chosen you, Waldo. He has charged you with the apostalate, in order to supply, together with your companions, what is lacking among the clergy and to struggle against error. (Durando de Huesca, *Liber antiheresis*) [2]

Introduction: Socio-Economic and Religious Context [3]

The Feudal System

The reforms carried out under Pope Gregory VII, 1073-1085, led to the increased institutionalization of the church. Early in 1077, the emperor, Henry IV, was humiliated during the struggle between the Roman Curia and the Empire. Church power was centralized as congregations lost the right to elect their bishops. Lay participation in the church was severely reduced. A century later, under Innocent III, the papacy reached its height of worldly power. The ecclesiastical hierarchy had absolute influence in the Empire.

The church did not reject the feudal system of the period, but became its patron and protector. Arable land was the most valuable asset of the time. The chain of feudal relationships guaranteed social cohesion. Serfs who worked the lands swore their allegiance to landed gentry, who swore allegiance to higher nobility. The entire social fabric was held together by oaths of allegiance, which were blessed by the church. Any rupture in these relationships was punished by religious and civil sanctions.

The populations of cities in southern France and northern Italy were swelling, and the center of gravity was shifting from rural areas to urban centers, where a new mercantile social class was growing. The church was unwilling to recognize or respond to these social and economic developments.

The Cathar Movement

The church saw its power questioned in the twelfth century, when the Cathar crisis in southern France threatened official Christendom. The Cathar movement had spread rapidly among the oppressed classes, and the lower nobility. The Third Lateran Council in 1179 was convened to combat the movement.

In its early stages, the Cathar movement was inspired by an ideal of apostolic poverty. Over time, its posture changed. The Albigenses, as the Cathars were known in southern France, denounced the superfluous riches of the church. However, the movement also enjoyed the support of the emerging mercantile class and the feudal nobility. To maintain this support, the Albigenses recognized the legitimacy of the former, something the church had not yet granted, and tolerated the latter, because their presence protected the movement in its dissent against the church.

By 1170, French Catharism had become strong enough, institutionally, to compete with the Catholic Church in its struggle for influence and power. However, by this time the ideal of apostolic poverty, on which the movement was originally founded, was no longer an important tenet of faith to the Cathars.[4]

The expansion of the Cathar movement in southern France coincided with social change. Feudalism was losing its exclusive hold on the rural population. The rural economy was becoming increasingly influenced by merchants and artisans. It was within this context that Peter Waldo, a rich merchant from Lyon, renounced his wealth. The church had long since institutionalized the expression of poverty, but Waldo was not interested in entering a monastery, nor was his renunciation an end in itself. Waldo renounced his wealth so that he might preach the gospel with integrity. He wanted to practice apostolic poverty.

Origins of a Movement: Peter Waldo

Why would a rich merchant from Lyon choose to renounce his wealth and preach the gospel, despite overwhelming opposition? Peter Waldo was no ordinary merchant, and several unusual experiences may have influenced his decision.

Translating Scripture

Around 1250, Stephen of Bourbon, the Dominican inquisitor in Lyon, described Waldo as a man who had somehow discovered the Gospels.[5] Indeed, in an effort to better understand the Gospels, Peter Waldo engaged a monk to translate a number of scriptural selections into the vernacular. The venture turned out to be costly, and the translator was partly compensated for his work with an oven. The popular Bible, entitled *Sentencias*, was composed of selections drawn from the Gospels. Waldo read them so often that he memorized the entire text. (1)

Peter Waldo's decision to read and interpret the Gospels for himself meant that

(1) **De Septem Donis Spiritu Sancti**
In the same way, they translated several books from the Bible and selections from the Church Fathers, all gathered together under the title, Sentencias. *By reading and rereading them, Waldo eventually memorized them.*[6]

he had to break from old loyalties and commitments. Waldo belonged to a new urban class of merchants and artisans, which was in the process of finding a niche for itself within the traditional feudal system. However, after learning the Gospels by heart, Waldo could not share in their struggle to obtain power. He was convinced that the gospel message could only be preached by those who embraced apostolic poverty.

The Legend of Saint Alexis

Several stories of Waldo's conversion were recounted two or three centuries after the event. One such story told how Waldo was greatly moved by the legend of Saint Alexis. One Sunday, Waldo and some of his fellow citizens listened to a traveling troubadour sing about the legend of Saint Alexis. Alexis had been born into a patrician Roman family. Although he had always been attracted to a life of chastity, his parents forced him to marry. On the night of their marriage, Alexis and his bride-to-be committed themselves to virginity, and Alexis fled to the Holy Land and became an anchorite.

After many years, Alexis returned to his paternal home as a beggar. He was emaciated due to his austere lifestyle, and his family did not recognize him. Nevertheless, they let him stay under the courtyard steps and eat scraps from their table. He was subjected to servants' taunts. Only in death did Alexis reveal his true identity to his family. It was too late for restitution.[7] As the story went, Waldo invited the troubadour home so that he could listen to the song more carefully. Utterly moved by the experience, Waldo set out to imitate the life of the saint.

It is improbable that the legend of Saint Alexis influenced Waldo's decision to convert. However, the story reflected the popular perception of Waldo, who was still alive in the people's memory generations later. The itinerant troubadour – a person without privilege or social standing, who chose to lead an adventurous, uncertain life – played an important role in this story. Perhaps in the popular imagination the troubadour's lifestyle inspired the itinerant ministry of Waldo and his disciples. Whether or not this was the case, Waldo believed that freely-assumed poverty was essential to the freedom of evangelical preaching.

The Convent of Fontevrault

Another story from the same source recounted that Peter Waldo entrusted his two daughters into the care of the convent of Fontevrault. The convent's founder, Roberto d'Arbrissel, strongly supported the poor. (2) He had organized groups of men and women who dedicated themselves to an itinerant ministry.

> **(2) Patrologia latina**
> *[Roberto d'Arbrissel] evangelized the poor, he invited the poor, the poor people are the ones who gathered about him.*[8]

D'Arbrissel wanted the groups' evangelical lifestyle to be a testimony in and of itself. However, the bishop would not permit him to pursue such a revolutionary course. D'Arbrissel was allowed to share his vision with peasant women, women from the streets, and women from the houses of ill repute. These women were his disciples, whom d'Arbrissel called the "poor ones of Christ."[9] D'Arbrissal offered the women a sense of dignity and self-worth unheard of in medieval Christendom.

The close connection between Peter Waldo and Roberto d'Arbrissel may or may not be apocryphal. However, the connection remained in the popular imagination long after Waldo's death, and certainly reflected the spirit of the early Waldensian movement. Female ministry was very important to the early life of the movement.[10]

Confrontation and Excommunication

Although their essential teachings were different, the Waldensian movement and the Cathar movement both opposed church wealth and advocated poverty. The established church did not approve of either movement. While the church could not reproach Waldo's choice to assume poverty, he had not done so under the institutional auspices of the church. Waldo did not become a monk; instead, he chose poverty so that he might preach the gospel with integrity. In truth, the church was indifferent to poverty, or its absence. What the church really opposed was lay preaching, particularly by the poor, the unlettered, and women. The church opposed Waldo because these people could actively participate in his version of Christian witness.

In 1178, Waldo appeared before the Papal Legate in Lyon where he was forced to sign an orthodox confession of faith, to prove that he did not share the heretical beliefs of the Cathars. In 1179, some of Waldo's followers appeared before the Third Lateran Council, which had been called to counteract the Cathar threat. The Waldensians were interrogated by a theological commission which did little more than ridicule their ignorance of the sophisms, so popular among medieval scholastic theologians.

Another attempt to end lay preaching occurred at the Council of Verona in 1184. Sanctions, including definitive excommunication, were approved for those who, without authorization, took "upon themselves the right to preach, even though the Apostle may say: 'How shall they preach unless they are sent?'"[11] Authorization, of course, could be granted only by the Apostolic See, or the resident bishop.

The established church confronted this apparent heresy with violent repression. The papacy and the Empire were united in their struggle against the dissidents. When the Waldensians returned to Lyon, after this final hearing before the Council, they were met by an official prohibition against public preaching. Despite the warning, they continued to preach. They were eventually excommunicated and expelled from the city. According to the tradition, Waldo is said to have invoked the words of Peter: "We must obey God rather than men."[12]

This itinerant ministry of preaching contrasted sharply with prevailing monastic attitudes, and the sporadic episcopal preaching. The Poor Ones of Lyon, as the itinerant preachers were known, traveled in pairs throughout the countryside, as had Jesus' followers in the Gospels. Waldo was remembered as a traveling pilgrim, who preached the gospel to the poor. He died around 1206 at an unrecorded place in France, leaving behind the Poor Ones of Lyon, heirs to his mission of gospel preaching.

Expansion of the Movement

Waldo's followers first pursued their missionary witness in Languedoc, a province in southern France which had been a hotbed of Cathar activity.

His disciples attempted to "restore to the Cathars a taste for the pure gospel."[13] According to their beliefs, anyone who could share God's word could join the mission.[14]

The church did not hold the same opinion. In medieval Christendom, preaching the gospel was the task of the bishop of a diocese, or of another person authorized by him. Even those in the Order of Preachers, known as the Dominicans, were strictly limited to preaching within their assigned territories. The Waldensian mission was in direct conflict with the feudal, civil, and ecclesiastical visions of Christendom. The bishop in Languedoc reported their civil disobedience to the secular authority, Alphonse II of Aragón, who ordered them to leave his territories.

Our understanding of the early Waldensian movement is mediated by the writings of their adversaries. The early Waldensian message arose out of the scriptures, especially the Sermon on the Mount. They prohibited the oath, condemned all violence and killing, and advocated a life of freely-assumed poverty. Their adversaries observed that the Waldensians had great success converting women, the weak, the naive, and the unlearned, clearly implying that strong, mature men were too wise to be swayed by the Waldensian message.

Despite vicious persecution by episcopal inquisitions initiated by bishops and papal legates, the Poor Ones of Lyon continued to preach. Moving about clandestinely, they preached throughout Europe, from the Balkans to the Low Countries, and from Spain to the shores of the Baltic. The canon of Notre Dame commented that he believed that a third of all Christendom had attended these Waldensian conventicles.

A Tributary of the Movement: The Poor Lombards

The Lombardian movement began among groups of lay Christians in Milan and other cities of Lombardy. They shared a common life of work and worship, and were drawn to message of the Poor Ones of Lyon.

The Poor Lombards held Waldo's missionary vision in high esteem, and decided to unite in a confraternity. However, they had a strong sense of community, and a profound respect for manual labor. The Poor Lombards were not, in short, traveling missionaries. They gave evangelical testimony as artisans and merchants, and refused to accumulate wealth for capital investment. It was said of them: "They do not buy houses or vineyards."[15] They created an alternative to feudal life, and resisted the dominant values of mercantilism.

After Waldo's death, the Poor Ones of Lyon and the Poor Lombards converged, although not without certain difficulties. In the long run, the Waldensian movement was enriched by the presence of both currents. While the Poor Ones of Lyon carried on the tradition of itinerant preaching, the Lombardian communities offered witness to a communitarian alternative to the materialism of the time. The Waldensian movement would eventually be organized on two levels: the "friends," who were dedicated to living in an alternative community, and the "Poor Ones," who were dedicated to a life of itinerant evangelization.

In 1215, at the height of his papal powers, Innocent III convened the Fourth Lateran Council. At this Council, the Waldensian movement was absolutely condemned. The Council declared that only the Catholic church could offer salvation. Anyone acting outside of the church's authority would be promptly excommunicated, and punished unless he showed penitence. (3)

> *(3) The Fourth Lateran Council, 1215*
> *All those who ... dare to usurp publicly or privately the office of preaching, without the authority of the Apostolic See, or of the Catholic bishop of the area, shall be bound by the ties of Excommunication, and, promptly, if he shows no penitence, be punished with another appropriate penalty.*[16]

Fundamental Characteristics of the Movement

Common People

During the early centuries of its existence, the Waldensian movement spread primarily through the lower social classes. Lay people preached to lay people, and freely assumed poverty in order to do so. The mission tended to attract common people: poor city dwellers, artisans, villagers, peasants, and a disproportionately large number of women. These people were victims of the feudal system. They distrusted the sophisms of scholastic theology, and were suspicious of the great universities at which the ecclesiastical authorities studied. Medieval Waldensianism was never an intellectual movement. Nevertheless, its message did not go unnoticed, and its influence was felt even in circles of power and culture.

Eventually, severe persecution limited the Waldensians to clandestine activities. The presence of the movement in urban centers became difficult to sustain. No longer able to preach publicly, the ongoing growth of the movement relied on the transmission of faith from parents to children. The witness of the Poor Ones became more pastoral and less missionary. But the movement survived. Their message was passed along by word of mouth, and confirmed by martyrdom. They were living witnesses to the gospel message.

It is impossible to determine how many people joined the Waldensian movement, but the number was considerable. In 1235, an adversary of the movement estimated that the Poor Lombards had 8,000 members.[17] Eighty years later, a Waldensian martyr estimated that the movement had 80,000 followers, although this was probably an exaggeration. During the time of Pope John XXII, 1316-1334, upwards of 500 people would gather in the valleys of northern Italy for the Waldensian assemblies. Near the end of the fourteenth century, the Waldensians recorded regular attendance of 700-1,000 people at their synods.[18]

The Free Assumption of Poverty

The economic practices of medieval Waldensians set them apart from contemporary society. Led by Peter Waldo's example, the Poor Ones of Lyon believed that by choosing to live in poverty, they would be freed from their servitude to money, and to the system it represented.

Many among the Poor Lombards were already poor, victims of a feudal system that valued them as mere instruments of agricultural production, and potential defenders of their lord's interests. For these people, the Waldensian movement offered an alternative to the feudal system. They could organize themselves into independent communities of artisans and workers, rather than submit to the values of the emerging mercantile system.

The poverty that characterized the Waldensian movement was a form of evangelical protest, directed against the economic attitudes and practices which prevailed in medieval Christendom. Without setting out to achieve this goal, the movement became a subversive element in society, an agent of liberation for the poor, its values in direct opposition to those of the church. (4)

---

(4) Observations made by inquisitors in central Europe, 1270
They live as laborers, from the work of their hands. Their teachers are weavers or shoemakers. They do not accumulate money, being content with only the necessities. ... They are hard workers, but they find time to teach and to study. They dedicate time to prayer. They attend church, participate in worship, go to confession, take communion and listen to preaching, but they do this in order to note the mistaken ideas of the preacher.[19]

In medieval society, the poor were not simply those who lacked material necessities. They included outcasts who had been deprived of their civil rights, manual workers, day laborers, peasants living in servitude, the handicapped, and single mothers. As far as we know, the majority of Waldo's followers came from these groups. The inquisitors referred to all Waldensians as a "race of damnable outcasts."[20]

Questioning the Established Order

Medieval Waldensianism radically questioned the established order. The movement offered a Christian presence and solidarity to those disinherited and oppressed by mainstream society. The Waldensians renounced not only their worldly goods, but also the political and economic power that accompany such things. They lived in anticipation of the coming rule of God. They knew from reading the gospel that God would have mercy on the "little ones" before the powerful.

The medieval church expected more of its monks than of Christians in general. The monks were to follow the counsels of perfection, which included teachings from the Sermon on the Mount, but lay Christians were not so obliged. However, the Waldensians believed that all Christians should follow these counsels. Therefore, they refused to swear oaths of loyalty, and avoided all use of the sword in the interest of establishing justice, be it civil or ecclesiastical.

The oath played an important role in medieval Christendom. The stability of the social hierarchy was based on oaths of loyalty. Refusing to swear an oath amounted to the rejection of the established religious and civil order. The Waldensians were severely persecuted for abstaining from swearing such oaths. However, they were simply acting in a manner consistent with the gospel message. They believed that life within the Christian community should be independent of political structures.

> **(5) Amedeo Molnar, 1981**
> *The Waldensians of the thirteenth and fourteenth centuries were rebels, but not revolutionaries, and their non-violence was not an abstract principle, theoretically rigid, but the consequence of an option assumed in favor of their little brothers in the Lord, of an active solidarity.*[21]

The Waldensian movement consistently renounced all forms of violence. (5) They protested the church's sacred right to co-opt temporal power for its own benefit. The Waldensians did not believe that scripture, such as Romans 13, justified the use of the sword to benefit the dominant authority. They heeded Jesus' warning against the misuse of power so commonly exercised by kings of the nations[22] (Luke 22:25-26).

The Role of the Bible

The Waldensian movement was based on reading and interpreting the Bible. They read the scriptures in the vernacular, and memorized entire passages. In the days before printing presses, manuscript copies were costly and rare, and the message was often passed on orally, by memory.

By reading and studying the Bible, the Waldensians developed a biblical spirituality which contrasted sharply with medieval Catholic spirituality. The Waldensians questioned much of church's liturgy: holy places, articles of worship, images of Christ, bells, organs, the veneration of Mary and the saints, and papal jurisdiction. Some Waldensians in central Europe even compared the liturgical chants of medieval Catholicism to "the barking of dogs."[23]

Biblical study led to doctrinal differences between the Waldensians and medieval Catholicism. The Waldensians no longer believed in purgatory, which played an important penitential role in the Catholic church. The

Waldensians rejected the practice of interceding through the saints. They didn't recite the church's prescribed prayers, but freely composed their own. In short, they protested the established church's claim that grace could only be found inside its sacramental institutions.

A typical Waldensian meeting was held out of doors, at nightfall, under the direction of an itinerant brother. An opening prayer was followed by a sermon based on text taken from the Gospels or the Epistles. The participants listened to the message, and invited the visiting brother into their homes for food and fellowship.

An official inquisitorial report, made in 1388, offered a description of one of these supper meetings. It described the blessing and breaking of a simple loaf of bread which was then shared among all who were present. The Eucharist was a deeply communitarian celebration shared by all members. In principle, any brother or sister might preside over the celebration. (6)

> **(6) Inquisition report, 1388**
> [O]ne of them placed a loaf of wheat bread in the hands of the minister who blessed it, broke it and gave it to each of those who were present ... and they, one by one, kissed the bread and then ate it. Next, an old woman, after she had taken the first sip, passed the cup to all.[24]

After studying the Bible, the Poor Ones of Lyon reclaimed their right to baptize, and even to repeat baptism if the earlier ritual had been administered by an unworthy priest. They followed the example of the early Donatists.

Communities of Faith

The Poor Ones of Lyon began as a community of traveling preachers. There was no immediate need to define the movement as an ecclesiastical institution. Its mission was purely charismatic. The Poor Lombards changed all that. Their communities of faith and work altered the shape of the Waldensian movement, providing the common social base needed to sustain the ministry. These communities came to be known as "friends," while the preachers continued to be called "Poor Ones," or simply "Brother" or "Sister." These simple names were found among Waldensians from Lombardy, in Italy, to the shores of the Baltic sea, in the north.

After persecution had forced the Waldensian movement into a clandestine existence, the Poor Ones became teachers charged with the instruction of the friends. With some variations, Waldensian communities spread throughout Europe, giving rise to a functional distinction between charismatic ministries and the laity.

In the fourteenth century, the Brothers were increasingly involved in pastoral roles, as confessors and spiritual counselors, and less given to evangelical preaching. They were called "the sandaled ones," "teachers," "apostles," "messengers," and "barbas." Barba comes from the Latin word, *barbanus*, meaning uncle, and became the customary title among Waldensians in the Alps. These titles reflected the variety of roles played by the preachers, and the affection the friends had for them.

In principle, there was equality among the Waldensian teachers. In practice, the Brothers who dedicated themselves to itinerant preaching were given more authority. The elders among the itinerant ministers gathered together each year to co-ordinate their mission, which was considered more important than the pastoral ministries, probably out of respect for the origins of the movement.

Conclusion: The Survival of the Waldensian Movement

Waldensianism survived a long period of clandestinity, with members living principally in the Alpine valleys of northern Italy. In the sixteenth century, a majority of Waldensians joined in the Protestant Reformation. The movement was aligned with the Reformed Calvinist tradition. This led to renewed persecution. During eleven days in June 1569, the Waldensian population of Calabria was decimated by Spanish troops. Over 2,000 Waldensians died, and 1,600 were taken prisoner. Many more were condemned to the galleys. Waldensians were not granted religious freedom in Italy until 1848.[25]

Today, Waldensian churches are found throughout Italy, from the Alps in the north, to Sicily in the south. Large groups of Waldensians emigrated to Uruguay and Argentina at the end of the nineteenth century, where they still exist today. The Waldensians have a theological seminary in Rome, located almost in the Vatican's shadow.

Notes

[1] Amedeo Molnar, *Historia del Valdismo Medieval* (Buenos Aires: Ediciones La Aurora, 1981), 21, 29. My translation. Walter Map was the English delegate before a commission of the Third Lateran Council.

[2] Molnar, 38. My translation. Durando de Huesca was one of Waldo's disciples.

[3] This section relies largely on the following source. Molnar, 11-12.

[4] Molnar, 28.

[5] Molnar, 13.

[6] Molnar, 13. My translation.

[7] Donald F. Durnbaugh, *The Believers' Church: The History and Character of Radical Protestantism* (Scottdale: Herald Press, 1985), 42.

[8] Amedeo Molnar, *Historia del Valdismo Medieval* (Buenos Aires: Ediciones La Aurora, 1981), 15. My translation.

[9] Molnar, 15-16.

[10] Molnar, 15-16.

[11] Molnar, 37. My translation.

[12] Molnar, 38.

[13] Molnar, 41. My translation.

[14] Molnar, 45. My translation. The Poor Ones of Lyon insisted that the evangelizing mission belonged to "all who were able to share with others around them, the Word of God."

[15] Molnar, 67. The statement was made by Juan de Ronco, a Lombard leader and spokesman.

[16] Enrique Denzinger, *El Magisterio de la Iglesia* (Barcelona: Editorial Herder, 1955), 154, 157. My translation.

[17] Amedeo Molnar, *Historia del Valdismo Medieval* (Buenos Aires: Ediciones La Aurora, 1981), 140. The adversary was Salvo Burci.

[18] Molnar, 141.

[19] Molnar, 161. My translation.

[20] Molnar, 151. My translation.

[21] Molnar, 159. My translation.

[22] Molnar, 94.

[23] Molnar, 179.

[24] Molnar, 180. My translation.

[25] Donald F. Durnbaugh, *The Believers' Church: The History and Character of Radical Protestantism* (Scottdale: Herald Press, 1985), 50.

Chapter 8

Medieval Movements: Francis of Assisi and the Little Brothers

The rule and life of these brothers is this: to live in obedience, in chastity, and without anything of their own, and to follow the teaching and the footprints of our Lord Jesus Christ, Who says: "If you wish to be perfect, go and sell everything you have and give it to the poor, and you will have treasure in heaven; and come, follow me." (The Earlier Rule, I, 1-2) [1]

Introduction: Francis of Assisi

Francis of Assisi, 1181-1226, was born Giovanni Bernardone in the town of Assisi, sixty miles northeast of Rome in the central part of the Italian peninsula. The son of a fairly well-to-do cloth merchant, he spent his early years working with his father. During his youth, Francis was known for his rebellious and spirited nature. At the age of twenty, he was conscripted into the armed forces, and called to defend his hometown against the commercial ambitions of the neighboring city, Perrugia.

In the course of this conflict, Francis was taken prisoner, and held hostage for several months. He spent this time reflecting on the mutually destructive rivalries between neighboring towns. When Francis was finally free to return home, he was in poor health, and deep in the throes of a personal crisis. His experiences in prison would lead him dedicate himself to an itinerant life of prayer, in service to the world's outcasts. [2]

During a visit to Rome, Francis was profoundly touched by the miserable condition of beggars on the steps of Saint Peter's Cathedral. He exchanged clothing with one of them and spent the day begging alms. After this experience, Francis increasingly dedicated himself to serving the needy, particularly lepers, for whom he felt special compassion. (1)

Francis also sought to repair Saint Damian chapel, near Assisi, which was in ruins. After Francis sold some of his father's merchandise to fund his service to the needy, he was disinherited.

> *(1) Francis of Assisi,* **The Testament**
> *When I was in sin, it seemed very bitter to me to see lepers. And the Lord Himself led me among them and I had mercy upon them. And when I left them that which seemed bitter to me was changed into sweetness of soul and body.*[3]

Francis spent the next four years traveling the countryside near Assisi, ministering to the needy, and restoring churches in need of repair. The Porciuncula chapel, located on the outskirts of Assisi, was his favorite. It was there, one Sunday, that he heard the same message that had moved Peter Waldo some thirty years earlier. (2) Both men were inspired by Christ's instruction of his apostles: "As you go proclaim the good news, 'The kingdom of heaven is at hand.' ... Freely you received, freely give" (Matt. 10:7-8).

> *(2) Francis of Assisi,* **The Testament**
> *The Most High Himself revealed to me that I ought to live according to the model of the holy Gospel.*[5]

Francis lost no time putting this vision into practice. He gave away his shoes and cane, and dressed in a long dark tunic tied at the waist with a cord. Francis freely assumed a life of poverty, and took on a ministry of itinerant evangelization.

The Little Brothers

Official Recognition

Francis was soon surrounded by a small band of men who had answered a similar call. Francis prepared a primitive rule to order the common life of the group. The rule was based on biblical texts that described Jesus teaching his disciples. Accompanied by a dozen companions, Francis took his rule to Innocent III, and requested official ecclesiastical recognition for the new movement. Innocent III represented the epitome of papal ambition and power in the medieval church. Nevertheless, recognition was granted in 1210. The new association was originally called "the Penitents of Assisi." Francis himself called them the Little – or humble – Brothers, or the Order of Friars Minor.

The Little Brothers were dedicated to the imitation of Christ. They travelled about two by two, preaching repentance, singing, helping peasants in the countryside with their labors, and poor village artisans with their tasks, and caring for lepers and others in need. (3)

Francis was able to recognize the gracious presence of the Lord in the midst of ordinary people who shared their bread with the hungry. This insight was radical at a time when Christian salvation was couched in the sacraments, and the sacraments were effectively unrelated to everyday existence.

> *(3) Francis of Assisi,* **The Testament**
> *Let those who know no trade learn one, but not for the purpose of receiving the price of their toil, but for their good example and to flee idleness. And when we are not given the price of our work, let us resort to the table of the Lord, begging our bread from door to door.*[5]

Social Significance of the Little Brothers

Francis of Assisi lived in a changing society. People sought to free themselves from the oppressive structures of feudalism, but the emerging system of mercantile capitalism, which was replacing feudalism, possessed its own dangers.

Medieval society was made up of "the little ones," or the *minores,* and "the great ones," or the *maiores*. The rural *minores* were victims of the feudal system, and the urban *minores*, victims of price inflation, lived under the constant threat of being conscripted into local and imperial warfare. Everyone feared new outbreaks of the plague. In contrast, the *maiores* were powerful, wealthy, and comfortable. Assisi itself was divided between these two social groups.

Francis's pilgrimage began when he rejected his family's emerging mercantile values, and chose to live in solidarity with the poor. He sought to restore dignity to the humiliation of poverty. However, his mission did not end there. Francis deeply respected all human beings, rich as well as poor. He did not judge those who did not renounce their material wealth. Francis considered himself a servant to all. He warned his rich brothers that a purely materialistic lifestyle would prevent the authentic liberation experienced through genuine sacrifice.

The Franciscans freely assumed poverty. They did so not only to experience inner, personal peace, but to promote social, common peace. The bishop of Assisi complained that the austerity assumed by the little brothers was exaggerated. Francis explained that the desire to acquire and accumulate and conserve worldly goods frequently led to violence against one's neighbor. (4) In Francis's view, choosing a life of poverty promoted social peace and justice.

Francis's selfless service to the poorest of the poor, and his compassion for the oppressor, as well as the oppressed, were expressions of a truly radical perception of human relationships, inspired by Jesus' teachings. Francis's loving concern extended to creatures of the natural order as well. His vision of God's love for all of creation was remarkable in its wholeness. Francis's *Canticle to Brother Sun* offers an example of this vision.[7]

> *(4) Francis to the bishop of Assisi*
> *My lord, if we should have possessions, we should need arms to protect ourselves. For thence arise disputes and law suits, and for this cause the love of God and of our neighbor is wont ofttimes to be hindered, wherefore we be minded to possess naught of worldly goods in this world.*[6]

Clare and the Poor Ladies of Assisi

In 1212, two years after the Little Brothers received papal approval for their mission, a women's branch, know as "the second order," was established.

Clare Sciffi of Assisi, 1194-1253, was the middle child of five, born into a wealthy family. Clare was twelve years younger than Francis. As a youth growing up in Assisi, she no doubt heard people talking about Francis, the strange young radical who had chosen such an unusual lifestyle. Clare was attracted to Francis's way of life. When her uncle arranged her marriage to a wealthy young man, Clare refused. With the help of a house servant, she sought out Francis to ask for his counsel.

On Palm Sunday, in 1212, the bishop of Assisi handed Clare a palm branch that symbolized martyrdom. The following day she was received at the Porciuncula chapel by Francis and the Little Brothers. There, she took vows to become his follower. Francis and the Brothers accompanied her to the Benedictine Convent, where she was soon joined by other like-minded women. Before long, the new movement was transferred to Saint Damian, the first chapel that Francis had restored. The group came to be known as the Poor Ladies of Assisi.

Francis and Clare shared a tender, respectful relationship which was not bound by the gender expectations of the period. Medieval society was strictly patriarchal, and women were treated as either idealized, romantic figures, or as objects of sexual conquest. The Franciscans were celibate and chaste, in part because this symbolized their respect for women.

Clare lived in the convent for forty-two years, and witnessed the growth of the movement. Within a relatively short period of time, daughter communities were established in Italy, France, and Germany. The women lived in greater austerity than was practiced in the Benedictine and Dominican communities. The daughter communities were less strict than the original community at Saint Damian, which observed its vows of absolute poverty until after Clare's death in 1253.

The Poor Ladies of Assisi were valued participants in the Franciscan community. Francis recognized that women had the same privilege and duty to participate in a community of apostolic poverty as did men.

The Franciscan Tertiaries

Participation of Lay People

A third order of Penitent Brothers and Sisters was established in 1221, upon the initiative of either Francis, or his friend and patron, Cardinal Ugolini of Ostia. Called the Tertiary Franciscan Community, it was organized so that lay people who were involved in the secular world could still participate in the movement. Many lay people in the medieval church were looking for a way to live out their faith in the spirit of the mendicant orders, but did not wish to abandon their families.

Men and women, living in normal family situations, could practice the way of justice and peace, and do works of mercy and charity. The Tertiaries sought to lead lives of evangelical perfection, despite the limitations placed on them by their secular vocations. It is not a coincidence that there were striking similarities between the Tertiary Penitents and the Waldensian friends, movements which took place during the same period of history. Each movement responded in its own way to a spiritual hunger not satisfied by the contemporary Christian church.

Cardinal Ugolini was probably chiefly responsible for organizing the Tertiary Penitents of Assisi, but Francis's example gave them inspiration. With him, they shared the simplicity of a common life, modest dress, the renunciation of dubious pleasures, and works of mercy.

Practices of the Tertiary Penitents

The Tertiary Penitents practiced a mystical spirituality of deep meditation, prayer, and confession. However, they expressed this spirituality through concrete works of mercy and charity. At their common assemblies, they read the Bible and took offerings for the needy among them. They exercised communitarian discipline, and did not appeal to ecclesiastical or civil authorities to resolve their conflicts.

The Tertiaries were forbidden to take up arms against their neighbor, no matter what the cause. Many lay people were attracted to the movement because of this pacifist privilege. They wished to free themselves from the feudal obligation of military service. Conscientious objection to military service was a right until 1289, when participation in the military was justified in defense of the fatherland, the church, and the Christian faith.

The Tertiary Penitents were forbidden to swear oaths of loyalty, with certain exceptions established by the Pope himself. This undermined the fundamental structure of the feudal system, which was based on such oaths. It is hardly surprising that this provision was severely attacked by civil authorities.

Conscientious objection to militarism proved impossible to sustain under the circumstances, and the Tertiaries yielded to the church's pressures. Nevertheless, the movement introduced a spirit of peace and unity into medieval society. Francis wanted all Christian brothers and sisters to share in a simple life, dedicated to serving society's outcasts.

The Early Franciscans and the Waldensian Movement [8]

The Franciscan Order and the Waldensian movement had similar origins. The Franciscans emerged in central Italy, and the Waldensians in southern France and northern Italy. The Waldensian movement preceded the Franciscans by scarcely thirty years.

Francis and Waldo were both members of the newly emerging mercantile class. Both men were inspired by the life of the Messianic community gathered around Jesus, as described in the Gospels. When confronted by the call to follow Jesus, both men reacted in similar ways. They believed that apostolic poverty was essential to the church's mission, and embarked on similar missions of itinerant preaching. The groups that they founded, The Little Brothers and the Poor Ones, sought to be incarnate examples of the gospel.

Attitudes Toward Ecclesiastical Authority

The most notable difference between the Franciscans and the Waldensians, was that the former was given a priestly character and status by the Pope, something the latter would never accept. Although Francis was personally reticent, the Franciscans willingly submitted to the Holy See, and obtained the church's approval. In 1210, Francis and his earliest followers were ordained as priests, and received their tonsures from ecclesiastical authorities. From that day onward, Francis never expressed doubts about the church's authority. In this way, the church was able to control what could have been a radical, dissenting movement, like the Waldensians had proven to be.

Francis and Waldo practiced evangelical obedience in different ways. Francis believed that Christ's authority was found in the church; therefore, he felt obliged to submit to ecclesiastical authority. Waldo distinguished between Christ's authority and the authority claimed by the ecclesiastical establishment. Waldo's attitude did not arise out of any sense of individualism, but reflected his criticism of contemporary Christendom's anti-evangelical social dimensions. Francis and Waldo were treated differently by papal authorities because they practiced evangelical obedience differently. It is probably too much to suggest, as has professor Albert Hauck, "that it was purely a matter of chance that Waldo became a heretic rather than a saint."[9]

"Protect Us From Heresy"

The Fransiscans and the Waldensians had a similar appreciation for honest and productive manual labor. Francis and Waldo never considered work a curse or a punishment for sin, but a valuable, worthy task. However, the decision to submit or not to submit to the church's authority would take the two groups in different directions. Around 1218, when the groups were in the process of making these decisions, some of Francis's disciples met up with some followers of the Lombardian Waldensians. The startled Franciscans are said to have exclaimed: "Lord, protect us from the heresy of the Lombards and from the barbarism of the Germans!"[10]

For the Franciscans, the recovery of evangelical poverty became the way to Christian perfection, reserved for small groups within the church's authority. For the Waldensians, the recovery of evangelical poverty became a way of identifying with the disinherited masses, and expressing solidarity with the oppressed poor. Only as a persecuted minority could the movement lead the church toward obedience to its Lord.

The Franciscans and the Waldensians shared a desire to incarnate the gospel within contemporary society. Both maintained contact with an increasingly urbanized society, while seeking to cultivate an intimate and direct relationship with God within their faith communities. Both movements protested the oppressive structures of the feudal system, and the alienating, materialistic values of new urban structures.

Conclusion

In 1230, four years after the death of Francis, the Testament that defined relationships within the order of the Little Brothers, or Minor Brethren, was modified by Pope Gregory IX, allowing them to hold property. This decision was not unanimously supported within the order, and led to the formation of a dissident group called the Spirituals. In 1318, in an attempt to resolve the conflict, Pope John XXII again authorized the order to hold property. At this time, many of the Spirituals left the order, and became known as the Fraticelli, or the little brothers.

Around the turn of the fifteenth century, after a period of laxity during which the Franciscans considerably increased their economic resources, a reformist Observant group broke from the main body. The Observants received ecclesiastical recognition at the Council of Constance in 1415. In 1517, after a century of co-existing with the Conventuals, the Observants were declared the true order of Saint Francis. Only a few years later, another reform movement led to the organization of the Capuchins, who sought to restore primitive simplicity to the order. A rule governing the common life of this new group was granted approval in 1529.

The Order of Saint Francis has always been dedicated to popular preaching and missionary service. Although it was not instituted as a scholarly order, it has produced many celebrated scholars throughout its history. In recent years, Franciscans in the third world have offered outstanding examples of service and scholarship. Among these, the brothers Leonardo and Clodovis Boff, of Brazil, are the best known.

Francis of Assisi, the Poverello or poor little one, was willing to risk everything, including his very life, to attain his ideals. He dared to confront materialism and socially-instituted violence. He was a prophetic voice, calling us toward the path of authentic human liberation.

Notes

[1] Regis J. Armstrong and Ignatius C. Brady, *Francis and Clare: The Complete Works* (New York: Paulist Press, 1982), 109.

[2] Armstrong and Brady, 121-122. "The Lord says: 'Behold, I am sending you as lambs in the midst of wolves.' Therefore, 'be prudent as serpents and simple as doves.' Therefore, any brother who, by divine inspiration, desires to go among the Saracens and other nonbelievers should go with the permission of his minister and servant. ... As for the brothers who go, they can live spiritually among [the Saracens and nonbelievers] in two ways. One way is not to engage in arguments or disputes, but to be subject 'to every human creature for God's sake' and to acknowledge that they are Christians. Another way is to proclaim the word of God when they see that it pleases the Lord. ... And all the brothers, wherever they may be, should remember that they gave themselves and abandoned their bodies to the Lord Jesus Christ. And for love of him they must make themselves vulnerable to their enemies, both visible and invisible, because the Lord says: 'Whoever loses his life for my sake will save it in eternal life.'" (*The Earlier Rule*, XVI, 1-3, 5-7a, 10-11).

[3] Armstrong and Brady, 154.

[4] Williston Walker, *A History of the Christian Church* (New York: Charles Scribner's Sons, 1959), 235.

[5] Walker, 235.

[6] Ray C. Petry, *Francis of Assisi: Apostle of Poverty* (New York: AMS Press, 1964), 62.

[7] Armstrong and Brady, 38-39. "Most High, all-powerful Lord, / Yours are the praises, the glory, the honor, and all blessing. / To you alone, Most High, do they belong, / and no man is worthy to mention Your name. / Praised be You, my Lord, with all your creatures, / especially Sir Brother Sun, / Who is the day and through whom You give us light. / And he is beautiful and radiant with great splendor; / and bears the likeness of You, Most High One. / Praised be You, my Lord, through Sister Moon and the stars, / in heaven You formed them clear and precious and beautiful. / Praised be You, my Lord, through Brother Wind, / and through the air, cloudy and serene, and every kind of weather /through which You give sustenance to Your creatures. / Praised be You, my Lord, through Sister

Water, / which is very useful and humble and precious and chaste. / Praised be You, my Lord, through Brother Fire, / through whom You light the night / and he is beautiful and playful and robust and strong. / Praised be You, my Lord, through our Sister Mother Earth, / who sustains and governs us, / and who produces varied fruits with colored flowers and herbs. / Praised be You, my Lord, through those who give pardon for Your love / and bear infirmity and tribulation. / Blessed are those who endure in peace / for by You, Most High, they shall be crowned. / Praised be You, my Lord, through our Sister Bodily Death, / from whom no living man can escape. / Woe to those who die in mortal sin. / Blessed are those whom death will find in Your most holy will, / for the second death shall do them no harm. / Praise and bless my Lord and give Him thanks / and serve Him with great humility." (*The Canticle of Brother Sun*).

[8] This section relies largely on the following source. Amedeo Molnar, *Historia del Valdismo Medieval* (Buenos Aires: Ediciones La Aurora, 1981), 71-74.

[9] Donald F. Durnbaugh, *The Believers' Church* (Scottdale: Herald Press, 1985), 45 n. 13.

[10] Amedeo Molnar, *Historia del Valdismo Medieval* (Buenos Aires: Ediciones La Aurora, 1981), 73.

Chapter 9

Medieval Movements: John Wyclif and the Lollards

And Jesus confirming his testament said to his apostles after his rising from death to life, my Father sent me and I send thee, that is to travail, persecution, and poverty and hunger and martyrdom in this world, and not to worldly pomp as clerics having secular lordship, with array of worldly vanity, being hugely cursed of God and man .... (John Wyclif, *Poor Priests*, B)[1]

This is clear: each one ought, to the limit of his ability, to follow Christ in his manner of life. (John Wyclif, *On the Pastoral Office*, I 2)[2]

Preaching the gospel exceeds prayer and administration of the sacraments ... it is the most precious activity of the Church. (John Wyclif, *On the Pastoral Office*, II, 2)[3]

Introduction: Turbulent Times

Black Death

John Wyclif, 1328-1384, was born in England during a time of social, political, economic, and religious turbulence. These factors undoubtedly affected the development of Wyclif's radical beliefs.

The bubonic plague, or black death, as it was popularly known, swept through Europe and reached the coast of England in 1348-49. An estimated one-third of the English population perished. At times there were scarcely enough able-bodied people to bury their dead. This created enormous demographic and economic imbalances in English society. The fear of imminent infection and death was so widespread that normal economic activity was brought to a standstill.[4] The plague decimated the population, and as the work force diminished throughout the countryside there was a severe short-term drop in the prices of agricultural products.

Anarchic Social Conditions

The short-term drop in prices of agricultural products created a dramatic increase in wages for many people, from clergy and craftsmen, to the most menial agricultural workers. The king froze wages to combat this imbalance. Many workers and craftsmen refused to comply with these regulations and were imprisoned for civil disobedience. Those who escaped fled to the forests. Social conditions became anarchic at the local level, and the cost of living skyrocketed. The price of food and other necessities soon became exorbitant.[5]

In 1349, King Edward III and the Council of Government made a royal decree that drastically countered the rise in wages and prices. The measure was aimed at freezing the wages of all workers and craftsmen at 1346 levels. In 1351, in another attempt to contain inflation, an even more drastic decree froze workers' wages. Thus, the burden of the economic crisis was shifted to those who occupied the lowest levels in English society.

During the proceeding decades, additional official attempts to freeze workers' wages were unsuccessful. People chose to become vagabonds rather than submit to such exploitative conditions. The disinherited and outcast shared a growing antipathy toward the landholding nobility, who were allies of the crown.[6]

The Burden of Taxation

A growing social and economic malaise troubled the English feudal system. Three more decrees, which imposed heavy personal taxes on the population, were implemented between 1377 and 1381. The crown was seeking to defray the costs of the nation's external wars. These taxes placed an onerous burden on the lowest social classes, exacerbated by abuses in tax collection. During the summer of 1381, there was an armed uprising against the nobility, who had used extortion and violence to collect taxes from the peasants. Fed by general discontent among the rural population, the conflagration spread throughout England until it was finally crushed by the king's army.[7]

John Wyclif's Ideas

John Wyclif studied at the University of Oxford. He received a master's degree in 1358, and a doctorate in 1372. His public career began when he was appointed to a commission charged with resolving a conflict relating to the Roman Curia. The conflict was over tributes levied by the Pope, who claimed feudal dominion over King John of England. Out of this debate, Wyclif first developed his theories on the nature of lordship. He later expounded these ideas in two works: *De dominio divino*, 1375, and *De civili dominio*, 1376.

Authority and Lordship

In *De dominio divino*, Wyclif expressed his opinion that divine lordship underpinned the exercise of all human authority. Divine lordship was not diminished when its exercise was delegated to humans, but authority was no more than a loan granted for the common good. It was neither permanent nor unlimited. Therefore, one who exercised authority should not be called lord, but rather a steward of the sovereign Lord. The exercise of authority over the world's resources, natural and human, was a gift of God's grace.

In *De civili dominio*, Wyclif concluded that all authority, exercised over humans or nature, was conditioned by the faithfulness of the one exercising it. Therefore, a poor, humble person who was faithful claimed a greater moral right to exercise lordship than did a pope or emperor who wielded power unjustly. Only the just could exercise lordship legitimately. Applying this theory to the exercise of ecclesiastical authority, Wyclif held that a Christian was lord only when he or she was servant of all.

Wyclif denied that the church had the authority to grant or accept bequests in perpetuity. Only God had the right to grant anything in perpetuity, and the church's dignitaries were not lords, but stewards. Principally, Wyclif argued that unjust ecclesiastical authorities lacked the right to exercise power over the properties to which they laid claim. These could therefore be confiscated by legitimate civil authorities.

Wyclif did not apply his theory to the state. In other words, he did not suggest that anyone had the right to revolt against an unjust civil regime. Wyclif forbade the use of force against the existing government, even if it were tyrannical. He advised subjects to submit to civil authority. Therefore, it would be unfair to hold Wyclif responsible for inciting or justifying the peasant rebellion of 1381.

Like many others, Wyclif believed that all members of the clergy should live in apostolic poverty. He argued that the source of the church's ills was to be found in the riches of prelates, priests, and monks. Wyclif enjoyed the early support of many among the mendicant orders. He traced the roots of the church's corruption to the donation of Constantine, on which the church based its claims to economic and secular power. (1)

> *(1) John Wyclif*
> *[Constantine] poured poison into the church.*[8]

Wyclif thought that the church should take primary responsibility for solving these ills, and through the exercise of ecclesiastical discipline, should strip unworthy clergy of their offices and wealth. However, the church's hierarchy was corrupt, and with rival claimants to the papacy in Avignon and Rome, was not inclined to discipline itself. Secular powers took on the duty of reforming the church.

Wyclif proposed that confiscated wealth be used to provide for the needs of the poor. As might be expected, the English monarch took advantage of Wyclif's proposals, and enriched the throne at the expense of his old enemy, the Roman Curia. Thus, the English peasants were freed from one set of tyrants, and delivered into the hands of another.

The Authority of Scripture

Wyclif espoused a vision for reform based on the authority of scripture. He honored biblical authority over scholastic theology and the papal claims of the period. He believed that the church's traditions, the decisions of the ecumenical councils, papal decrees, and all other doctrinal formulations should be measured against the biblical norm. This explains Wyclif's interest in translating the scriptures into the vernacular.

Wyclif insisted that everyone dedicated to the ministry of the church lead a life modeled on scripture. All messengers of God must live in apostolic poverty. A life unworthy of the gospel invalidated a minister's sacramental activity. Spiritual authority grew out of an authentically evangelical life and service, rather than an ecclesiastical appointment. An ethic inspired by the gospel also guided the lifestyle practiced in Lollard communities. For example, in 1395, eleven years after John Wyclif's death, the Lollards presented a pacifist petition to the English parliament. They claimed that homicide in battle or at the hands of the law was contrary to the New Testament teachings of grace and mercy.

The True Church: An Invisible Community

Despite his obvious respect for biblical authority, Wyclif had an Augustinian understanding of the church. The true church, he said, was an invisible community made up of those predestined for salvation, and known only by God. Therefore, participation in the institutional church was no guarantee of salvation. This view allowed him to criticize severely the ecclesiastical institution of his time. From 1380 onward, Wyclif was convinced that the pope was really the Antichrist.[9]

Wyclif's ecclesiology was not entirely consistent. Wyclif actively supported the Lollard movement of itinerant evangelization, which contributed to the formation of concrete ecclesial communities. The Lollard conventicles were highly visible in their practices. Wyclif had developed his theory of the true church as an invisible entity during his struggle with Roman Catholicism, but his practical understanding of the church arose out of his participation in the visible mission of the English Lollards. Wyclif did not acknowledge the inconsistencies between his theory and practice.

A Heterodox View of the Sacraments

Wyclif criticized the eucharistic doctrine of the medieval church. Looking to the practices and teachings of the primitive church, Wyclif maintained that the consecrated elements – the bread and the wine – were symbols of the body and blood of Christ. Christ was figuratively, sacramentally, and effectively present in the elements, but not in the material or fleshly sense claimed by the modern church.[10] (2) These heterodox arguments cost Wyclif the support of many of his English defenders, including the king, John of Gaunt, scholarly colleagues at Oxford, and friends in the mendicant orders.

These views reflected the practices of the Lollard communities. The last years of Wyclif's life were dedicated to forming a community of poor preachers. The Lollards' primary mission was evangelization, not the administration of sacraments. Until the day of his death in 1384, Wyclif maintained that the Scriptures were a sufficient basis for the life of the church.

> *(2) John Wyclif,* **The Eucharist**
> *The modern church proposes transubstantiation of bread and wine into the body and blood of Christ; but the primitive church did not hold this; therefore they disagree in opinion.*[11]

In 1415, the Council of Constance condemned 267 errors found in Wyclif's writings, and ordered them destroyed by burning. It also ordered that Wyclif's body be exhumed, his remains burned, and the ashes scattered to the far reaches of the oceans. This order was carried out in 1428.

The Lollards[12]

The Lollard movement developed in England during the fourteenth century, and its members were poor preachers dedicated to an itinerant ministry. They traveled the country barefoot, dressed in rustic robes, and spreading an evangelical message. In the minds of the English people, a Lollard was associated with John Wyclif. However, it is not clear whether or not Wyclif was actually responsible for formation of the movement.

It is certain that the relationship between Wyclif and the poor preachers was close. The Lollards were largely responsible for spreading Wyclif's ideas. They realized Wyclif's great dream: the evangelization of the English people in their mother tongue.

As he grew older, Wyclif became increasingly indifferent to the philosophical aspects of theology, and interested instead in the practice of authentic faith. In his latter years at Oxford, Wyclif ceased to worry what his colleagues might think of him. He was solely interested in bringing the living Christ into the lives of common people.[13] Using his professorship at Oxford as his base of operation, he prepared theological tracts and sermons for the poor preachers who would popularize his ideas in the English villages and countryside.

Practices of the Lollards

Lollard preachers included Nicholas of Hereford, dedicated to translating the Vulgate version of the Scriptures into the English vernacular, and John Aston, known for his fearless preaching. Lollard preaching consisted of a simple exposition of the Scriptures, and occupied a central place at the gatherings of conventicles. The Sermon on the Mount, the Lord's Prayer, the Ten Commandments, and the Apostles' Creed, all spoken in the mother tongue, were mainstays of the meetings. There were reports of participants learning vast amounts of scripture by heart.[14]

We do not know how many people participated in the Lollard movement. Few members were detained by secular authorities, but there is reason to believe the movement was widespread and that multitudes attended the secret meetings. Areas of England where the Lollard movement was strongest were the same areas in which the dissident Anabaptist movement took root most rapidly in the sixteenth century.[15]

Principal Characteristics of the Lollard Movement

Rejection of Catholic Practices

Their beliefs firmly immersed in the Scriptures, followers of the Lollard movement rejected many popular Catholic practices. These practices included the Catholic teachings on purgatory, pilgrimages, prayers to the saints, works of merit, the use of images, ornaments, and costly vestments in worship, holy water, ceremonies, and the custom of recognizing ranks of honor among the clergy. Testimony recorded from those in the Lollard communities showed their opposition to Catholic forms of spiritual expression. (3)

---

(3) Thomas Bilney, a Lollard preacher who met a martyr's death
[H]e says that it was but folly for a man to go on pilgrimages for saints; for they are but stocks and stones ... men should pray only to God, and to no saints .... [H]e has oftentimes spoken against fasting ... also against holy days ... [and] against pardons, saying, and affirming that pardons granted by the Pope, or other men of the Church, are of no effect. [16]

In line with Wyclif's beliefs, Lollards opposed the medieval Catholic doctrine of transubstantiation. (4) They viewed Eucharist celebrations as idolatrous, but didn't advance a formal theological critique of the Catholic practices. It was clear to the Lollards that the corporeal presence of Christ was not to be found in the sacramental bread on the altar. Lollard parents taught their children not to worship the sacrament of the altar as if it were divine, because it was only a symbol of the body of Christ.

---

(4) "Wycklyffe's Wycket"
Therefore all the sacraments that are left here in earth are but reminders of the body of Christ, for a sacrament is no more to say, but a sign or reminder of a thing passed or a thing to come. [17]

At first glance, the Lollards' rejection of the Eucharist might appear to be a theoretical matter relating only to doctrinal definition. However, by rejecting transubstantiation, the Lollards were effectively undoing the clerical elite's monopoly over the means of sacramental grace, and restoring them to the common people of God.

Reading Scripture in the Vernacular

The Lollards vehemently claimed the right to read the Bible in their mother tongue. They believed that biblical authority was more potent than secular or ecclesiastical authority, and this led to significant social and religious changes in medieval England. Unable to read the scriptures, many illiterate poor memorized them instead. One dissident woman was found to have memorized the entire Epistle of James, with the help of a Lollard preacher.

In these circles, the Epistle of James was favored over other New Testament books, pointing to a major difference between the Lollard vision and the theology of Protestant reformers on the European continent. Martin Luther, in an effort to establish his vision of salvation by faith alone, virtually removed the Epistle of James from his working canon. The Epistle of James emphasized a faith which expressed itself through good works.

In judicial proceedings against the Lollards, charges levelled by their adversaries underscored the powerful attraction of the scriptures in Lollard communities. A carpenter and two companions were accused of having spent the entire night in their house reading the Bible. English translations of the books of the Bible were surreptitiously passed from member to member in the Lollard communities. A stone mason was accused of hiding a man in his house who was working on a translation of the book of Revelation. In another case, a woman had been overheard in her house reciting from memory passages from the Epistles and the Gospels.

The success of the Lollard movement depended largely on the popularization of the New Testament. Inspired by John Wyclif, Lollards based the doctrinal content of their preaching on scripture, opposing traditional Catholic doctrines such as transubstantiation, indulgences, auricular confession, and purgatory.

The Lollard movement anticipated the extraordinary popularity of Tyndale's translation of the New Testament, which arrived in England after its publication on the continent in 1526. The successors of the Lollards, particularly in London and eastern England, had long treasured their handwritten copies of the New Testament, gathering in their homes to read and pray together.

The Written Word

The Lollards spread their ideas through other writings as well, primarily authored by John Wyclif. Wyclif's ideas were passed on in university debates, sermons, tracts, books, and scriptural translations. Records of judicial proceedings reported that the Lollards were accused of heresy "for carrying about certain books in English ... [and] other sheets of paper written in English, containing a matter against the Romish religion."[18] This literature, passed from hand to hand in the Lollard communities, answered questions raised by common people about the faith and life of Christians, and was forbidden by church authorities.

Conclusion

John Wyclif was the principal source behind the Lollards' ideas. With him, the Lollards shared a serious concern for the moral integrity of the Christian life. Like the Donatists eight centuries earlier, they believed that the ministry of a priest living in mortal sin was invalidated. Like the Waldensians, they believed that the divine call to preach was more meaningful than academic preparation or ecclesiastical authorization. The Lollards refused to take oaths of allegiance which perpetuated oppressive relationships within the feudal system.

The English Lollards were not simply Protestants before Luther. In many ways, they were more radical than Luther. Following the lead of Wyclif, they did not appeal to the Protestant principle of *sola fide* (faith alone), as Lutherans would later do. The Lollards were radical Christians, their beliefs and practices born out of the turbulence of their times.

Notes

[1] Herbert E. Winn, *Wyclif: Select English Writings* (New York: AMS Press, 1976), 34-35. My adaptation from Middle English.

[2] Matthew Spinka, ed., *Advocates of Reform: From Wyclif to Erasmus* (London: SCM Press, 1953), 33.

[3] Spinka, 49.

[4] R. B. Dobson, *The Peasants' Revolt of 1381* (London: Macmillan and Co., 1970), 60.

[5] Dobson, 60-63.

[6] Dobson, 63-68.

[7] Dobson, 123-131.

[8] Matthew Spinka, ed., *Advocates of Reform: From Wyclif to Erasmus* (London: SCM Press, 1953), 24.

[9] Spinka, 27.

[10] Spinka, 30.

[11] Spinka, 73.

[12] This section relies largely on the following source. John Stacey, *John Wyclif and Reform* (Philadelphia: Westminster Press, 1964), 128-147.

[13] Stacey, 129.

[14] Stacey, 135.

[15] Stacey, 137.

[16] Stacey, 141.

[17] Stacey, 141-142.

[18] Stacey, 145.

Chapter 10

Medieval Movements: Peter Chelčický and the Czech Brethren

Nor can it be truly argued that the apostles divided the Holy Church into three parts and commanded one part to work, so that the two others might be maintained by its labor, and rest on it as though on a bed, in idleness. ...

[Paul] teaches that equality is to be preserved among those who compose the Holy Church, equality of the kind that the limbs of a natural body have, and he says: "There should be no division in the body ...." And the truth is greater than the example; it requires undivided equality among the limbs of the body so that without envy they serve each other ....

And since the limbs of the Holy Church have this relation to each other, one will not make others pay excessive rent ... so that he can sit in the cool shade and ridicule the "louts" and "boors" roasting in the heat, or drive them out into the bitter cold in their smocks to trap hares, and himself sit in the warm indoors. (Peter Chelčický, *On the Holy Church*).[1]

Introduction: Peter Chelčický

Peter Chelčický, *c.*1380-*c.*1460, was the spiritual father, ideologue, prophet, and teacher of the Unity of Czech Brethren, or the Unitas Fratrum. Although he was little known outside his native Bohemia, Chelčický was one of the most original, radical Christian thinkers of the period, not only in Hussite reformation circles, but in all of medieval Europe.

Chelčický was born into a family of modest means in southeastern Bohemia, in the rural village of Chelcice. His father, who owned a small farm, died shortly after Peter's birth, and his mother died during his childhood. Relatives cared for the orphaned child, giving him a rudimentary education that included some Latin, an introduction to scholastic theology, and an opportunity to read widely at the local parish library. One of Chelčický's maternal uncles was a priest in a nearby parish.

Social Climate: The Concentration of Arable Land

Wealth and political power were concentrated in the hands of the nobility and the medieval church in fifteenth century Bohemia. At the turn of the fifteenth century, the church held title to an estimated one-third of all arable land in Bohemia.[2] Under the constant threat of warfare, taxes were high, as was military conscription, and the rural labor force was reduced. This resulted in a decrease in arable land for food production. Those who owned arable land exerted absolute control over the peasants who cultivated it.[3]

By birth, Peter Chelčický held a small plot of rural land. While he did not figure among even the lower nobility, his plot of land, and the freedom that came with it, distinguished him from the common peasant class. Moved by a deep Christian conviction, Chelčický lived in solidarity with these peasants, who were controlled by the feudal lords and clerics. Chelčický remained a layman his entire life, and was identified with the laity who were exploited by those in power in medieval Christendom.[4]

Peter Chelčický's Hussite Background [5]

The Hussite century – that is, the fifteenth century – was an unsettled period, marked by deep transformations in all spheres of life: religious, cultural, economic, social, and political. Running in Prague's university circles, John Huss and his colleagues unleashed a moral revolution aimed at correcting abuses in the medieval church. Their theological position had its basis in the writings of John Wyclif, which had recently arrived in Prague from England, and in the Czech reform movement.

John Huss, *c*.1373-1415, a man of modest origins, was named rector of the University of Prague in 1402. An enthusiastic disciple of John Wyclif,

Huss used Wyclif's ideas in his own university lectures, sermons, and writings. Huss was a gifted, charismatic preacher, and a staunch Czech patriot. He hoped that the church might be reformed through the intervention of secular authorities. Before long, the Hussite party in Prague was at the center of a nationalist revolution against imperial and papal forces.

The Utraquists

The right wing of the Hussite reformation was occupied by a conservative party called the Utraquists, who insisted on the laity's right to receive communion in both the cup and the bread. The chalice came to symbolize Bohemia's struggle for independence from Rome. Apart from this, the group did not depart much from the doctrinal positions espoused by the Catholics. They took a minimalist approach in their appeal to biblical authority and forbade only those practices which were explicitly forbidden in the Bible.

The Moderates

Huss identified most closely with the party at the center of the Hussite movement. The Four Articles of Prague, formulated in 1420, laid out the Hussite program for reform. The Hussites called for the following changes: free preaching of the Word of God; communion in bread and wine for all faithful followers; the confiscation of secular properties under the control of monks and priests; and the punishment of mortal sins and transgressions, including simony, which is the purchase and sale of church offices.

The moderate party's program called for a national reformation that would cleanse both church and state of their immorality and abuses of power. The Hussite movement's vision for reform was essentially Constantinian: they believed that these changes would be effected by the authority of the magistracy.

The Taborites

The left wing of the Hussite movement was occupied by the Taborites. Members of this group came mainly from southeastern Bohemia. Followers of the medieval Waldensians could still be found among Czechs living along the Austrian border. Like the Waldensians before them, the Taborites in this area were non-violent and withdrew from dominant society.

In contrast to the Utraquists, the Taborites rejected everything not expressly permitted by the Bible. They opposed any compromise with Rome. Their program for reform called for the formation of a theocratic society without Catholic participation. Like Wyclif, the Taborites rejected specific Catholic doctrines: purgatory; ostentatious ceremonies; clerical vestments; and five of the seven sacraments, excepting baptism and communion.

In 1420, the Taborites broke with the Catholic tradition of apostolic succession and elected their own bishop, who related to his fellow ministers as *primus inter pares*, or first among equals. Smaller and more extremist groups emerged among the Taborites. Some practiced a community of goods. Some understood communion in a strictly commemorative sense, denying the Taborite doctrine of consubstantiation which held that Christ's body and blood was spiritually present in the bread and wine.

Initially, the Taborites were non-violent, but apocalyptic expectations soon led to active militancy. The vision of Christ's imminent return probably originated with an anarchist group in Bohemia known as the Picards, and it incited the Taborites to violence. Peter Chelčický was distressed by these excesses, warned the Taborites against them, and finally distanced himself from the movement.

Some Taborite radicals put aside their apocalyptic expectations and attempted to establish their own autonomous Christian nation. The group set up fortifications on a mountain near Tabor, in southeastern Bohemia. The principal sector of the Taborite movement did not support the splinter group, who were influenced by the Picards. Irreconcilable differences erupted into open conflict. A bloody battle in 1421 virtually destroyed the extremist group.

In their ongoing struggle with government and church forces, the Taborite army was twice able to defeat the combined powers of the Empire and Rome. However, in May 1434, the Czech nobility and the Utraquist party in Prague joined with the Catholic forces to create a coalition against the Taborite army. The ferocious battle left twelve thousand Taborites dead on the battlefield. The Taborite movement was decimated, and this marked the end of its armed resistance.

Society of Bohemian Brethren

In the wake of this disastrous armed confrontation, a new popular movement was taking shape. Members of the moderate and leftist parties, committed to a radically evangelical position, rallied around Peter Chelčický's vision. In 1467, the radical movement would cohere into the Society of the Bohemian Brethren, or Unitas Fratrum.

Chelčický's Writings: The Church and Secular Power

One of Peter Chelčický's best-known writings was entitled *The Net of Faith*, an allegorical treatise about the damage inflicted onto Christian communities by the abuses of church and state. (1) The net of faith, cast into the sea by Peter, represented God's law, which guided the faithful toward lives of commitment and fidelity, like the lives of those in the early church. Those in Peter's net were called by the grace of God. But they were endangered by the violent actions of two whales – the pope and the emperor – who entered the net and tore it to shreds. The damage done by these whales was so great that the net of the early apostolic church was scarcely recognizable.

> *(1) Peter Chelčický,* **The Net of Faith**
> *Peter's net was horribly torn when two whales forced their way into it, namely the highest priest with royal dominion to whom is given more honor than the Emperor, and the second, the Emperor with pagan dominion, with pagan offices and pagan power, who sneaked in under the cover of faith.*[6]

In his writings, Chelčický argued for total separation between church and state. A vicious cycle existed in which various parties seized secular power and asserted their right to exercise dominion.[7] In Chelčický's opinion, this ongoing power struggle was entirely secular, and could not reflect Christ's order of love: the two were in no way related, and would never be. Power was based on acquiring material goods using any means, while faith was fulfilled only through loving actions and goodwill. (2)

> *(2) Peter Chelčický,* **On the Triple Division of Society**
> *The order of Christ and the secular order cannot exist together .... Power is not regulated by faith, and faith does not need power ....*[8]

Secular Authority and the Christian Community

Chelčický recognized that God had established secular authority to restrain evil. Civil authorities often depended on coercion to maintain order in society, but this order nevertheless fulfilled God's purposes. However, Chelčický held that the Christian community did not require the assistance of secular authority in its exercise of internal discipline. The Christian church maintained order through acts of love, not by coercive means. (3)

Utraquist theologians in Prague said that "among Christians the best Christian would have to be the king."[9] But Chelčický could not conceive of a true Christian fulfilling the coercive and repressive functions of secular government, because such functions were fundamentally opposed to Christ and to his people.[10]

Despite the pagan nature of secular power, Christians should freely submit to its authority. Christians who enjoyed the benefits of civil order should respect the state's authority. However, obedience to civil authority had its limits. Christians must refuse obedience to any order contrary to the law of God. Secular commands to bear arms, swear oaths of allegiance, and participate in the judicial process must be resisted in a non-violent manner. The faithful were called to bear patiently the sufferings brought on them by civil disobedience.

> *(3) Peter Chelčický,* **The Net of Faith**
> *According to the ordinances of Christ, the wicked shall not be coerced in any way, neither shall any kind of vengeance be practiced against them, but they shall be improved only through brotherly good [will] and be led to penitence.*[11]

Chelčický's Critique of Medieval Socio-Economic Structures

Divine Ordination

Medieval European society was divided into three classes. (fig.1) The magistrates occupied a privileged place at the top of the social pyramid. This group included the secular nobility and the high clergy, who, in medieval Europe, fulfilled more of a secular function than a spiritual one. The middle of the social pyramid was occupied by the Roman Catholic clergy, whose services were considered essential to the welfare of medieval Christendom. The common people occupied the lowest place in the pyramid, and were mainly peasants who worked the land and struggled to survive. This group was made up serfs, completely subjugated to their feudal lords, farmers who owned small plots of land, which they cultivated for survival, as well as laborers, artisans, and small merchants.

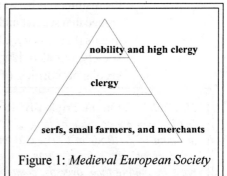

Figure 1: *Medieval European Society*

According to church doctrine, the hierarchy was divinely ordained. The head of the mystical body of Christ was represented by the nobility, who governed. The clergy provided the peasants with spiritual consolation and administered the sacramental means for eternal salvation. They represented the hands of the mystical body of Christ. The peasants worked to support those in a higher position, and their position corresponded to the feet of the mystical body. The hierarchy was considered sacrosanct in medieval Christendom. No one in their right mind dared question this tripartite division of society.

Chelčický's Protest

Peter Chelčický dared to question the hierarchy. He identified deeply with the suffering of common people. The indolent nobles were subjects of his most biting satire. Chelčický was a common man of uncommon courage. A brilliantly original thinker, he was capable of impressing the powerful, and might have chosen to become a social climber. Instead, he remained faithful to his radical spiritual vision and his social roots.

Chelčický did not only oppose the actions of the feudal nobility, but also those of the Taborite clergy. The Taborite oligarchy promised to be a democratic regime, yet continued to exact onerous rents and taxes from the peasants, treating them no differently than had their previous masters.[12] Chelčický accused the Taborite priests of being "proud, greedy, [and] carnal."[13] The priests did not care for their flocks, but fed off of them.

Both John Wyclif and theologians of the Hussite reformation had defended the validity of the tripartite division of medieval society, endorsing the distinctions between secular nobility, clergy, and peasants. Wyclif even argued that secular authorities had the right to reform the church, by coercive means if necessary. Chelčický not only rejected the traditional division of society, but also denounced the violent treatment of the lowest class by secular authorities. (4)

---

(4) Chelčický, **On the Triple Division of Society**
But I ... will not concede as long as I live that this meaning of the Body of Christ is a true one. Nor will I grant such a large estate to the two upper parts by putting them over the common people so that they can ride the latter at their own pleasure, and even consider themselves thereby better members of the Body of Christ than the common people whom they ride, and whom they subject to themselves not as limbs of their own body but as beasts whom they think nothing of tearing apart.[14]

Chelčický argued that the clergy, by colluding with secular nobility, were guilty of abusing their power. He wrote scathingly of the idle clergy, surrounded by silken cushions and expensive food and drink. The labor of the common people supported their contemptible lifestyles. Chelčický condemned the clergy's attitude toward its flock, who were treated not as limbs of a common body, but as beasts of burden. He did not mince his words, calling the clergy "accursed sons" ... "to whom the Whore who sits on the Roman throne has given birth."[15]

Nonviolent Resistance

Contradictory Church Policy

Peter Chelčický approved of John Huss's defiant opposition to the pomp and triviality of the Roman clergy. Nevertheless, Chelčický thought Huss's conclusions were somewhat misled. In *The Net of Faith*, Chelčický wrote: "It seemed to John Huss as though Christians were not henceforth obliged to follow the apostles of the Holy Primitive Church in suffering, because now kings [had] entered the church."[16]

Chelčický recognized that the teachings of the church were fundamentally contradictory. The church called on the innocent faithful to endure their sufferings for Christ, but it also justified the nobility's use of violence when defending Christ's apparent cause. Chelčický believed that

Christians were not called to be both the perpetrators and the victims of violence. Christians were called to live peacefully, even when threatened by violence, and to give willingly, never to steal.[17]

Chelčický's Pacifist Stance

Peter Chelčický was a pacifist at a difficult time. The Utraquists, believing the survival of the nation was at stake, accused him of heresy because he objected to their claim that it was right to defend themselves with arms. Chelčický's pacifist convictions remained unshaken. In his opinion, the theological justification of revolution was as abominable as the theory of just war, which supported violently defending the status quo.

Disillusioned and bitter, Chelčický wrote to the bishop of the moderate Hussite party. He demanded to know how any kind of murder could be considered heroic. Chelčický saw the issue of pacifism with a great moral clarity: there could be no grey areas, because all murder, in any form, went against Christ's teachings. (5)

Chelčický believed that Christian warfare could only be waged spiritually, with faith in the power of non-resistance. Under no circumstance could one be saved by using the sword. He could imagine no worse violation of Jesus' teachings than

> **(5) Chelčický to the Hussite bishop**
> *But if a nobleman gathers a great army of peasants and makes of them warriors who can kill someone with the power of an army, they will in no way be murderers, neither will it be held against the conscience; but it can be boasted that they make of themselves brave men and heroes by murdering heretics. And this poison is poured out among Christians by doctors who ... did not have the counsel of Jesus the Meek, but the counsel of the Great Whore ....*[18]

Christians killing one another in the name of Christ. Chelčický did not support the use of violent protest against oppressors. Salvation would come through suffering, not violence.

Chelčický did not distinguish between defensive warfare and military aggression. He refused to support either the Utraquists or the Taborites, both of whom tried to justify their use of defensive violence. Chelčický believed that a Christian's only true defense was spiritual. He maintained this conviction despite the horrifying suffering of many countrymen at the hands of their enemies. One chronicle from the period recorded that 1,600

Czechs were captured and turned over to Germans who operated silver mines in the area. All were thrown into the mine shafts, "some alive, some first decapitated ... the executioners often being exhausted by the fatigue of slaughter."[19] Despite all this, Chelčický's convictions remained firm.

Radical Biblical Interpretation

Scholastic theologians of the time were content to repeat traditional interpretations of Biblical texts, but Chelčický was an original thinker with the independence to challenge the most sacrosanct positions. Chelčický was familiar with Wyclif's writings, and there is evidence that he was influenced by John Huss and his successors in the Hussite reformation. He also showed familiarity with the traditions of western Christendom. However, none of these influences determined the evolution of his thought.

The Bible was a primary source for Chelčický's radical thought. He moved in circles in which the scriptures were read in the vernacular, and the New Testament interpreted literally. Many of these people came to doubt, or reject outright, the sacrosanct doctrines of medieval Catholicism. There is little question that Chelčický's reformist ideas arose out of his reading of the Bible, but on what did he base his hermeneutics?

Firstly, Chelčický may have been influenced by a succession of Czech preachers who advocated popular reform and denounced social and ecclesiastical abuses by the upper echelons of medieval society. Secondly, Chelcicky would have been familiar with Wyclif's suggestions for doctrinal reform, which were promoted by the teachers in Prague, and by Taborite priests. Thirdly, he had the example of Waldensian ideology, which rejected coercive power and preached apostolic poverty.[20]

But Chelčický's principal hermeneutical key was undoubtedly the faith he confessed and upon which he acted. Chelčický believed that a true Christian would courageously follow Christ, even to martyrdom. This conviction freed Chelčický from the illusory hope of possible political salvation, and he approached the Bible without the Constantinian biases of his contemporaries.

A Church of the Poor; A Church without Power

Wyclif had argued that the true church was the congregation of the elect. Using Wyclif's definition, John Huss declared that the Roman church was not the true church. Even after the Hussite reformation created a national state-church, which replaced imperial Christendom, Huss continued to maintain that the true church was invisible, known only to God.

Chelčický agreed with Huss, but believed that the members of the true church could be recognized by their lives of justice. The true church was visible in the discipleship of the faithful. In fifteenth-century rural Bohemia, Chelčický set out to establish communities modeled on the New Testament church. These conventicles would be places where believers could live together in Christian love and holiness. The tripartite division of medieval society would have no validity there.

Rather than judging the actions of Christians according to the norms of social class, Chelčický used the model found in the Messianic communities of the New Testament. The only visible sign of election was one's faithfulness to that model. Chelčický's proposed that the apostolic church be restored in the villages of southeastern Bohemia. The true church would be both an invisible congregation chosen by God, and a visible community of the faithful, living in the world.

Indeed, Chelčický was able to adapt Wyclif's theory into a living vision of the church. He established contemporary versions of the apostolic church in places like Chelcice.[21]

Conclusion: Romans 13

Chelčický's interpretation of Romans 13 provides us an example of his radical vision. In Romans 13, Paul offered counsel to Christians living in Rome under a pagan emperor. Paul recognized that the Roman state maintained a necessary social order, and urged Christians to submit to its authority. Since Augustine, the orthodox interpretation of this passage had granted apostolic approval to secular authority. The church used the text to support the divine right of secular and ecclesiastical powers.

Chelčický could not accept this interpretation, and offered an almost unheard of reading of the text. Chelčický argued that Paul was addressing particular Christians living under particular pagan rulers, and that there was no textual basis for formulating an absolute Christian doctrine on the exercise of civil power. The Roman Christians were being asked to submit to Roman rule as their conscience permitted them, but this did not rule out the possibility for non-violent resistance. Chelčický accused Christian apologists of devising their doctrines by "milking the Scriptures," and fabricating "despicable things, very offensive to God."[22]

Chelčický's beliefs clearly went against the traditional doctrines of the church. He protested unjust social structures, but did not believe that violence was the Christian solution to earthly injustices. His moral teachings were based on the Synoptic Gospels, and particularly the Sermon on the Mount. Chelčický believed that Jesus' persecution had unveiled the true character of political powers, which were demonic, violent, and uncontrolled. He believed that such powers, by their very nature, would inevitably persecute the faithful church. The true church must therefore be prepared to follow Jesus' example and suffer; and by suffering to achieve eternal salvation.

Notes

---

[1] William M. Bowsky, ed., *Studies in Medieval and Renaissance History*, vol. 1 (Lincoln, NE: University of Nebraska Press, 1964), 171-173.

[2] Peter Brock, *The Political and Social Doctrines of the Unity of the Czech Brethren* (The Hague: Mouton and Co., 1957), 22.

[3] Brock, 23.

[4] Murray L. Wagner, *Petr Chelčický: A Radical Separatist in Hussite Bohemia* (Scottdale, PA: Herald Press, 1983), 38-41.

[5] This section relies largely on the following source. Peter Brock, *The Political and Social Doctrines of the Unity of the Czech Brethren* (The Hague: Mouton and Co., 1957), 12-13.

[6] Murray L. Wagner, *Petr Chelčický: A Radical Separatist in Hussite Bohemia* (Scottdale, PA: Herald Press, 1983), 132.

[7] Wagner, 132.

[8] William M. Bowsky, ed., *Studies in Medieval and Renaissance History*, vol. 1 (Lincoln, NE: University of Nebraska Press, 1964), 143.

[9] Murray L. Wagner, *Petr Chelčický: A Radical Separatist in Hussite Bohemia* (Scottdale, PA: Herald Press, 1983), 135.

[10] Wagner, 135.

[11] Wagner, 135.

[12] Wagner, 89.

[13] Wagner, 89-90.

[14] William M. Bowsky, ed., *Studies in Medieval and Renaissance History*, vol. 1 (Lincoln, NE: University of Nebraska Press, 1964), 163.

[15] Bowsky, 162. Quoted from Peter Chelčický, *On the Triple Division of Society.*

[16] Murray L. Wagner, *Petr Chelčický: A Radical Separatist in Hussite Bohemia* (Scottdale, PA: Herald Press, 1983), 70.

[17] William M. Bowsky, ed., *Studies in Medieval and Renaissance History*, vol. 1 (Lincoln, NE: University of Nebraska Press, 1964), 153.

[18] Murray L. Wagner, *Petr Chelčický: A Radical Separatist in Hussite Bohemia* (Scottdale, PA: Herald Press, 1983), 78-79.

[18] Wagner, 78-79.

[19] Wagner, 88.

[20] Wagner, 45.

[21] Wagner, 94.

[22] Wagner, 98.

Chapter 11

Medieval Movements: Juan de Valdés and Catholic Evangelism

And just as the light cannot be separated from the flame, that burns of itself, neither can good works be separated from faith, that of itself justifies. (Benito of Mantua, *Del Beneficio de Jesucristo Crucificado*, 99). [1]

By what right and according to what system of justice do you subject those Indians to such cruel and horrible servitude? With what authority have you waged these detestable wars against these peoples living meekly and peacefully in their lands ...? Why do you oppress and exhaust them without giving them adequate food or treating their illnesses and because of the hard labor which you exact from them they die, or in reality, you kill in your efforts to extract more gold every day? ... Are they not humans? ... Are you not obliged to love them just as you love yourselves? (Antonio Montesinos in Bartolomé de las Casas, *Historia de las Indias*, III, 4). [2]

Introduction: Catholic Evangelism

Catholic Evangelism is the term given by modern historians to a group of related movements which emerged in Latin Europe early in the sixteenth century.[3] Catholic Evangelism was in decline by 1542, the year in which the Papal Inquisition was reinstated. In France, the movement was called Evangelism, because it took its inspiration from the Gospels. In Spain, the movement was known as Illuminism, and was found in the conventicles of the Spanish Alumbrados, and in Valdesianism, named for Juan de Valdés. In Italy, around 1540, the movement flourished in Naples, where it was known as Evangelism or Valdesianism. Juan de Valdés spent the last decade of his life in Italy, and played a central role in the emergence of the Italian movement.

In Opposition to Inquisitional Tactics

The Catholic Evangelist movement was pacifist, and reacted against the Inquisition's imposition of religious and political uniformity onto entire populations. The movement was non-dogmatic at a time when orthodoxy was the norm. Catholic Evangelism was a religion of the spirit, not of right doctrine. The movement was anti-clerical during a period when clergy exercised a monopoly over almost every aspect of people's lives, including their apparent means to salvation.

The movement attracted people of Jewish and Islamic descent, who were persecuted by a Spanish nationalism defined by Catholic Christianity. In Spain and Italy, women enjoyed full participation in the life of Evangelist conventicles. Catholic Evangelism rejected coercive means of evangelization, and did not support imperial conquest being justified under such terms.

Illuministic, or Catholic, Evangelism was a movement of outsiders. Foreigners, strangers, lay persons, women, the unlettered, the poor, and those not accepted by the institutional church were able to find a merciful God, and a place of belonging, within the movement.

The Spanish Alumbrados

The Origins of Alcaraz's Beliefs

The Spanish Alumbrados were an indigenous movement that emerged early in the sixteenth century. Pedro Ruiz de Alcaraz was one of the principal proponents of the movement's illuministic spirituality. Alcaraz began his mission around 1511, clearly preceding Lutheranism in Europe.

Alcaraz was influenced by Isabel de la Cruz, a Spanish mystic. Testifying before the Inquisition, Alcaraz stated that he had been devoted to Our Lady until de la Cruz "advised him to read the Bible, to stop his devotions, and drop the idea that by his meritorious works God would grant him grace."[4] The environment was ripe for Alcaraz to study the Bible on his own, and he embraced de la Cruz's suggestion.[5] The Gospels and the Epistles had been translated into Spanish in 1486 by a layman from Zaragoza. From 1512 onward the text was revised and reprinted repeatedly until, in 1559, the Spanish Inquisition forbade the translation of scripture into the vernacular.[6]

Alcaraz was born around 1480, in Guadalajara, to a family of "New Christians," who had recently converted from Judaism. In 1523, the Marquis of Villena, Diego López Pacheco, invited Alcaraz to his castle in Escalona to serve as lay preacher. There, Alcaraz dedicated himself to teaching the Bible to small groups of people in their homes. The meetings were informal, and everyone participated, both men and women. Participants were generally social outsiders, and a disproportionately large number were of Jewish descent. The sermons were simple, and were supplemented by scriptural readings in the vernacular.[7]

Alcaraz read as many biblical translations as he could find. He possessed a prodigious memory and could recite entire passages from the Bible. Life in the Alumbrado conventicles was characterized by a radical ethic, inspired by the Sermon on the Mount. Among the ideas condemned by the Inquisition in 1525 were the words of Jesus: "That one should swear not at all."[8] These words became a commonly-held conviction among movements of radical Christian renewal.

Alcaraz's Ecclesiological Vision

Alcaraz's vision did not depend on the mysticism of Christianity or Islam, nor on Erasmian or Lutheran influences. His Jewish religious consciousness freed him from medieval influences in his reading of the Bible. God loved his people, as was manifest in their history of salvation.[9] Alcaraz did not harbor ambitious visions of church reform. Nevertheless, the doctrinal conclusions he formulated at these informal meetings were fundamentally opposed to the sacraments and hierarchy of the traditional church.

Alcaraz's ecclesiological vision was affected by his reading of the Bible. In the Bible, he found a people among whom God was continually present. The sacramental, hierarchical, and doctrinal structures, so crucial to the definitions of medieval Catholicism, were dispensable. Alcaraz came to believe in God's essential freedom, and the radical need for divine grace. His theology was based on his belief in God's matchless love.

Alcaraz's theology led him to oppose systems of religious piety that claimed God's grace could be earned. He rejected the worship of the sacrament, works of charity, fasts, prayers, and indulgences. He also denied the doctrine of Christ's real presence in the Eucharist. Alcaraz saw the clerical office as being unimportant: Christ was present not in the altar, but in the soul of the righteous.[10] Participants in the Alumbrado conventicles were aware that Alcaraz's biblical interpretation was a "new doctrine."[11]

Alcaraz had an appreciation for the Holy Spirit's role in scriptural interpretation. Alcaraz distinguished between human understanding, and understanding inspired by the Holy Spirit. He did not discount serious reflection on the Bible, but had little regard for the study of other books or traditions. Among the Alumbrados, abandonment was an important concept. Abandonment meant surrendering oneself to God, and owing all knowledge to His divine initiative. Christian liberty meant absolute dependence on God, and absolute liberation from institutional means of salvation.[12]

In 1524, after two years of activity in Escalona, Alcaraz was arrested by the Inquisition. Following five years of imprisonment, torture, and interrogation, Alcaraz's radical vision of the gospel was condemned by the Inquisition in July 1529.

Juan de Valdés in Spain

In 1523, Juan de Valdés participated in one of Alcaraz's conventicles. Valdés, a young man of Jewish ancestry, was destined to become the principal spokesman for Catholic Evangelism in Spain and Italy. His later writings showed evidence of Alcaraz's influence.

Juan de Valdés, c.1500-1541, was born into a family of New Christians in Cuenca. The Valdés family understood the suffering inflicted on outsiders in Spain under the Inquisition. A maternal uncle, Fernando de la Barreda, a parish priest accused by the Inquisition of reverting to Judaism, had been burned at the stake early in the sixteenth century. After Alcaraz was arrested in Escalona, Valdés probably returned hurriedly to his paternal home in Cuenca where he spent the next two years in biblical study.

In 1526, Valdés entered the University of Alcalá where he would be a student for the next four years. He probably studied Hebrew, Greek, and Latin, as well as biblical subjects. The cardinal and primate of Spain, Jiménez de Cisneros had established the University of Alcalá in an attempt to reform the intellectual life of the Spanish church. The university was a center for the study of biblical sciences. Little is known of Valdés' studies. He was certainly no ordinary student. On January 14, 1529, barely into his third year of study, Valdés' first book, *Diálogo de Doctrina Cristiana*, was published by the press of Miguel de Eguía in Alcalá de Henares.

Diálogo de Doctrina Cristiana

In 1525 and 1526, several of Erasmus' writings were translated into Spanish, specifically, *Paráfrasis de los Evangelios* and *Enchiridion*. Some have noted similarities between Erasmus' writings and Valdés' first book. Both severely critiqued medieval monasticism and clericalism; both criticized popular religious practices such as Marian devotion and auricular confession; and both held a high appreciation for practical Christianity.

However, Valdés' writing also expressed the convictions he had learned from Alcaraz, and from his own biblical reflections on the New Testament. For example, Valdés took his concept of faith further than did Erasmus. He argued that faith combined absolute trust in God with real works of charity. True faith was manifested spiritually and physically. (1)

Valdés used traditional categories to structure his catechism: the Apostles' Creed, the Ten Commandments, the Seven Capital Sins, the Three Theological Virtues, the Seven Gifts of the Spirit, and the Lord's Prayer. However, his treatment

> *(1) Valdés,* **Diálogo de Doctrina Cristiana**
> *We understand that faith is trust, as for example, when we hear some of God's words ... we have complete confidence that God will fulfill them. Then we have living faith, which is the root of works of charity. ... From all this we may well conclude that for a Christian to possess faith, he must believe "in God" and "believe God."*[13]

of these categories was decidedly non-traditional. The most unusual aspect of his catechism was the compendium of Holy Scriptures. Valdés looked at Christian faith through the biblical salvation story narrated in the Old and New Testaments. This was a radical way of viewing faith, because it did not depend on the dogmatic or ritualistic categorizations assigned by medieval ecclesiastical institutions. Instead, Valdés saw faith as a living history, acted out in the story of God's people.[14]

Valdés believed that church reform required change from within, starting with the clergy. He insisted that a ministerial candidate should have integrity, and the ability to read. Further, a candidate must renounce all ambitions to wealth and power. (2)

The catechism closed with a translation of the Sermon on the Mount, which was essentially a summary of Christian doctrine. The description of the kingdom of God would help Christians orient their lives.[16]

The *Diálogo de Doctrina Cristiana* was read widely throughout Spain. Despite precautions taken by the author, the book soon came to the attention of the Spanish Inquisition. In 1531, *Diálogo de Doctrina Cristiana* was confiscated, and reading it forbidden. The measures of the Inquisition were so thorough that the book completely disappeared. It wasn't until 1929, exactly four hundred years after its publication, that Marcel Bataillon discovered the only copy known to have survived, in the National Library in Lisbon, Portugal.

> *(2) Valdés,* **Diálogo de Doctrina Cristiana**
> *As clerics and also friars increase, so does disorder and evil living among them. Laymen see in it a reason for wickedness, and so all is lost. ... I sincerely urge and charge you that you first determine to be truly and completely Christian. ... For this it'll be necessary for you to rid yourself of all your desires for worldly honors ....*[15]

Juan de Valdés in Italy

The Inquisition launched an investigation against Juan de Valdés, who had fled for safety to Italy in August 1531. In Rome, he found employment as chamberlain in the service of Pope Clement VII, known for his benevolence toward Christians of Jewish descent.

Little is known of the first three years of Valdés' life in Italy. Apparently, he made several trips to visit his brother Alfonso, secretary of Emperor Carlos V, who was with the imperial court in Europe. Valdés no doubt continued his reflective study of the Bible, applying it to contemporary Christian faith and life. In 1534, Valdés moved to Naples, a center of Spanish influence in Italy, where he would spend the most intense years of his literary and ecclesial activity, until his early death in 1541.

In 1535, Valdés wrote *Diálogo de la Lengua,* which established his reputation as a Spanish philologist. The following year he wrote *Alfabeto Cristiano.* This book outlined the rudiments of Christian life, in response to spiritual concerns raised by Julia Gonzaga, a patrician renowned for her spirituality and her extraordinary beauty. The book was a practical guide to Christian maturity. Valdés believed that maturity manifested itself most clearly in concrete deeds of charity. The Christian's maturity was grounded in God's grace.[17]

Valdesian spirituality was grounded in practical experience. Christians were urged to read the scriptures, not to increase their doctrinal understanding, but to learn how to live.[18] Following her encounter with Valdés, Julia entered a convent of the second order of Franciscans.

Valdés continued writing, producing *Ciento y Diez Consideraciones Divinas,* a collection of biblical reflections on specific themes. This book was probably used during meetings of the community that had formed around Valdés in Naples. A few other writings escaped the eye of the Papal Inquisition, which was reinstated in 1542, the year after Valdés' death. These included translations and commentaries on the Psalms, Romans, 1 Corinthians, and the Gospel of Matthew.

Valdés' interest in reading and interpreting scripture was rooted in his experience in Spain, in the Alumbrado conventicle. He argued that one could not know God through scripture alone. Time and again Valdés' commentaries urged the interpretation of biblical texts through personal experience. (3)

> *(3) Valdés,* **Comentario a la primera epístola de San Pablo a los Corintos** *[U]ntil a man comes to know God in and through Christ, he cannot know him in the Scriptures.*[19]

The Valdesian Community in Naples

Among the participants in the Valdesian community which formed in Naples were persons of renown in the Italian social and religious world. Among these were the humanist, Marco Antonio Flaminio; the papal secretary, Pietro Carnesecchi, Secondo Curione, who secretly smuggled the text of *Ciento y Diez Consideraciones Divinas* out of the Inquisition's reach to Basel where it was published in 1550; Pietro Martire Vermigli and Bernardino Ochino, renowned preachers of the period; and Jacobo Bonifadio, to name only a few.[20] Participants were united by their interest in prayer and Bible study, and their remarkable social sensitivity, particularly their concern for the poor.[21]

Sunday meetings were held in private homes, including Valdés' own house. *Ciento y Diez Consideraciones Divinas* and Valdés' other biblical commentaries reflected the themes treated at these meetings, and the communitarian way in which they were approached. Religious instruction was offered for new believers and the children of participating families. Valdés' ideas were so widely disseminated that tanners in the market-place were overheard discussing the Pauline Epistles.[22]

Although many among the social elite were attracted to Valdés' message, his interests were neither elitist nor speculative. He sought an authentic spiritual renewal of Christianity for the masses. Two of the most popular Italian preachers of the period, Pietro Martire Vermigli and Bernardino Ochino, the Capuchin, were among the members of the Valdesian community. Emperor Carlos V was said to have commented that Ochino's eloquence could draw tears from the cobblestones of the street. According to testimony at Carnesecchi's trial, Ochino received outlines for his public sermons from Valdés.[23] Valdesian ideals were being thus disseminated through the popular preaching of the Capuchins.

It is difficult to estimate how many people were associated with the Valdesian movement in Italy. According to the testimony of Caracciolo at the trial of Carnesecchi, approximately 3,000 people were associated with the movement in Naples.[24] Today, we know the names of only about forty participants. Many of these were of elite origin, and others were radicals, but all were united in their concern for the poor.[25]

Valdés died in the summer of 1541, at around forty years of age. Many people offered testimony about the purity and holiness of Valdés' life and conduct. (4) The archbishop of Oranto, who attended him at his death, said, "Valdés simply confessed that he died in the same faith by which he had lived."[26] One of Valdés' disciples, Curione, later wrote that he had lived with "a sweetness of doctrine and a holiness of life that won many disciples to Christ."[27]

The biblical radicalism of the Italian Valdesians flourished behind the back of official Catholicism in Italy. However, soon after the Papal Inquisition was reinstated, the Valdesian movement all but disappeared. Some fled Italy to save their lives. Pierpaolo Vergerio joined the Lutherans. Pietro Martire Vermigli and Celio Secondo Curione identified themselves with the Calvinists. Bernardino Ochino joined the radicals.

> **(4) Jacobo Bonifadio's letter to Pietro Carnesecchi**
> *Where shall we go since Signor Valdés is dead? This has been truly a great loss for us, and for the world, for Signor Valdés was one of the rare men of Europe, and these writings he has left on the Epistles of Paul and the Psalms of David will fully confirm it. He was, without doubt, in his speech, and in all his conduct a perfect man.*[28]

Among those who remained in Italy, only Pietro Carnesecchi paid the price of martyrdom. Following a long judicial process, he was accused of heresy for having "believed 'the false dottrina e institutioni' taught by the said Giovanni Valdesio, 'tuo maestro.'"[29] Carnesecchi was condemned to death by decapitation, and his body was burned on a pyre in Rome on September 30, 1567.

After Valdés' death, an Italian Valdesian community continued for some time in Viterbo. Only the names of the group's most influential members remain, recorded in surviving letters, and in the Inquisition's records. Prominent members in Viterbo included Julia Gonzaga, Pietro Carnesecchi, Vitoria Colonna, and Cardinals Pole and Contarini.

Two Italian editions of *Alfabeto Cristiano* were published in Venice, in 1545 and 1546. Another tract, *Il Beneficio di Giesu Christo*, written by a monk, Benito de Montova, and edited by Flaminio, appeared in 1543 and was reprinted in Venice until its prohibition in 1549. During this time,

40,000 copies were sold in Venice alone, according to Pierpaolo Vergerio, bishop of Capodistria.[30] The latter volume was a compendium of Valdesian thought using the forms and metaphors employed by Valdés. In this way, Valdés' vision continued to inspire the populace.

Valdés' Influence in Spain

Although Juan de Valdés spent the last ten years of his life in exile, he continued to influence the life and ideas of religious conventicles in Spain. These conventicles arose in and around Seville and Valladolid, and were characterized by their evangelical spirituality. The communities were later destroyed by the Spanish Inquisition, in 1558-1560.

The Conventicle in Seville

In Seville, three of the community's leaders, Francisco Vargas, Doctor Egidio, and Constantino Ponce de la Fuente, had studied with Valdés at the University of Alcalá. Only Ponce de la Fuente left any significant writings, and these reflected Valdés' central ideas, and showed the author's familiarity with Valdés' *Diálogo de Doctrina Cristiana*, which had been written during his student years at Alcalá.

There is evidence that other writings by Valdés found their way to Seville. Juan Pérez de Pineda, an exile from Seville, published Valdés' commentaries on Romans and 1 Corinthians in Geneva under the pseudonym, Juan Philadelfo of Venice. These books were smuggled into Spain by Julianillo Hernández, a member of the Valdesian community in Seville. Both books were included in the index of forbidden books published by the Inquisition in Seville in 1559.[31]

The Valdesian community, centered in the Convent of San Isidro del Campo on Seville's outskirts, was crushed by two autos-de-fé. Autos-de-fé were the public trials of suspected heretics, used by the established church to reaffirm orthodoxy. The first of these was held on September 24, 1559, and the second on December 22, 1560. Among the victims was

Constantino Ponce de la Fuente, burned in effigy because he had succumbed earlier in prison. A dozen monks escaped to Geneva, among whom were Casidoro de Reina and Cipriano de Valera, who would be remembered as the first Protestants to translate the Bible into Castilian Spanish.[32]

The Conventicle in Valladolid

Valdés influenced the evangelical community in Valladolid even more directly. Carlos de Seso, an Italian aristocrat in government service on the Iberian peninsula, was the principal link between Valdés and the community. Seso had been Valdés' disciple, and an intimate friend of several members of the conventicle in Naples. In 1550, Seso brought copies of *Ciento y Diez Consideraciones Divinas* and *Il Beneficio di Giesu Christo* to Valladolid. There is evidence that both texts were circulated widely throughout the community.

Carlos de Seso converted many prominent figures in the community. Among these were members of the Cazalla family, originally of Jewish descent. These included Pedro de Cazalla, the parish priest, and Doctor Agustín de Cazalla, who was one of Carlos V's favorite preachers. The Dominican scholar, Domingo de Rojas, and a number of sisters from the Cistercian and Dominican convents also embraced the movement. The new conventicle in Valladolid probably had about fifty-five to sixty members.

Within two or three years, the community had been betrayed to the Inquisition, which proceeded to repress the movement. On May 21, 1559, Doctor Agustín de Cazalla was burned at the stake at an auto-de-fé in Valladolid. On October 8, 1559, Carlos de Seso, Pedro de Cazalla, and Domingo de Rojas were among those who perished in a second auto-de-fé.

Valdés' Vision of the Church

The established church did not consider the conventicles of the Alumbrados in Spain and of the Valdesians in Naples to be legitimate churches. However, Valdés and his brothers and sisters considered themselves to be part of a kingdom community. Valdés' writings, and testimony given at the trial of Carnesecchi, clearly indicate that Valdesians thought of themselves as authentic participants in God's kingdom, in contrast to the established Catholic church.[33]

The Valdesians, influenced by the New Testament and particularly by Paul's writings, understood the church to be neither institutional nor hierarchical. (5) Valdés believed that the church needed a concrete spiritual base, rather than an institutional one. Therefore, a church was a community of Christ's followers, who lived as Christ had lived. Within a church, love was expressed through fraternal counsel and mutual discipline. Unity was sacred to the community.[35]

Juan de Valdés did not explicitly reject the institutional church of his time. However, his actions and writings implicitly pointed followers in another direction. The true church was to be found in the experience of communion. Valdés gave the conventicles of the Spanish Alumbrados and the Valdesian community in Italy an ecclesial identity. Christians in these communities read and interpreted scripture, prayed together, sought solutions to common problems, and shared responsibility for each other's welfare.

---

(5) Valdés, Dialogue on Christian Doctrine
There is here in the world one Church, that is, an assembly of the faithful who believe in one God, the Father, who place all their confidence in His Son, and who are ruled and governed by the Holy Spirit. ... Anyone who commits mortal sin is separated from this congregation.[34]

The Sacraments: Baptism and the Eucharist

Valdés was faithful to scripture and affirmed the importance of baptism and the Eucharist. Baptism represented the renunciation of worldly desires, the promise to be faithful to Christ, and to live in his example. Valdés overcame traditional distinctions between the two levels of Christian spirituality. The institutional church demanded a deeper level of commitment from those in the monastic orders than it did from ordinary lay Christians. Valdés restored to baptism the commitment to discipleship which the early church had assigned to the rite. All baptized Christians bore responsibility to the same commitments. (6)

Valdés lamented the loss of purity and simplicity in the church's practice of the Eucharistic sacrament. The Lord's Supper no longer held the meaning which Christ had intended. Valdés believed that this problem could be solved by returning to the original institution, and adhering to its intentions and practices "without adding or taking away anything from what Christ had done, or said, or commanded."[37]

> **(6) *Valdés*, Dialogue on Christian Doctrine**
> *[Those baptized] renounced Satan with all his pomp and evil desires and ... they also renounced the world, that is to say, appetites and worldly desires. And they promised to be perfect in the Order of Jesus Christ, to have faith and love toward Him, and to follow His most holy doctrine and imitate His most perfect life.*[36]

On Divine Satisfaction

Valdés recognized that Christ had died for the sins of humankind. But he was resistant to the traditional sacrificial interpretation proposed by Anselm some 300 years earlier. Anselm argued that Christ's death had satisfied the divine demand for justice, and made atonement possible. Valdés was not so sure. He was not comfortable with the idea that God had been "satisfied" by Christ's death. (7)

Valdés reflected on this theme often in his writings. He emphasized forgiveness over Anselm's theory of divine satisfaction. Valdés' more radical followers, like Bernardino Ochino, also taught that forgiveness came through justification and sanctification.[39]

Anselm's theory of atonement through divine satisfaction was based on medieval penitential practices, and focussed exclusively on the benefits to the Christian individual. Valdés also considered the cosmic dimensions of Christ's sacrifice, and concluded that creation, as well as humanity, was the beneficiary of his atonement. Christ's restoration of humanity would atone for Adam's corruption, and all of creation would be restored.[40]

> **(7) *Valdés*, El Evangelico segun San Mateo**
> *I understand that Christ intended to impress upon our spirits his death ... in order that, wherever in the Gospel it speaks of the remission of sins and reconciliation with God which is like an amnesty or a general pardon, we can be assured of pardon, considering that Christ is justified and seeing that his blood has been shed. And here it is good to repeat what I have said many times, that God in the execution of the rigors of his justice upon Christ, had in mind my assurance more than his own satisfaction.*[38]

Justification by Faith

Valdés affirmed justification by faith, a view which differed from the traditional Catholic position. The established church offered the mechanisms for justification, or salvation, through acts of penance, or prayers to the saints, to give two examples. Valdés did not believe that these mechanisms were necessary, and argued that spirituality and faith were the fruit of justification, not vice versa. In other words, Christ's death justified all of humanity, so that humanity might be righteous. (8)

> *(8) Valdés,* **Ziento i Diez Consideraciones**
> [T]hose who understand justification as the fruit of their spirituality follow Plato and Aristotle. And those who understand their spirituality to be the fruit of justification, justification being the fruit of faith, follow St. Paul and St. Peter. ... The principal thing to understand is this: that [God] put all our sins on his most precious Son Jesus Christ our Lord, in order to put in us the righteousness of Jesus Christ our Lord Himself.[41]

The typically Protestant phrase "by faith alone" rarely appeared in Valdés' writings. Valdés so emphatically denied the saving efficacy of works of merit, that it would seem he believed in salvation by faith alone. But Valdés did not identify completely with the Lutheran position. He believed that an authentic saving faith was a "living faith," or an "inspired" or "revealed faith."[42] In contrast to Luther, Valdés was drawn to the concept of faith expressed in the Book of James. Faith justified humanity, but it had to be a living faith, expressed through works of charity.[43]

A Non-Violent Church

Juan de Valdés lived during a time when the established church openly relied on its coercive powers to defend and promote Christian interests. In Spain, fanaticism fanned by incendiary but orthodox preachers among the Old Christians led to violence against New Christians of Jewish descent. The Spanish Alumbrados and the Valdesians in Naples were targets of this violence, but responded non-violently, guided by their evangelical convictions.

Their understanding of the Gospel led them to reject coercion in social relationships. Christians were called to be peacemakers, following

Christ's example. Even victims of severe persecution should not respond with violence, but "enjoy peace with God, an inner peace."[44]

At a time when Imperialism was being justified in the name of evangelization, Valdés wrote, "I ought to guard myself as from fire against persecuting anyone in any manner, pretending thereby to serve God."[45] Neither religious intolerance nor coercive defense of the truth were acceptable to Valdés. Christians should act mercifully, not severely, toward those who had done wrong, or who believed differently. (9)

> *(9) Valdés,* **Ziento i Diez Consideraciones**
> *One must not allow oneself to be blinded by violent passions which lead to sin against God out of an ignorance born of malice.*[46]

Conclusion

Juan de Valdés understood the meaning of a church differently than did established medieval Catholicism. His views also stood in contrast to the Protestantism emerging in Europe during this time. During the sixteenth and seventeenth centuries, Valdesian influence spread throughout Europe.

Shortly after the Italian publication of *Ciento y Diez Consideraciones Divinas*, three French editions appeared between 1563 and 1565. The text was well-received by French Evangelists, particularly those in the southern part of the country. But the text was not popular with the Calvinists. The dogmatic rationalism of Calvinism, which had been established by this time, left little room for the Valdesian emphasis on the Spirit. Theodore Beza, Calvin's successor, may have felt personal admiration for Valdés, but he nevertheless energetically opposed the publication of Valdés's works. Beza wrote that they "should never have been published, because they were full of errors and blasphemies against the Scriptures" and "were in many places not unlike the Anabaptist spirit."[47]

A Calvinist pastor in Holland translated and published *Ciento y Diez Consideraciones Divinas* in 1565 without the permission of authorities in Geneva. He was summarily suspended from his pastoral duties and the edition was confiscated. An English version was published at Oxford in

1638, and awakened little response from the established church, although John Wesley may have been familiar with it. But dissidents like the Quakers and the Familists came to treasure the book. In fact, the modern recovery of Valdesianism, spearheaded by nineteenth century Quakers, began with the discovery of *Ciento y Diez Consideraciones Divinas* in the library of an elderly English Quaker.

[1] José A. Pistonesi, *Del Beneficio de Jesucristo Crucificado* (Buenos Aires: Libería "La Aurora," 1942), 99. My translation.

[2] Juan Pérez de Tudela Bueso, *Biblioteca de Autores Españoles: Obras Escogidas de Bartolomé de las Casas, II* (Madrid: Ediciones Atlas, 1961), 176. My translation.

[3] George Huntston Williams, *The Radical Reformation* (Philadelphia: The Westminster Press, 1962), 1-4.

[4] José C. Nieto, *Juan de Valdés and the Origins of the Spanish and Italian Reformation* (Geneva: Librairie Droz, 1970), 64.

[5] Nieto, *Juan de Valdés and the Origins of the Spanish and Italian Reformation*, 92. "Alcaraz, an exotic plant growing in Castilian soil which was heavily fertilized with ascetic and mystical ideas, decided to put his own roots in the Bible and nourish himself from it. This, the source and root of his heresy, does not need to be explained by appealing to remote sources or sociological or psychological theories."

[6] John Driver, *The Religious Thought of Juan de Valdés*, diss., Southern Methodist U, Texas, 1966, 22.

[7] Marcel Bataillon, *Erasmo y España: Estudios sobre la Historia Espiritual del Siglo XVI* (México: Fondo de Cultura Económico, 1966), 178-179. A participant at Escalona recalled that following one sermon, María de Casalla took out a book written in the vernacular – undoubtedly a copy of The Gospels and the Epistles – and read a Pauline Epistle.

[8] Bataillon, 173.

[9] José C. Nieto, *Juan de Valdés and the Origins of the Spanish and Italian Reformation* (Geneva: Librairie Droz, 1970), 91.

[10] Marcel Bataillon, *Erasmo y España: Estudios sobre la Historia Espiritual del Siglo XVI* (México: Fondo de Cultura Económico, 1966), 171. My translation. A Spiritual Franciscan, Francisco Ortiz, preached a sermon in Burgos during Lent, in 1524, in which he declared that "Christ is more perfectly present in the soul of the righteous than he is in the holy sacrament of the altar."

[11] José C. Nieto, *Juan de Valdés and the Origins of the Spanish and Italian Reformation* (Geneva: Librairie Droz, 1970), 73.

[12] Nieto, *Juan de Valdés and the Origins of the Spanish and Italian Reformation*, 84.

[13] José C. Nieto, *Valdés' Two Catechisms: The Dialogue on Christian Doctrine and the Christian Instruction for Children* (Lawrence, KS: Coronado Press, 1981), 110.

[14] Nieto, *Valdés' Two Catechisms: The Dialogue on Christian Doctrine and the Christian Instruction for Children*, 142-151.

[15] Nieto, *Valdés' Two Catechisms: The Dialogue on Christian Doctrine and the Christian Instruction for Children*, 155-156.

[16] Nieto, *Valdés' Two Catechisms: The Dialogue on Christian Doctrine and the Christian Instruction for Children*, 159. "Because ... the three chapters of the Gospel written by St. Matthew, ... are so often praised in the Dialogue, I resolved to translate them into our Romance Castilian and to set them down here, so that if your lordship, after having read the Dialogue and having heard them praised in it, should want to see them for himself, he could satisfy his desire."

[17] John Driver, *The Religious Thought of Juan de Valdés*, diss., Southern Methodist U, Texas, 1966, 52.

[18] Driver, 53.

[19] Driver, 55. My translation.

[20] José C. Nieto, *Juan de Valdés and the Origins of the Spanish and Italian Reformation* (Geneva: Librairie Droz, 1970), 145 n. 26.

[21] George Huntston Williams, *La Reforma Radical* (México: Fondo de Cultura Económica, 1983), 577.

[22] Williams, *La Reforma Radical*, 586.

[23] John Driver, *The Religious Thought of Juan de Valdés*, diss., Southern Methodist U, Texas, 1966, 57.

[24] Driver, 200 n. 126.

[25] George Huntston Williams, *La Reforma Radical* (México: Fondo de Cultura Económica, 1983), 586.

[26] John Driver, *The Religious Thought of Juan de Valdés*, diss., Southern Methodist U, Texas, 1966, 60.

[27] Driver, 60.

[28] Driver, 202 n. 149.

[29] José C. Nieto, *Juan de Valdés and the Origins of the Spanish and*

Italian Reformation (Geneva: Librairie Droz, 1970), 146.

[30] John Driver, *The Religious Thought of Juan de Valdés*, diss., Southern Methodist U, Texas, 1966, 167.

[31] Driver, 160-161.

[32] Marcel Bataillon, *Erasmo y España: Estudios sobre la Historia Espiritual del Siglo XVI* (México: Fondo de Cultura Económico, 1966), 705 n. 2.

[33] José C. Nieto, *Juan de Valdés and the Origins of the Spanish and Italian Reformation* (Geneva: Librairie Droz, 1970), 148-149, 164.

[34] José C. Nieto, ed., *Valdés' Two Catechisms: The Dialogue on Christian Doctrine and the Christian Instruction for Children* (Lawrence, KS: Coronado Press, 1981), 73.

[35] Luis de Usoz i Rio, ed., *Ziento i Diez Consideraziones de Juan de Valdés* (1863), 418.

[36] José C. Nieto, ed., *Valdés' Two Catechisms: The Dialogue on Christian Doctrine and the Christian Instruction for Children* (Lawrence, KS: Coronado Press, 1981, 65.

[37] John Driver, *The Religious Thought of Juan de Valdés*, diss., Southern Methodist U, Texas, 1966, 142-143.

[38] Eduardo Boehmer, ed., *El Evangelio según San Mateo Declarado por Juan de Valdés* (Madrid: Librería Nacional y Extranjera, 1880), 484. My translation and emphasis.

[39] George Huntston Williams, *La Reforma Radical* (México: Fondo de Cultura Económica, 1983), 582-583.

[40] Luis de Usoz i Rio, ed., *Ziento i Diez Consideraziones de Juan de Valdés*(1863), 305, 307. My translation. "Just as man in his depravation corrupted all of creation, so also in the restoration of man, all creation shall be restored; in the first Adam all humanity being subjected to suffering and death, all creation was flawed; in the second Adam, Jesus Christ our Lord, all humanity was brought to happiness and eternal life, all creation will be restored. ... All creation will recover that being, that disposition, and that order for which it was created, to make humanity in its restoration immortal and happy."

[41] Usoz i Rio, 356-357. My translation.

[42] John Driver, *The Religious Thought of Juan de Valdés*, diss., Southern Methodist U, Texas, 1966, 97.

[43] José C. Nieto, ed., *Valdés' Two Catechisms: The Dialogue on Christian Doctrine and the Christian Instruction for Children* (Lawrence, KS:

Coronado Press, 1981), 110. "This faith I'm speaking of ... is like a living fire in the hearts of the faithful ... [J]ust as it is impossible for (the fire not to burn, so also it is impossible for) this faith to exist without works of charity. If there were none it would cease to be true faith. ... [I]t is necessary for reason to be subjected to the obedience of faith." (Valdés, *Dialogue on Christian Doctrine*). The words in parentheses appear in the original Spanish version but are missing from the English translation.

[44] Eduardo Boehmer, ed., *El Evangelio según San Mateo Declarado por Juan de Valdés* (Madrid: Librería Nacional y Extranjera, 1880), 66, 79, 81. My translation. "Those who belong to the kingdom of heaven, Christ calls to be peacemakers .... Even though they are the victims of persecution and death at the hands of the world, they enjoy peace with God, an inner peace as well as with others. They do violence to no one. ... Those who receive the gospel and enter the kingdom of heaven give themselves to a life of purity as Christ teaches. ... His intention for his disciples, those who are born again by the gospel, is that they live in this world with the same meekness with which he lived, as sheep in the midst of wolves."

[45] Luis de Usoz i Rio, ed., *Ziento i Diez Consideraziones de Juan de Valdés* (1863), 265. My translation.

[46] Usoz i Rio, 204, 391. My translation.

[47] John Driver, *The Religious Thought of Juan de Valdés*, diss., Southern Methodist U, Texas, 1966, 172. See also Domingo Ricart, *Juan de Valdés y el Pensamiento Religioso Europeo de los Siglos XVI Y XVII* (México: El Colegio de México, 1958), 50-55.

Chapter 12

Sixteenth-Century Movements: Radicalism in a Lutheran Context

The third kind of service should be a truly evangelical order and should not be held in a public place for all sorts of people. But those who want to be Christians ... should sign their names and meet alone in a house somewhere to pray, to read, to baptize, to receive the sacrament, and to do other Christian works. According to this order, those who do not lead Christian lives could be known, reproved, corrected, cast out, or excommunicated, according to the rule of Christ, Matthew 18 [:15-17]. Here one could also solicit benevolent gifts to be willingly given and distributed to the poor, according to St. Paul's example, 2 Corinthians 9. Here would be no need of much and elaborate singing. Here one could set up a brief and neat order for baptism and the sacrament and center everything on the Word, prayer, and love. ...

In short, if one had the kind of people and persons who wanted to be Christians in earnest, the rules and regulations would soon be ready. But as yet I neither can nor desire to begin such a congregation or assembly or to make rules for it. ... For if I should try to make it up out of my own need, it might turn into a sect. (Martin Luther, *Preface to the German Mass and Order of Service.*)[1]

Introduction

Martin Luther's vision of an evangelical church order, not dependent on secular powers, was never realized under the auspices of Lutheranism. Lutheranism's most radical elements were limited to several outspoken preachers, and to the peasant movement which, with Luther's approval, was crushed by the forces of Protestant and Catholic princes in 1525.

Neither the initiative of the rogue preachers, nor that of the peasant uprising, produced a community which could survive without the support of secular authorities.

During the early years of the Lutheran Reformation, which began in 1517, institutional structures allowed a prince to authorize a priest or monk to preach. Three Lutheran preachers, authorized in such a way, proved to be too radical for Luther's taste. He requested that secular authorities withdraw their support for Andreas Carlstadt, Jacob Strauss, and Thomas Müntzer, the preachers in question.

Andreas Bodenstein von Carlstadt

Liturgical and Social Innovations

Andreas Carlstadt, *c.*1477-1541, was Luther's teacher and colleague at the University of Wittenberg, and from 1516, served as dean of the theological faculty. During 1521-1522, when Luther was at Wartburg, Carlstadt became the leader of the reform movement in Wittenberg. His vision for reform was more radical than Luther's. On Christmas Eve, 1521, he celebrated what has been called "the first Evangelical Eucharist." The liturgy for the mass was in German, it was officiated without priestly vestments, omitted all references to sacrifice and the elevation of the host, and offered both cup and bread to the entire congregation.

Behind these innovations was Carlstadt's growing biblicism. Carlstadt was anxious to put the priesthood of believers into practice. He encouraged lay people to read the Bible, and supported the lay celebration of communion in private homes. Believing that the rite of baptism incorporated the baptized into the body of Christ, Carlstadt suppressed the practice of infant baptism. As early as 1520, he expressed concern about a lack of moral seriousness in the Lutheran Reformation. Carlstadt said, "I am grieved by [Luther's] bold deprecation of James. ... Beware that you do not take a paper and loveless faith for the greatest work."[2]

Responding to popular demand, Carlstadt chose to celebrate communion with both bread and wine. However, it was a daring act, and contrary to the prince's orders. Despite opposition from authorities, Carlstadt continued to celebrate the "Evangelical Eucharist" throughout January. He ordered images removed from the churches in Wittenberg. Furthermore, acting on his convictions regarding the celibacy of the clergy, Carlstadt married a young woman from his congregation. In addition to these liturgical reforms, he initiated several social changes. He forbade prostitution and begging, and established welfare and educational programs for the poor.

Official reprisals were not long in coming. Carlstadt's permission to preach was withdrawn. Luther returned to Wittenberg, reversed Carlstadt's initiatives for reform, and restored traditional liturgical practices. Carlstadt was exiled to Orlamünde where he became pastor in the village's parish church.

Concrete Expressions of Solidarity

Meanwhile, Carlstadt's radical convictions continued to evolve. He was a fervent proponent of the priesthood of believers. He renounced his title of "Doctor," and asked to be called "brother Andreas." He did not wear clerical vestments, and assumed the role of a peasant farmer. Carlstadt's concrete expressions of social solidarity were well-received by the common people; however, the authorities perceived them as a threat. In September 1524, Luther himself had Carlstadt expelled from Saxony. Carlstadt became a pilgrim and an outcast in a nation troubled by social agitation and discontent among its peasant population.

In Rottenberg, the artisan class, which was hostile toward the patrician upper class, had declared its support for the peasants' demands. In March 1525, there was great social agitation in the city. At first, Carlstadt refused to take sides in the confrontation, preaching a message of social justice and counseling evangelical moderation. However, in the face of growing agitation, Carlstadt joined the peasants as chaplain and counselor. He sought to contain the movement's demands within their claims for social justice, but his warnings fell on deaf ears. Carlstadt was finally forced to escape in a basket lowered over the city wall. After a period in Strassburg, Carlstadt took up residence in Basel where he spent the last ten years of his life, from 1530-1541, teaching in Reformed circles.

Two Tracts

Carlstadt's writings contained radical ideas which he never put into practice, never having the community basis for experimentation. Carlstadt wrote two tracts, *On the Removal of Images* and *There Should Be No Beggars among Christians*, on January 27, 1522, just after he had instituted his surprising innovations in Wittenberg. *There Should Be No Beggars* recalled Luther's intention, expressed as early as 1519, to ban begging. Carlstadt applied the New Testament vision of Jubilee to contemporary situations of social injustice. Referring to Deuteronomy 15 and Leviticus 23, Carlstadt argued that cities were required, by God, to care for their inhabitants. Everyone had a responsibility to the poor, particularly those in positions of authority. (1) Compassion and generosity were essential to both social justice and Christian witness.[4]

---

(1) *Andreas Carlstadt,* There Should Be No Beggars

This passage teaches us that each city should care for its inhabitants. Therefore, if someone falls into poverty, all – and the authorities in particular – should have pity on the poor ....[3]

In 1524, in Orlamünde, Carlstadt wrote *Whether One Should Proceed Slowly and Avoid Offending the Weak in Matters that Concern God's Will*. The tract was addressed to the town clerk of Joachimsthal, and contained criticism of the conservative caution that characterized the Lutheran Reformation. Carlstadt believed that this conservatism sprang from a dangerous acquiescence to the opinion of the majority. Carlstadt warned that the majority should not be favored over God's word. (2)

Carlstadt perceived that the "weak" were the authorities, both secular and religious, not the poor. He did not accept the excuse that change should be delayed out of deference to the weak. He recognized the logical inconsistencies in the argument that "For the sake of the weak, one should not fulfill God's command quickly, but rather tarry until they become intelligent and strong."[6] Such rhetoric clearly favored those already in power.

---

(2) *Andreas Carlstadt,* Whether One Should Proceed Slowly

I must therefore tell you that neither in this case nor in other matters concerning God should you consider how the great crowd speaks or judges, but rather look only at God's Word. For at the least it is clear that the princes of the biblical scholars and the whole crowd formerly have erred and can err.[5]

Jacob Strauss

We do not know much about the spiritual pilgrimage that led Jacob Strauss, *c.*1483-*c.*1533, to became a radical within Lutheranism. A Dominican monk with a doctorate in theology, Strauss was among the first to bring the Reformation to miners and commoners in Tyrol, in the south of Germany. He was expelled from the Dominican order because of this activity. Strauss found protection under the Lutheran umbrella in Saxony, and was named pastor in Eisenach by the Prince Protector of Lutheranism. He rejected violence, and advocated dialogue in its place. In fact, Strauss served as a mediator in the conflicts between Luther and Luther's critics. Luther's protection allowed him to flee into exile following the horrible massacre of peasants at Frankenhausen.[7]

The Practice of Usury

Among Strauss's extant writings are a sermon *On Simoniacal Baptism*, which questioned traditional baptismal practices, and another on usury. Basing his argument on clear biblical foundations, Strauss rejected the practice of usury, in which money is lent at interest. This was not a particularly radical position – it had been traditionally assumed by the medieval church – but it was articulated at a time when capitalistic mercantilism was on the upsurge. Many were attempting to justify usury, but Strauss argued against it on biblical and humanitarian grounds. Luther and Zwingli also rejected usury until 1524, but did not go as far as Strauss did. Strauss suggested that people actively resist paying interest.

Strauss believed that the church was a loving, caring community. Relationships within the church should not be guided by material concerns, and usury had no place there. (3) Strauss condemned the church's

> **(3) Jacob Strauss, On Usury**
> *Every Christian should keep ... the commandment of God ... to freely and willingly help his neighbor in need, with no concern for material gain. To receive one cent above the amount of the loan is usury. By its very nature, usury is contrary to love for one's neighbor and is forbidden by God.*[8]

> **(4) Jacob Strauss, On Usury**
> *The person who in his poverty continues to pay interest is unfortunately and completely disoriented in his faith. ... The poor victims, who are ignorant of the gospel and seduced by the example and the teachings of the anti-Christ and all the anti-Christian priests, doctors and monks, should by order of no one pay interest now that they have come to know the truth.*[11]

revision of its traditional policy on usury. Responding to pressure from interest groups, the church now allowed Christians to charge each other interest.[9] Protesting the church's hypocrisy, Strauss suggested that Christian debtors discontinue their interest payments, and "obey God rather than men."[10] (4) For their part, Christian creditors should follow the word of God and stop charging interest.[12]

Knowing that creditors might forcibly seek to collect their interest, Strauss counseled the poor to respond with non-violent resistance. "You must be willing to lose body, goods, life and honor in order to hold to Christ and his Word."[13] Strauss also counseled those burdened by interest payments inherited from previous generations to practice civil disobedience. He argued that one was not bound by another's commitment.[14] However, Strauss was not naive, and anticipated that taking such a radical stance would elicit negative reactions from those who benefitted from the practice of usury. He warned: "It is commonly said among the money lenders and those who participate in the system that anyone who preaches against usury is guilty of sedition."[15]

Thomas Müntzer[16]

Itinerant Preaching

Thomas Müntzer, *c*.1488-1525, was by far the most controversial of the Lutheran radicals. Like Luther, he was an Augustinian monk, and on Luther's recommendation he was named to a pastorate in Zwickau. The parish had many weavers, day laborers, and miners, and Müntzer's radical social beliefs soon took active shape. His denunciation of the opulent lifestyle of local Franciscan monks won him popular acclaim. Müntzer soon joined forces with Nicholas Storch, a weaver, Thomas Dreschel, and Marcus Thomas Stübner, men who held similar beliefs. The group opposed infant baptism, but did not call for the rebaptism of adults. They based their argument on the text, "Whoever believes and is baptized will be saved." (Mark 16:16.6). Luther referred to the group as "the prophets of Zwickau," because of their spiritual interpretation of the Bible.[17]

Müntzer was expelled from Zwickau on April 15, 1521 because of his participation in this revolutionary group. He surfaced in Prague two months later, where he preached and published a tract. Müntzer believed that all classes had been betrayed by the scholars and priests. All classes were suffering from spiritual impoverishment. Quoting the early writer, Hegesippus, Müntzer showed that the early church had been prostituted by religious authorities. He believed the contemporary situation could be remedied if congregations were permitted to elect their own pastors. During his stay in Prague, Müntzer apparently came to believe that recourse to violence, on the part of the elect, was justified if it established a new order.

After travelling and preaching throughout Germany, Müntzer was named to a temporary pastorate in Allstedt. There, he inaugurated a new German liturgy which allowed the congregation to participate actively in worship. He also counseled that baptism be postponed until adulthood, but stopped short of proposing that adult members be rebaptized. In Allstedt, Müntzer formed a secret society charged with executing, at the opportune moment, "the eternal covenant of God."[18] He warned that the elect must carry a cross of suffering.

A Call to Arms

On July 13, 1524, Müntzer preached the most important sermon of his life before princes John and John Frederick, and a select group of provincial and municipal authorities. Müntzer exhorted the princes to fulfill God's will by pouring wrath on the godless and defending His holy revolutionaries. He asked that they not be misled by hypocritical clergy, but listen instead to the peasants and lay people. The church must be returned to its roots, either in an orderly fashion or through violent means. If the princes refused to "wipe out the godless," then Müntzer warned that the sword would be passed over into the hands of the people.[19]

Müntzer hoped that an apparently imminent agreement between miners and authorities might herald the realization of his dream for a community of goods. Müntzer dreamed of an earthly restoration of the primitive church in which there was both spiritual and material equality. Müntzer believed that a community of goods would satisfy people's material needs and free them from worldly anxiety. (5) All of this was too revolutionary for the princes, and the authorities promptly issued a warning. Müntzer could no longer stay in Allstedt. On August 7, 1524, he fled under cover of darkness to join the peasant uprising in Mühlhausen.

> *(5) Müntzer*
> *In the face of usury, taxes, and rents no one can have faith.*[20]

Mühlhausen soon became the center of revolutionary activity. Müntzer's preaching gave the miners and peasants a sense of their mission as instruments of divine judgment. The princes had refused to fulfill God's will, so the peasants must do so instead. While Müntzer was not responsible for the organization of the movement, it probably could not have continued without his preaching. Following the tragic outcome of the battle of Frankenhausen, Müntzer was captured, brutally tortured, executed, and his remains placed on exhibit.

Müntzer attempted to participate in a counter-cultural alternative community. However, by resorting to violence, he betrayed his own original vision of a community of the poor which did not require force to establish nor to sustain. Even some of Müntzer's followers expressed their doubt. For example, a group of radical Zwinglians, identifying themselves as "seven new young Müntzers against Luther," wrote to Müntzer in the fall of 1524, and questioned his activities. (6)

> *(6) Letter from "seven new young Müntzers against Luther"*
> *Moreover the gospel and its adherents are not to be protected by the sword, nor are they thus to protect themselves, which, as we learn from our brother, is thy opinion and practice. True Christian believers are sheep among wolves.*[21]

Andreas Carlstadt, Jacob Strauss, and Thomas Müntzer did not create any lasting social changes nor viable communities. However, their examples and their writings inspired other radical European thinkers.

The Peasants' War[22]

The Twelve Articles

There had been outbreaks of peasant rebellion in central Europe throughout the Middle Ages. In German-speaking lands, the peasants struggled to conserve ancient common law provisions. New legal structures threatened the traditional liberties of rural peasants. The situation was particularly critical in areas where feudal serfs worked the vast landholdings of monasteries. The church had tightened its control over its sources of cheap labor. In such situations, the peasants appealed to traditional provisions of Germanic common law, under which the rights and duties of commoners were respected.

In the spring of 1521, Balthasar Hubmaier, 1481-1528, was named parish priest in the city of Waldshut. However, by the summer of 1522, Hubmaier had begun a spiritual pilgrimage, sparked by his reading of Luther's writings. Eventually, he would join the Anabaptist movement. In June 1524, the Great Peasant War broke out near Schaffhausen, in the Black Forest in southwestern Germany. The peasants found the Waldshut congregation to be sympathetic to their cause. Indeed, Hubmaier, their pastor, had been forced by authorities to flee Waldshut, because of his evangelical sympathies. During the last four months of 1524, Hubmaier sought refuge in Schaffhausen, among the peasants.

The *Twelve Articles*, published on March 12, 1525, summarized the peasants' demands. The demands were supported by the peasants' interpretation of the gospel, and reflected the teachings of Martin Luther. Balthasar Hubmaier, the Anabaptist pastor from Waldshut, spent four months exiled in their midst, and assisted them with the revision of the *Twelve Articles*. The final edition was the work of an artisan-furrier from Swabia, named Sebastian Lotzer.

The Christian Union of peasants, organized under the leadership of Sebastian Lotzer, declared that it would not resort to violence. This declaration mitigated a potentially explosive situation, and on April 17, 1525, a peace agreement was signed. The agreement met some of the peasants' demands, and put an end to the first phase of the war.

Twelve Articles,[23] **published March 12, 1525**

The First Article – Appointment of Minister

First, it is our humble petition and desire ... that the entire community should choose and appoint a minister, and that we should have the right to depose him should he conduct himself improperly. The minister thus chosen should teach us the holy gospel pure and simple, without any human addition, doctrine or ordinance.

The Second Article – Tithing

Since the right tithe is established in the Old Testament and fulfilled in the New, we are ready and willing to pay the fair tithe of grain. ... We will in the future collect the tithe through our church elders, appointed by the congregation and distribute from it, to the sufficient livelihood of the minister and his family elected by the entire congregation. ... The remainder shall be given to the poor of the place.

The Third Article – Freedom

It has been the custom hitherto for men to hold us as their own property, which is pitiable enough considering that Christ has redeemed and purchased us without exception, by the shedding of His precious blood, the lowly as well as the great. Accordingly, it is consistent with Scripture that we should be free and we wish to be so. Not that we want to be absolutely free ... but that we should live by the commandments, love the Lord our God and our neighbor.

cont.

Carlstadt in Rottenburg

On March 21, 1525, the second phase of the war broke out in an outlying district of Rottenberg, an imperial city in Franconia. Andreas Carlstadt, who had taken refuge in the city, refused to participate in the social tumult. He preached social justice and counseled moderation. Carlstadt hoped to mitigate excesses within the peasant movement, but a growing excitement among the peasants deafened them to his counsels. Finally, fearing for his life, he fled the city. Meanwhile, in Frankfort, Gerhard Westerburg had shown solidarity with the peasants' cause, and bloodshed had been averted. The authorities in Frankfort made some concessions to the peasants, in exchange for Westerburg's exile.

Disaster at Frankenhausen

In Mühlhausen, in the region of Thuringia, Thomas Müntzer proclaimed the advent of a new order, which would be preceded by the destruction of the godless. Müntzer saw himself as a warrior-priest, signing his letters, "Thomas Müntzer with the sword of Gideon."[24] In his sermons, Müntzer predicted a glorious victory for the elect, and encouraged the peasants to "let not the sword of the saints get cold."[25]

By mid-May 1525, a large contingent of Thuringian peasants had gathered at nearby Frankenhausen. A military confrontation appeared unavoidable when Philip of Hesse mobilized his troops against the assembled peasants. The morning of May 15, Thomas Müntzer preached to the peasant warriors, assuring them of God's favor. After an initial skirmish in which the peasants appeared to have the upper hand, Philip offered peace in exchange for Müntzer. The peasants refused the overture. Taking advantage of the peasants' indecision and confusion, Philip's troops unleashed a withering attack that decimated the peasant army. This marked the climax of a campaign which cost the lives of some 100,000 peasants.

Luther had written a letter blaming both the princes and the peasants for the situation. He called on both sides to mediate their differences. Faced with the growing threat of peasant rebellion, Luther wrote a second and more severe letter, in which he condemned the rebels in no uncertain terms: "Let everyone who can, smite, slay, and stab, secretly or openly, remembering that nothing can be more poisonous, hurtful, or devilish than a rebel. It is just as when one must kill a mad dog; if you do not strike him, he will strike you, and a whole land with you."[26] After the disaster at Frankenhausen, Luther wrote a third letter that responded to people's protests and doubts in the wake of the slaughter of so many peasants.

The Fourth Article – Ownership of Fish

[I]t has been the custom heretofore that no poor man was allowed to catch venison or wild fowl, or fish in flowing water, which seems to us quite unseemly and unbrotherly, as well as selfish and not according to the word of God. ... Accordingly, it is our desire that if a man holds possession of waters that he should prove from satisfactory documents that his right has been wittingly acquired by purchase.

The Fifth Article – Ownership of Woods

We are aggrieved in the matter of woodcutting, for our noble folk have appropriated all the woods to themselves alone. ... It should be free to every member of the community to help himself to such firewood as he needs in his home.

The Sixth Article – Excessive Services

Our sixth complaint is in regard to the excessive services demanded of us, which increase from day to day. We ask that this matter be properly looked into, so that we shall not continue to be oppressed in this way, ... since our forefathers served only according to the word of God.

The Seventh Article – Oppression by Lords

Seventh, we will not hereafter allow ourselves to be further oppressed by our lords. What the lords possess is to be held according to the agreement between the lord and the peasant.

cont.

The Eighth Article – Fair Rent

We are greatly burdened by holdings which cannot support the rent exacted from them. The peasants suffer loss in this way and are ruined. We ask that the lords may appoint persons of honor to inspect these holdings and fix a rent in accordance with justice, so that the peasant shall not work for nothing, since the laborer is worthy of his hire.

The Ninth Article – The Law

We are burdened with the great evil in the constant making of new laws. We are not judged according to the offense but sometimes with great ill will, and sometimes much too leniently. In our opinion we should be judged according to the old written law, so that the case shall be decided according to its merits, and not with favors.

The Tenth Article – Appropriation of Land

We are aggrieved that certain individuals have appropriated meadows and fields which at one time belonged to the community. These we will take again into our own hands unless they were rightfully purchased.

The Eleventh Article – Custom of Heriot

We will entirely abolish the custom called 'Todfall' [heriot], and will no longer endure it, nor allow widows and orphans to be thus shamefully robbed against God's will.

cont.

Conclusion: The Peasants and the Anabaptists[27]

The peasant protest of 1524-1525 was a Christian plea for social justice. The movement had roots in Protestant doctrines of biblical authority and evangelical freedom. When attempts at dialogue and evangelical moderation failed, violence erupted and was repressed with even greater violence. In the end, the feudal system remained intact, and clergy and civil authorities maintained their monopoly over issues of faith and life.

Among Christian groups of the period, the Anabaptists were linked most closely to the peasant movement. Anabaptist leaders, including Hubmaier, Carlstadt, Strauss, Westerburg, Melchior Rinck, from Hesse, Clement Ziegler, a lay preacher and peasant leader in the Alsace region, and Hans Hut, the itinerant Anabaptist evangelist, all showed compassion and sympathetic solidarity toward the peasants.

Following the brutal suppression of the peasant uprising, many people sympathetic to the peasant cause seem to have joined clandestine conventicles of Anabaptists. Anabaptist congregations arose in the same areas in which the peasant movement had flourished. Within these free, albeit persecuted, communities, the survivors of the peasant struggle were able to realize many of their aspirations for social justice. There were many similarities between the peasant and Anabaptist movements.

Both groups believed that the gospel was socially and economically relevant. In fact, Luther had reproached the peasants for basing their claims for justice on the gospel. Both groups protested against paying tithes which increased the riches of an already powerful church. Both protested the practice of usury, which further oppressed the poor. The peasants were willing to continue paying tithes, but only in support of their own

> ### *The Twelfth Article – Conclusion*
>
> *In the twelfth place it is our conclusion and final resolution, that if any one or more of these articles should not be in agreement with the word of God, which we do not think, we will willingly recede from such article when it is proved to be against the word of God by a clear explanation of Scripture. ... The peace of God abide with us all.*

chosen pastor, and their poor. The Anabaptists gave tithes in this manner, through their free church structures. Both groups opposed the social structures that perpetuated inequality. The peasants believed that meadows and streams should be open to all in need, not just the nobility. In a similar protest, the Anabaptists rejected all titles of honor.

Both groups claimed the right to freedom: the peasants wished to be free from servitude, and the Anabaptists believed in uncoerced freedom of thought and action. Both groups sought freedom from the control of the established church. The peasants claimed the right to name and depose their own pastors. The Anabaptists not only claimed this right, but practiced it in their clandestine congregations.

Both movements resisted established authority, secular and ecclesiastical. The peasants opposed economic oppression by their feudal lords. The Anabaptists opposed authorities, both Catholic and Protestant, who demanded an oath of loyalty and absolute allegiance. In their protests, both groups committed acts of civil and ecclesiastical disobedience.

Both groups had hoped to achieve social and economic equality through non-violent means. The peasants were incited to violence by apocalyptic visionaries in their midst. With the disaster at Münster being the one exception, Anabaptists held to their conviction that the survival of Christ's community was not dependant on the power of coercion.

Like radical movements which preceded them, the peasants and the Anabaptists struggled against violent repression, and formed alternative communities which were witnesses to a new social and religious vision.

Notes

[1] Ulrich S. Leupold, ed., *Liturgy and Hymns*, vol. 53 of *Luther's Works*, ed. Helmut T. Lehmann (Philadelphia: Fortress Press, 1965), 62-64.

[2] George H. Williams, *The Radical Reformation* (Philadelphia: Westminster Press, 1962), 40.

[3] John Howard Yoder, ed., *Textos Escogidos de la Reforma Radical* (Buenos Aires: Editorial La Aurora, 1976), 52-53. My translation.

[4] Yoder, 57-58. "God desires that you look upon the tribulations, the needs and the sufferings of your brothers; and what's more, of all men, and that through your generous benevolence you make begging unnecessary. [In this] you will help no one more than you do your own pocketbook." My translation.

[5] Ronald J. Sider, ed., *Karlstadt's Battle with Luther: Documents in a Liberal-Radical Debate* (Philadelphia: Fortress Press, 1978), 50.

[6] Sider, 64. Carlstadt's opinion pleased the Zwinglian radicals in Switzerland. In the autumn of 1524 they wrote that "thou and Carlstadt are esteemed by us the purest proclaimers and preachers of the purest Word of God. ... We have good hopes of Jacob Strauss and a few others, who are little esteemed by the slothful scholars and doctors at Wittenberg. We too are rejected by our learned shepherds." "Letters to Thomas Müntzer By Conrad Grebel and Friends," George H. Williams, ed., *Spiritual and Anabaptist Writers* (Philadelphia: Westminster Press, 1957), 78.

[7] John Howard Yoder, ed., *Textos Escogidos de la Reforma Radical* (Buenos Aires: Editorial La Aurora, 1976), 16-17.

[8] Yoder, 90. My translation.

[9] Yoder, 91. My translation. "The five per cent interest, permitted – as they claim – by the Council of Constance, is usury. ... The nobility by birth and the citizenry have obtained the Pope's approval for their usurious practices. It is easy to detect the melody of the anti-Christ in this usury, because the bonds of riches are thereby disguised."

[10] Yoder, 91. My translation.

[11] Yoder, 91-92. My translation.

[12] Yoder, 92. My translation. "All kings, princes and Christian lords, as well as their noble counsellors, should keep in mind the Word of God, so that

they do not force their subjects to charge interest, nor should they encourage or practice it themselves."

[13] Yoder, 92. My translation.

[14] Yoder, 92-93. My translation. "Jurists who, finding their justification in written law, teach and counsel the payment of usury, understand nothing in their dull and anti-Christian minds. ... No one is bound to keep promises and commitments which are not his. You have committed yourselves to God and his Word; and no obligation to pay interest assumed by your parents, or by you yourself, can obligate you."

[15] Yoder, 93. My translation.

[16] This section relies largely on the following source. George H. Williams, *The Radical Reformation* (Philadelphia: Westminster Press, 1962), 44-58.

[17] Williams, *The Radical Reformation*, 46.

[18] Williams, *The Radical Reformation*, 51.

[19] George H. Williams, ed., *Spiritual and Anabaptist Writers* (Philadelphia: Westminster Press, 1957), 63-64, 68. "O beloved lords, how handsomely the Lord will go smashing among the old pots with his rod of iron. (Ps. 2:9). Therefore, you much beloved and esteemed princes, learn your judgments directly from the mouth of God and do not let yourselves be misled by your hypocritical parsons nor be restrained by false consideration and indulgence. For the Stone [made] without hands, cut from the mountain [which will crush the fifth kingdom, (Dan. 2:34)], has become great. The poor laity [of the towns] and the peasants see it much more clearly than you. Yea, God be praised, it has become so great [that] already, if other lords or neighbors should wish to persecute you for the gospel's sake, they would be driven back by their own people! ... In just this way the sword is necessary to wipe out the godless. (Rom. 13:4). That this might now take place, however, in an orderly fashion, our cherished fathers, the princes, should do it, who with us confess Christ. If, however, they do not do it, the sword will be taken from them. (Dan. 7:26f.). ... Otherwise the Christian church (*Kirche*) cannot come back to its origin."

[20] George H. Williams, *The Radical Reformation* (Philadelphia: Westminster Press, 1962), 56.

[21] George H. Williams, ed., *Spiritual and Anabaptist Writers* (Philadelphia: Westminster Press, 1957), 85, 80.

[22] This section relies largely on the following source. George H. Williams, *The Radical Reformation* (Philadelphia: Westminster Press, 1962), 59-84.

[23] Lowell H. Zuck, ed., *Christianity and Revolution* (Philadelphia:

Temple University Press, 1975), 14-16. The Twelve Articles are excerpted from this source.

[24] George H. Williams, *The Radical Reformation* (Philadelphia: Westminster Press, 1962), 76.

[25] Williams, *The Radical Reformation*, 77.

[26] Robert C. Schultz, ed., *The Christian in Society*, vol. 46 of *Luther's Works*, ed. Helmut T. Lehmann (Philadelphia: Fortress Press, 1967), 1950.

[27] This section relies largely on the following source. Juan Driver, *Contra Corriente: Ensayos Sobre una Eclesiología Radical* (Santafé de Bogotá and Ciudad de Guatemala: Ediciones Clara-Semilla, 1994), 141-144.

Chapter 13

Sixteenth-Century Movements:
Anabaptism in a Zwinglian Context

[The Anabaptist movement] began in Switzerland, where God brought about an awakening. First of all a meeting took place between Ulrich Zwingli, Conrad Grebel ... and Felix Mantz. ... They started to discuss matters of faith and realized that infant baptism is unnecessary and moreover, is not baptism at all....

After the prayer, Georg Blaurock stood up and asked Conrad Grebel in the name of God to baptize him ... [H]e knelt down, and Conrad baptized him, since at that time there was no appointed servant of the Word.[1] Then the others turned to Georg in their turn, asking him to baptize them, which he did. ... This was the beginning of separation from the world and its evil ways. ...

So the movement spread ... Zwingli began to write and preach with fanaticism that baptism of adult believers was false and should not be tolerated. This was contrary to his earlier confession, when he himself had taught that not one clear word from God justified infant baptism. ... He persuaded the authorities to use the imperial law[2] to behead as Anabaptists those who were truly dedicated to God, those who out of conviction had made the bond of a good conscience with him. (Kaspar Braitmichel, *The Beginnings of Anabaptism*, 1565).[3]

Introduction: Anabaptist Beginnings in Zurich[4]

The roots of evangelical Anabaptism were to be found in the circle of radical disciples surrounding Ulrich Zwingli in Zurich. Late in 1518, Zwingli, a Swiss priest of Erasmian orientation, had been appointed parish priest in Zurich. Committed to biblical study, he soon came to the conclusion that only the gospel could provide spiritual authority. This conclusion led him to question traditional Catholic practices. In November 1522, he formally broke with the papacy, renouncing his papal commission and salary. The Zurich city council quickly moved to reinstate him as parish pastor, thereby forming an established congregation independent of Roman Catholicism.

Zwingli and His Followers

Among Zwingli's closest followers was Conrad Grebel, son of a patrician family in Zurich. While studying at the universities of Vienna and Paris, Grebel had wasted time and money living dissolutely. He was finally forced to return home with broken health and without an academic degree. During the spring of 1522, Grebel experienced a profound conversion. Inspired by Zwingli's evangelical preaching, Grebel became an admiring follower.

Felix Mantz also followed Zwingli. Mantz, the illegitimate son of a Catholic priest, was well-versed in the biblical languages. Others in Zwingli's circle included Johannes Brotli and Simon Stumpf, the parish priests of two churches located in outlying districts around Zurich. Balthasar Hubmaier, pastor of the church in Waldshut on the German border, shared the group's interest in church reform based on the gospel, and was thus drawn to the Zwinglian circle.

Through his personal study, Zwingli rediscovered the gospel, and he shared his new vision in his preaching. His preaching inspired the common people to voice their demands for changes in official taxation policies, and in the church's liturgical forms. Zwingli taught that charging interest was contrary to the gospel, and peasants from surrounding villages began to call for the elimination of taxes and tithes. City council was unmoved, and ordered the peasants to meet their economic obligations to the city, and to the monasteries. By the middle of 1523, Zwingli urged that the Lord's Supper be changed to reflect the gospel. City council, fearing problems with other members of the Swiss Confederation, refused to give their approval to such sweeping reforms.

The common people were growing increasingly restless. Pressed by public opinion, Zwingli declared that by Christmas of 1523 evangelical communion practices would be instituted in Zurich. However, city council once again rejected the proposed changes. Zwingli had to retract his promise indefinitely, in order to maintain a working relationship with secular authorities. During this process, Zwingli's followers, committed to his program for evangelical restoration, became disillusioned. In a public debate staged before city council, Conrad Grebel again called for changes to the Mass. Zwingli demurred to the council, invoking an angry response from Simon Stumpf. (1) At stake was a congregation's freedom to interpret and follow God's word as they chose, without the intervention of secular or ecclesiastical authorities. Zwingli did not appear prepared to defend this. His followers' confidence in him diminished.

> *(1) Zwingli to his followers*
> *My Lords [the Council] will decide how to proceed henceforth with the Mass.*
> **Simon Stumpf, responding**
> *Master Ulrich: You have no authority to place the decision in the hands of My Lords, for the decision is already made, the Spirit of God decides.*[5]

During 1523, discussions between Zwingli and his followers focussed on the eucharistic celebration. Would they continue to celebrate a traditional Mass, or would they adopt more evangelical forms of communion? In 1524, the theme of their discussions changed to infant baptism. Both questions implicitly addressed the nature and exercise of spiritual authority. Would authority continue to be exercised by an ecclesiastical or secular elite, or would it be restored to a believing and obedient people?

Infant Baptism

Early in 1524, two Zurich priests, Wilhelm Reublin and Johannes Brotli, began to preach against the practice of infant baptism, and refused to baptize infants in their parishes. They did so without Zwingli's sanction. The Zurich city council had difficulty maintaining uniformity in the religious practices in the region, mainly because rural villagers refused to be compliant. Over the course of the summer, city council failed to prevent the dissident priests from continuing their activities.

In September 1524, the dissident group wrote letters to Martin Luther, Andreas Carlstadt, and Thomas Müntzer. Only the letter to Thomas Müntzer is extant. This letter detailed the dissidents' understanding of baptism. Baptism signified a commitment to live according to God's word. However,

> **(2) From the dissidents' letter to Thomas Müntzer**
>
> *Scripture describes baptism for us as signifying that through faith and the blood of Christ our sins are washed away ... It signifies that one should be and is dead to sin, and walking in newness of life and spirit ... But the water does not strengthen nor increase faith ... Furthermore, it does not save.*[6]

the act of baptism was not meaningful in and of itself. The act alone would not cleanse, nor increase faith. Rather, baptism was the foundation for a new church, free from dependence on civil authority. Its members were mutually committed to giving and receiving fraternal counsel, and sharing in this new spiritual reality. (2)

Meanwhile, the social unrest increased, exacerbated by the suspension of infant baptism, and city council was forced to intervene. They ordered Zwingli and his followers to resolve their differences. After several unfruitful attempts, Zwingli terminated the efforts at mediation, stating: "it would be not only inadvisable but also dangerous to have further debate with them."[7]

On January 18, 1525, Zurich city council ordered that all children be baptized within the week. Parents who refused to comply with the order would be exiled. Three days later, Reublin, Haetzer, Brotli, and Castelberger, who were not residents of Zurich, were expelled from the city. Grebel and Mantz were ordered to discontinue the meetings of "schools" which were the focus of growing unrest.

> **(3) From the letter to Thomas Müntzer**
>
> *Common bread should be used. ... Also a common drinking vessel ... The supper is an exhibition of unity. It is not a mass nor a sacrament. Therefore no one shall receive it alone ... and no one shall take for his own individual use the bread of those in unity. ... It shall be observed often and much.*[8]

Actually, these "schools" were evening meetings held in private homes, at which biblical passages were shared by readers, followed by open discussion. The readers were itinerants who also visited the regions surrounding Zurich. In all probability, they also celebrated the Lord's Supper during these clandestine house meetings. In their letter to Thomas Müntzer four months earlier, Grebel and his brethren had argued that the Supper did not belong in a mass, because it was a simple meal representing unity. It was not to be administered, but shared. (3) The authorities forbade the meetings of "schools" in an attempt to curtail the informal beginnings of Anabaptist congregations.[9]

On January 21, 1525, despite city council's order, the dissident group met in the "school" that gathered at Felix

Mantz's house. They prayed for guidance during this difficult time. That night, they were all baptized. The gathering on January 21, 1525 determined the group's mission. Those who were expelled from the city returned to their cities of origin where they shared their message.

The Spread of Swiss Anabaptism[10]

Within six months, the baptizing movement had spread to neighboring towns and cities. From Zurich, the movement spread to nearby Zollikon and then into other regions in the Swiss Confederation. The movement also spread north, to Waldshut, Schaffhausen, and Hallau, in South Germany, even as peasant unrest was brewing in these regions.[11]

Itinerant Ministry

On January 22, 1525, Johannes Brotli baptized a new believer by sprinkling him with well water. The ceremony took place just outside of Zurich, in the presence of onlookers. During the following week, Georg Blaurock, Conrad Grebel, and Felix Mantz organized an informal group into an Anabaptist congregation, in Zollikon, a village near Zurich. There, they baptized about thirty-five believers, along with their wives and hired hands.

Wilhelm Reublin and Johannes Brotli traveled twenty miles north to Waldshut, which had been recently affected by peasant unrest. Zwingli characterized Reublin as "simple of mind, foolishly bold, garrulous, and unwise."[12] Brotli was an ex-priest who had left his parish to join Zwingli. He had married and become a small farmer in Zollikon, where he spoke against infant baptism. The two men were on itinerant missions to spread the word. Near Waldshut, Reublin convinced members of Balthasar Hubmaier's reformed congregation to receive baptism. During Holy Week, most of the congregation, along with Hubmaier, were baptized.

In 1525, the Peasant's War had flared to life again in this region. The town of Waldshut was already aligned politically with the peasants when Hubmaier and his congregation received baptism. As a reformer in

(4) Snyder, **Anabaptist History and Theology**
This early Anabaptist movement was closely involved with the movement of social reform represented by the peasants.[13]

Waldshut, Hubmaier became involved in both the Anabaptist movement and the peasant movement. (4)

Conrad Grebel fled to Schaffhausen, but his witness was largely unsuccessful. He did baptize Wolfgang Ulimann, a native of St. Gall, by immersion in the icy waters of the Rhine. Two years earlier, Hubmaier had preached near Appenzell and St. Gall, in the eastern part of Switzerland. Ulimann's father was the leader of a trade union in St. Gall, and when Ulimann returned to the city he preached to the weavers. When Grebel arrived in St. Gall that April, he received a sympathetic hearing. On Palm Sunday, he baptized nearly two hundred people at the river's edge.

Persecution and Martyrdom

After Grebel had moved on, Bolt Eberli, a peasant and eloquent Anabaptist preacher, arrived on the scene. During Easter, almost everyone from the town and neighboring countryside gathered to hear Eberli "proclaim repentance and the baptism of the reborn."[14] Soon thereafter, Eberli was arrested by authorities in the nearby region of Schwys. He was burned at the stake on May 29, 1525, becoming the first martyr among the Swiss Anabaptists.

The Anabaptist movement achieved greater success in rural areas near St. Gall and Appenzell, which enjoyed a degree of political autonomy. The Anabaptists were uniformly opposed to the levying of tithes and taxes for pastoral support, and many peasants believed that the movement would improve social conditions and relieve their financial burdens.

Alarmed by the surge of popular Anabaptist support among peasants, Zurich authorities intervened. Hans Krüsi, a rural Anabaptist leader, was arrested under cover of darkness by the Bishop of St. Gall's troops, and executed in Lucerne. An official edict forbade gatherings within the city and all outlying districts. Heavy fines were imposed on those guilty of rebaptism. A special militia was created to repress threats of rebellion.

Ulimann refused to stop preaching, and was condemned to exile. Three years later, he was arrested and executed for guiding Anabaptist refugees to a safe haven in Moravia. Meanwhile, in the summer of 1526, Conrad Grebel died of the plague, while preaching in some unknown place in eastern Switzerland. He had spent six months in prison with Blaurock and Mantz, and his remaining life had been that of a fugitive.

On November 19, 1526, Zurich city council passed a measure which imposed the death penalty on anyone caught attending an Anabaptist meeting. A few weeks later, Mantz and Blaurock were arrested. They were accused of forming ecclesial communities, of teaching non-violence, and of practicing rebaptism. But authorities were most concerned about the social unrest which Anabaptism appeared to inspire among the people.

Mantz was sentenced to death by drowning. Blaurock, not a citizen of Zurich, was sentenced to perpetual exile, after first being whipped through the city streets. Mantz was drowned in the Limmat River, the first dissident martyr to die at the hands of established Protestantism. Mantz's mother and sister witnessed his execution, and loudly urged him to remain faithful. The authorities were in a decidedly unpopular position.

The Schleitheim Consensus

By early 1527, the Anabaptist movement seemed doomed to disintegration. The peasant uprising in and around Waldshut had failed, leaving the fledgling Anabaptist movement with no political support in the South German and Swiss territories.[15] With its principal spokesmen either dead, or fugitives, the movement faced both external and internal threats.

Externally, the established church attacked the Anabaptist movement with violent repression, and systematically exposed its divisive doctrines. Internally, the movement lacked the homogeneous character that would give it a clear sense of identity. Many sympathizers took the safe route, and participated only spiritually, regarding concrete expressions of discipleship as relatively unimportant – and dangerous.

Determined to deal with these threats, Anabaptist leaders met in the village of Schleitheim near the German-Swiss border, in February of 1527. There, the leaders formally defined the movement's essential identity. Their first task was to deal with the meaning of "freedom in the Spirit of Christ."[16] Some Anabaptists interpreted freedom to mean unrestrained fanaticism and moral license. Others believed it meant that the spiritually illumined were free to participate in the practices of the established churches, partaking of their sacraments, swearing loyalty to the authorities, and bearing arms under their orders. The brethren at Schleitheim rejected both alternatives.

Seven Articles

The Schleitheim consensus created seven articles which described the principal characteristics of the Anabaptist community, or those "who desired to walk in the resurrection of Jesus Christ."[17] Baptism was a freely assumed pact with God, and with one's community. The community was committed to sustaining those within it. The Lord's Supper was a symbol of communion with Christ. Pastors were called and supported by their own congregations, and should have the "good report of those who are outside the faith."[18] The document dedicated much space to the last two articles, which treated violent coercion and the swearing of oaths. Here, the differences between Anabaptism and established Protestantism were most visible. The Anabaptists believed that while coercion might be used in the secular sphere, it did not belong in the Kingdom of Christ. Further, relationships within the community of Christ were undertaken with love, rendering the oath meaningless.

The Swiss Brethren approached the Bible with a freedom that opened them to the vision of a God who acts on behalf of the oppressed. The Anabaptists believed that salvation was possible without relying on sacraments, or

(5) From the document accompanying the Scheitheim Articles

1. The brothers and sisters should meet at least three or four times a week, to exercise themselves in the teaching of Christ and His apostles and heartily to exhort one another to remain faithful to the Lord as they have pledged.

2. When the brothers and sisters are together, they shall take up something to read together. The one to whom God has given the best understanding shall explain it, the others should be still and listen, so that there are not two or three carrying on a private conversation, bothering the others. The Psalter shall be read daily at home.

3. Let none be frivolous in the church of God, neither in words nor in actions. Good conduct shall be maintained by them all also before the heathen.

cont.

submitting to the unjust structures of Christendom, which featured an unholy alliance of ecclesiastical and civil authorities. The Anabaptist movement sought to restore the church of God to the outcast.

The Schleitheim articles were circulated among Swiss and South German Anabaptist communities, accompanied by another document, written in the same hand. The document was a brief rule for ordering congregational life. (5) It stated that Bible study should occur frequently, to remind the brothers and sisters of their duties. Their behaviour should always reflect their beliefs, and they must be watchful of each other, and admonish those who erred. Everything was held in common, and the community should live austerely.

Within a month, Michael Sattler, the guiding spirit behind the Schleitheim Articles, was arrested by Austrian authorities, along with thirteen brothers and sisters. After a puppet trial, all were sentenced to death. Sattler had been prior of a Benedictine monastery in the Black Forest in South Germany. In March, 1525, he had been imprisoned with the group in Zurich. Upon his release, Sattler had returned with Wilhelm Reublin to shepherd the Anabaptist conventicles in southwest Germany.

Among the accusations against Sattler was that he had "initiated a new and unheard-of usage in the Lord's Supper, with wine and bread crumbled in a basin, and eating the same."[20] This probably referred to the suppers that Anabaptists celebrated in peasant homes. Three charges accused Sattler of civil disobedience,

4. When a brother sees his brother erring, he shall warn him according to the command of Christ, and shall admonish him in a Christian and brotherly way, as everyone is bound and obliged to do out of love.

5. Of all of the brothers and sisters in this congregation none shall have anything of his own, but rather, as the Christians in the time of the apostles held all in common, and especially stored up a common fund, from which aid can be given to the poor, according as each will have need, and as in the apostles' time permit no brother to be in need.

6. All gluttony shall be avoided among the brothers who are gathered in the congregation; serve a soup or a minimum of vegetable and meat, for eating and drinking are not the kingdom of heaven.

7. The Lord's Supper shall be held, as often as the brothers are together, thereby proclaiming the death of the Lord, and thereby warning each one to commemorate, how Christ gave His life for us, and shed His blood for us, that we might also be willing to give our body and life for Christ's sake, which means for the sake of all the brothers.[19]

non-violence, and refusing to swear the oath of loyalty, all of which were deemed subversive. (6)

The severity of the sentence reflected the authorities' perception that Anabaptism posed a serious threat to social order. Anabaptism was not merely about new doctrines and rituals. It was a new vision of the church that restored power to the people. Popular opposition to the arrest and trial of Sattler was overwhelming. Authorities had to reinforce the guard, and transfer the trial first to Binsdorf, and finally to Rottenberg.

---

(6) Yoder, **The Legacy of Michael Sattler**
In the matter of the prosecutor of the imperial majesty versus Michael Sattler, it has been found that Michael Sattler should be given into the hands of the hangman, who shall lead him to the square and cut off his tongue, then chain him to a wagon, there tear his body twice with red hot tongs .... When this is done to be burned to powder as a heretic.[21]

Hutterian Anabaptism in Austria and Moravia

Tyrolean Anabaptism

On January 7, 1527, one hour after the execution of Felix Mantz, Georg Blaurock was whipped out of Zurich. Shaking the dust off his feet, he traveled home to the mining country in the Tyrol, in eastern Switzerland. Many foreigners had come into the area to work in the mines. Massive immigration had destabilized traditional social and parochial structures, and there was political unrest.

During May of 1525, a coalition of peasants, miners, and artisans, under the leadership of Michael Gaismair, a miner's son, had attempted to form a workers' alliance. Negotiating with the authorities, the alliance had been granted some of its requests. Despite this success, many among the rural peasantry and the urban poor rebelled, and the movement was crushed by imperial power.[22] Tyrolean Anabaptism arose out of this context.

The Anabaptist ministry responded to these social concerns, and attracted followers from all social classes. Many new Anabaptists were artisans and miners, as well as peasants.[23] Hans Hut, the zealous and apocalyptic Anabaptist evangelist, was active in the area. He baptized the new leaders of the movement: Leonard Schiemer, an ex-Franciscan monk, and Hans Schlaffer, an ex-priest. Both leaders were arrested and executed only six months later.

When Georg Blaurock returned home, he baptized new converts and established new congregations. In September, 1529, Blaurock was arrested, tortured, and burned at the stake. Under Archduke Ferdinand, the authorities in Tyrol repressed Anabaptism with extreme severity. A special militia of "Anabaptist hunters" was commissioned, and special courts were charged with applying the death sentence to all who stood accused.[24] An exodus of refugees fled into Moravia, where the nobles were more tolerant of Anabaptists.

In the summer of 1526, after traveling for a long time, Balthasar Hubmaier and his wife found relative security and tolerance among these refugees, under the lords of Lichtenstein. In Nicholsburg, Hubmaier dedicated himself to converting a Lutheran congregation to Anabaptism, to accommodate the stream of Anabaptist refugees who were constantly arriving. In less than a year, Nicholsburg had become one of the movement's centers, with a population of some 12,000 Anabaptists.

The Turkish Threat

Facing the threat of a Turkish invasion in Eastern Europe, the Austrian and German authorities prepared to defend themselves. In this uncertain climate, the Anabaptists' non-violence seemed like sedition. The matter of war taxes also became a contentious issue. Hubmaier's Anabaptist career had begun under the protection of secular authorities in Waldshut, and he was inclined to support authorities who were sympathetic to the Anabaptist cause. Therefore, Hubmaier did not object to these new taxation policies. However, upon his arrival in Nicholsburg, Hans Hut denounced the payment of war taxes. The congregation was divided.

In May, 1527, other matters were debated in the Nicholsburg congregation. Refugees arriving from the Tyrol had radical political and economic views. Some favored a community of goods, and separating themselves from the world. They took a non-violent stance, which the authorities found insupportable, given the Turkish threat. Hut sympathized with the Tyrolean refugees. The Count of Lichtenstein responded by incarcerating Hut, and backing Hubmaier. Hut escaped with the help of his sympathizers. However, the congregation had become divided between the *Schwertler*, those who bore a sword, and the *Stabler*, those who carried only a staff.

Hans Hut influenced the Anabaptist movement more than any other leader. During the last two years of his ministry, Hut probably brought more people into the Anabaptist movement than all of the other Anabaptist itinerants combined.[25] Exiled from his home in the German village of Bibra for refusing to allow his children to be baptized, he dedicated four years to itinerant evangelization, until he died at the hands of Augsburg authorities in December, 1527. Hut had witnessed the peasant massacre at Frankenhausen in 1525. In May, 1526, he was baptized by Hans Denk. Hut's apocalyptic expectations added urgency to his message. A student of Thomas Müntzer, Hut believed that following Jesus meant surrendering all worldly goods, and sharing a deep compassion for others.[26]

Late in 1526, Archduke Ferdinand was elected ruler of Moravia. Concerned about the Turkish threat, Ferdinand was determined to eradicate the pacifist Anabaptist movement. In the fall of 1527, Hubmaier was arrested, and not even his friend and protector, the Count of Lichtenstein, could defend him. Hubmaier was tortured and interrogated before being condemned for heresy and sedition, and sentenced to a public execution. He was burned at the stake on March 10, 1528. To show "mercy," the executioner rubbed gunpowder into Hubmaier's hair and beard to hasten his death. Hubmaier's wife, faithful to the end, was drowned a few days later. With the death of their spiritual leader, the *Schwertler* party was destined to disappear.

The Hutterites

In the spring of 1528, the Count of Lichtenstein exiled the *Stabler* party from his lands. The group of two hundred adults, and their families, were thrown into precarious circumstances. They wandered for three weeks until the lords of Kaunitz granted them lands in Austerlitz, and later in Auspitz, where they could live and work.[27] In 1529, Jacob Hutter, a leader of the radical Tyrolean movement, came to Moravia in search of refuge for his persecuted people. Favorably impressed, Hutter sent groups of Anabaptist refugees to the area, and settled in Auspitz himself.

However, repression was so severe that the Hutterian communities had to break into small groups to escape the attention of imperial authorities. At times, they survived by hiding in caves dug in the earth. By 1533, the persecution had become so intense that the community asked Jacob Hutter to leave, as his presence threatened their safety. Hutter returned to the Tyrol, hoping that persecution there had diminished. However, he and his wife were surprised by imperial agents. Arrested, tried, and tortured, Hutter was burned at the stake on February 25, 1536. His wife was drowned a few days later.

The communal economic practices of the Hutterian Brethren were inspired Michael Gaismair's vision, by Hans Hut's radical message, and by Georg Blaurock's link to the Anabaptist beginnings in Zurich. The communal economic practices had begun as an

> *(7)* **The Chronicle of Hutterian Brethren**
> *They practiced Christian community of goods as Christ taught it and lived it with his disciples and as the first apostolic church practiced it. ... Those who earlier had been rich or poor now shared one purse, one house, one table.*[28]

emergency measure during a time of need and exile, but these practices would become definitive for the group. The community of goods had strong biblical and theological foundations, and the Hutterites lived out that ideal. (7) The Hutterites believed in *Gelassenheit,* or surrender, to God, and, by extension, to one's fellow beings. Commitment to others included surrendering property, which was considered an extension of oneself. (8) In the community of goods, differences between social classes were effectively overcome. Everybody shared in the labor required to sustain the community, no matter what his or her social position.[30]

> *(8)* **The Chronicle of the Hutterian Brethren**
> *Every brother and sister should be fully surrendered to God and to the church, in body and soul. All gifts received from God should be held in common, according to the practice of the first apostolic church community of Christ, so that the needy can be supported.*[29]

A Period of Peace

Between 1555 and 1595, the Anabaptist communities in Moravia flourished. They lived relatively free from persecution, although radicals in other parts of Europe were subjected to the pressures of the Catholic counter reformation. During those years, the Hutterites sent missionaries throughout Europe. An estimated eighty per cent of those sent met a martyr's death.[31] Nevertheless, the Moravian communities grew as new converts joined, and refugees from other parts of Europe arrived. They formed new colonies in Moravia, Slovakia, and Hungary. By the end of the sixteenth century, there were nearly one hundred Hutterite colonies, with a total membership of between 20,000 and 30,000 people.

During this peaceful period, the Hutterite communities created an authentic alternative to contemporary social structures. A century before Commensuis's educational innovations, the Hutterites instituted a system of popular education which resulted in universal literacy. Their system of production anticipated the innovations of the Industrial Revolution by two centuries. Culturally, they contributed significantly to the field of medicine. Hutterites were the personal physicians of Emperor Rudolph II, in 1582, and of Cardinal Francis von Dietrichstein.[32] Artistically, their ceramics were prized throughout Europe. In short, the Hutterites' contributions proved so valuable that the Catholic princes declined to persecute them, even going so far as to exempt them from the payment of war taxes.[33]

The Chronicle of the Hutterian Brethren, published during this peaceful period, described production in the Hutterite communities using the analogy of the workings of a clock, or of a beehive. Each person was part of a larger whole, and all activity supported that larger purpose. (9)

---

(9) The Chronicle of the Hutterian Brethren

Everyone ... worked for the common good to supply the needs of all and to give help and support wherever it was needed. It was indeed a perfect body whose living active members served one another. Think of the ingenious works of a clock, where one piece helps another to make it go, so that it serves its purpose. Or think of the bees ... working together in their hive ... until their noble work of making sweet honey is done, not only for their own needs but enough to share with man. That is how it is among the brothers.[34]

Conclusion

The relative peace came to an end at the close of the sixteenth century when the authorities renewed their efforts to repress heresy. During the first half of the seventeenth century, the Hutterite communities were persecuted by both Turks and Christians, particularly the Jesuits. The communities that were able to survive did so by emigrating to the east, to Transylvania and the Ukraine. Vestiges of the once-flourishing movement found their way to North America during the 1870s, and formed colonies in the United States and Canada.

Notes

[1] Although the text implies that no one had yet been commissioned to a pastoral ministry, it should be noted that there were at least four ordained Catholic priests in the group: Georg Blaurock, Wilhelm Reublin, Johannes Brotli, and Simon Stumpf. In addition to being a movement of "anabaptists," or rebaptizers, the movement was also "re-ordinationist." The group's understanding of ordination, and baptism, was not sacramental, in the traditional sense of the term, but symbolic. The symbols were meaningful only within the context of a disciple community.

[2] To justify the use of extreme measures to repress the movement, authorities appealed to the fifth century Justinian Code which had established the death penalty to combat "rebaptism" among Donatists in North Africa. The practice was not viewed as simply a religious matter of baptizing, or being baptized, or of attending Anabaptist meetings. Authorities considered it to be an act of sedition, of civil disobedience of imperial law, and in the case of repeated offenses, of perjury. Thus, the practice of religion was considered a civil offense.

[3] The Hutterian Brethren, eds. and trans., *The Chronicle of Hutterian Brethren*, vol. 1 (Rifton, NY: Plough Publishing House, 1987), 41-47.

[4] This section relies largely on the following source. Cornelius J. Dyck, ed., *An Introduction to Mennonite History* (Scottdale, PA: Herald Press, 1967), 26-35.

[5] Dyck, 29.

[6] J. C. Wenger, trans., *Conrad Grebel's Programmatic Letters of 1524* (Scottdale, PA: Herald Press, 1970), 29-31.

[7] George H. Williams, *The Radical Reformation* (Philadelphia: The Westminster Press, 1962), 120.

[8] J. C. Wenger, trans., *Conrad Grebel's Programmatic Letters of 1524* (Scottdale, PA: Herald Press, 1970), 21-23.

[9] George H. Williams, *The Radical Reformation* (Philadelphia: The Westminster Press, 1962), 122.

[10] This section relies largely on the following source. Cornelius J. Dyck, ed., *An Introduction to Mennonite History* (Scottdale, PA: Herald Press, 1967), 36-43.

[11] C. Arnold Snyder, *Anabaptist History and Theology: An Introduction* (Kitchener, ON: Pandora Press, 1995), 55.

[12] George H. Williams, *The Radical Reformation* (Philadelphia: The Westminster Press, 1962), 121.

[13] C. Arnold Snyder, *Anabaptist History and Theology: An Introduction* (Kitchener, ON: Pandora Press, 1995), 56.

[14] George H. Williams, *The Radical Reformation* (Philadelphia: The Westminster Press, 1962), 129-130.

[15] C. Arnold Snyder, *Anabaptist History and Theology: An Introduction* (Kitchener, ON: Pandora Press, 1995), 60.

[16] John H. Yoder, ed. *The Legacy of Michael Sattler* (Scottdale, PA: Herald Press, 1973), 35.

[17] Yoder, *Michael Sattler*, 36.

[18] Yoder, *Michael Sattler*, 39.

[19] Yoder, *Michael Sattler*, 44-45.

[20] Yoder, *Michael Sattler*, 70.

[21] Yoder, *Michael Sattler*, 74-75.

[22] George H. Williams, *The Radical Reformation* (Philadelphia: The Westminster Press, 1962), 81.

[23] Williams, 166-167.

[24] Cornelius J. Dyck, ed., *An Introduction to Mennonite History* (Scottdale, PA: Herald Press, 1967), 53.

[25] Dyck, 48.

[26] George H. Williams, *The Radical Reformation* (Philadelphia: The Westminster Press, 1962), 165. For example, in Augsburg, under Hut's influence, the Anabaptist community organized a program of mutual aid that responded to the needs of immigrants arriving from other parts of Europe, and contributed to the rapid growth of the congregation.

[27] Cornelius J. Dyck, ed., *An Introduction to Mennonite History* (Scottdale, PA: Herald Press, 1967), 54. Along the way they laid a coat on the ground and "everyone willingly laid his fortune down without compulsion or urging for the support of the needy."

[28] The Hutterian Brethren, eds. and trans., *The Chronicle of Hutterian Brethren*, vol. 1 (Rifton, NY: Plough Publishing House, 1987), 404.

[29] The Hutterian Brethren, 78.

[30] The Hutterian Brethren, 406. "In short, no one was idle; each did what was required and what he was able to do, whatever he had been before – rich or poor, aristocrat or commoner. Even priests who joined the community learned to work."

[31] George H. Williams, *The Radical Reformation* (Philadelphia: The Westminster Press, 1962), 426.

[32] Cornelius J. Dyck, ed., *An Introduction to Mennonite History* (Scottdale, PA: Herald Press, 1967), 58.

[33] John H. Yoder, *Textos Escogidos de la Reforma Radical* (Buenos Aires: Editorial La Aurora, 1976), 280.

[34] The Hutterian Brethren, eds. and trans., *The Chronicle of Hutterian Brethren*, vol. 1 (Rifton, NY: Plough Publishing House, 1987), 406.

Chapter 14

Sixteenth-Century Movements: Anabaptism in the Low Countries

Therefore let us – all of us who fear God in truth – earnestly pray to God that we may be saved through Christ Jesus from having to think beyond what is the will, the truth and the command of the Lord to the end that we hold not our own opinion .... (Melchior Hofmann, *The Ordinance of God*, 1530).[1]

Melchior ... departed for Strassburg ... to heed the prophecy of an old man of East Frisia who had prophesied of him that he would sit a half year in prison in Strassburg and thereafter would freely spread his ministry over the whole world with the help of his ministers and supporters. ... When Melchior saw that he was going to prison, he thanked God that the hour had come and threw his hat from his head .... And with this he went willingly, cheerfully, and well comforted to prison. (Obbe Philips, *A Confession*).[2]

Then I, without restraint ... renounced all my worldly reputation, name and fame, my unchristian abominations, my masses, infant baptism, and my easy life, and I willingly submitted to distress and poverty under the heavy cross of Christ. (Menno Simons, *Conversion, Call and Testimony*).[3]

Introduction: The Sacramentarian Movement[4]

In the Low Countries, during the late Middle Ages, there was widespread opposition to the sacramental eucharistic theology of medieval Catholicism. The origin of this movement is unclear, but contemporary ecclesiastical and secular authorities were threatened by its implications. They called the movement "Sacramentarianism," and its proponents "Sacramentists." The movement opposed the clerical monopoly over sacramental rites. Sacramentarianism viewed the Eucharist as a commemorative and symbolic communion with the body of Christ, not a sacrificial rite. The movement believed that baptism should be instrumental in creating a community of the new covenant, not in maintaining the monolithic character of medieval society. In short, the movement questioned the church's essential nature.

Early in the twelfth century, Tanchelm, the Dutch heretic, urged his followers not to participate in the sacraments of the clergy, nor to pay the tithes imposed by priests and bishops.[5] The works of Wessel Gansfort, Erasmus, and others associated with the Brethren of the Common Life contributed to widespread dissatisfaction with official eucharistic theology.

In 1517, Wouter, an ex-Dominican monk and Sacramentist, traveled throughout the Low Countries preaching "the truth of the Gospel."[6] One of Wouter's followers, a lawyer from The Hague named Cornelius Hoen, later wrote that the significance of the Lord's Supper was purely symbolic. Hoen argued that the phrase "this is my body" was properly translated as this "signifies" my body.[7] He questioned the sacrificial conception of the Mass, in which a ritual of expiation was repeated indefinitely. Hoen believed that the supper was commemorative, and signified the faith commitment that joined Christ and his people.

Sacramentarianism began as a popular movement of the common people. Lay preachers disseminated the iconoclastic message among commoners, while the Erasmian biblico-humanist tradition was spread mainly among the privileged classes. Both groups joined in common opposition to the foreign political control exercised by Spain and traditional Roman Catholicism.

Between 1525 and 1530, the Sacramentarian movement grew considerably. The proponents of the movement were often lay preachers without formal theological preparation. These preachers embraced their faith with courage and personal abandon, as exemplified by Weynken de Monickendam, the first Sacramentist martyr. In 1527, Monickendam was taken before the authorities and questioned about her beliefs. (1) Under severe questioning, she held firmly to her convictions, speaking not only for herself, but on behalf of her community. Seven years after Monickendam was executed, her native village became predominantly Anabaptist.

(1) Weynken de Monickendam responding to the authorities
On the nature of the sacrament: *I hold your sacrament to be bread and flour, and if you hold it as God, I say that it is your devil.* On extreme unction: *Oil is good for salad, or to oil your shoes with.* On the crucifix: *This is not my God; the cross by which I have been redeemed is a different one. This is a wooden god; throw him into the fire and warm yourselves with him. ... my Lord God is in me, and I in Him.*[8]

Many Sacramentists would join the Melchiorite movement, which added its own apocalyptic flavor to the iconoclastic protest. Medieval Sacramentarianism, widely disseminated throughout the Low Countries, prepared the way for the Melchiorite and Anabaptist movements which flourished during the fourth decade of the sixteenth century, and attracted a following among the common people.

The Melchiorite Movement [9]

Melchior Hofmann, *c.*1495-1543, was a native of Swabia and a furrier by trade. Around 1522, Hofmann embraced the Lutheran cause and became an itinerant evangelist. He traveled throughout northern Europe, particularly in the Scandinavian and Baltic countries. Hofmann's radical views on church liturgy were influenced by Andreas Carlstadt. In Stockholm, he took part in an iconoclastic outbreak, for which he was incarcerated, forbidden to preach, and eventually expelled from the country. Hofmann continued his preaching in Germany, but by 1528 he had abandoned Lutheranism and become a Sacramentist.

Hofmann maintained contact with Carlstadt, the Strassburg reformers, and others. He began to develop his own spiritualistic interpretation of the Bible, and was particularly drawn to the apocalyptic apocryphal books, and to prophetic millennial visions. Hofmann identified Rome as the Babylon of the Apocalypse, and Strassburg as the New Jerusalem. His apocalyptic visions were influenced by Leonard and Ursula Jost, whom Hofmann had met in the Low Countries. The Josts' spiritual visions not only made a profound impression on Hofmann, but on many other people in the Rhine region.

In April 1530, not an Anabaptist himself, Hofmann asked Strassburg city council to recognize officially the city's Anabaptists. The local authorities promptly ordered his arrest, but he anticipated their actions and fled to Emden. It is uncertain whether or not Hofmann himself was ever rebaptized. However, he became a proponent of Anabaptism, insisting that "inner spiritual" baptism must precede external baptism.[10]

Hofmann's Influence in Emden

In Emden, there were many Dutch Sacramentists who had also fled the repression of imperial authorities. The Low Countries proved to be fertile ground for Hofmann's message. In a short time, he had baptized nearly 300 of the Sacramentists, and established a Melchiorite Anabaptist congregation.

Among Hofmann's converts in Emden were Jan Trijpmaker and Sicke Snijder. Snijder was sent to Leeuwarden in West Frisia, where he established a new Sacramentist Anabaptist conventicle. He was arrested, and on March 20, 1531, became the first Anabaptist martyr in the Low Countries. During Snijder's execution, a drummer broke ranks and shouted protests at the authorities before disappearing into the crowd of sympathizers. The execution would decisively influence the spiritual journey of Menno Simons, who at that time was parish priest in a nearby village.

Obbe Philips, a barber-surgeon, and Dietrich Philips, a Franciscan monk, were the illegitimate sons of a local Catholic priest. The Philips brothers secretly sympathized with Snijder's cause. The brothers had read Martin Luther's writings, and were seeking alternate ways to live out their faith. The brothers met with other Sacramentists in the area and resolved to "serve God in ... quiet simpliticity ... without preacher, teacher, or any external assembly."[11]

Meanwhile, Trijpmaker had been expelled from Emden. He fled to Amsterdam and promptly organized another Anabaptist conventicle. Trijpmaker was arrested by authorities and put on trial at The Hague, where he and nine of his followers were sentenced to decapitation. After

Trijpmaker's death, Hofmann was shaken and uncertain. Hoping that the persecution would wane, Hofmann ordered his followers not to perform rebaptims for two years. However, his followers had already scattered throughout the Low Countries. The rampage of plague, floods, and famine, caused by blockades and warfare, increased apocalyptic expectations among peasants, and Melchiorite Anabaptism flourished.

A Split in the Movement

In contrast to Hofmann's growing caution, his follower, Jan Mathijs, a baker from Haarlem, intensified his activity. Mathijs continued to baptize new members, and named twelve apostles, among them Jan Beukels of Leiden. Meanwhile, Hofmann, inspired by visionaries in the movement, became convinced that a new Elijah and a New Jerusalem were about to be revealed. In fact, to precipitate the coming of the kingdom, Hofmann had turned himself over to municipal authorities in Strassburg, in 1533. He sent notes of warning to his followers in the Low Countries, concerned about the militant apocalyptic stance being introduced into the movement.

Under Mathijs's influence, the Melchiorite movement became increasingly militant. Obbe Philips's experience exemplifies the split between the movement's two wings. Philips, who had gone to Leeuwarden, was mistakenly identified as a militant after an incident in that city. One of Mathijs's apostles had appeared there, proclaiming that the destruction of all tyrants was imminent. Although innocent, Philips was accused of insurrection on February 23, 1534, and was forced to flee to Amsterdam.

In Amsterdam, Philips witnessed a public demonstration which had been organized by some of his own followers. People marched in the streets, carrying swords and shouting slogans: "The new city is given to the children of God."[12] Five days later, on March 26, 1534, Philips witnessed the execution of all the demonstrators. Horrified, he definitively separated himself from the militant Dutch wing of Melchiorites.

In the following year, differences between the two wings of the Dutch Melchiorite movement became increasingly clear. On May 10, 1535, a group of forty Melchiorites attempted to take over Amsterdam city hall by force, without Philips's support. Disillusioned, Philips lost hope for the restoration of a new apostolic church. He began to doubt the validity of his ordination, which had been performed by Mathijs. Philips even questioned the ordinations he had performed himself, including those of his own brother, Dietrich Philips, and Menno Simons. In 1539, Philips would withdraw entirely from the movement.

The Theocratic Kingdom of Münster [13]

Bernard Rothmann

The theocratic kingdom of Münster arose out of a restorationist vision, accompanied by apocalyptic expectations. In Münster, the Anabaptist vision for an apostolic church was transformed into an oppressive, militant society, which drew its inspiration not from the Gospels, but from the Old Testament Patriarchs and the Maccabeans.

Münster was an important urban center in Westphalia, in northwest Germany. It had an estimated population of 15,000 residents. Before the arrival of the Melchiorites, an ecclesiastical reformation had already begun in the city. In 1529, Bernard Rothmann, *c*.1495-1535, the cathedral preacher, had left the city to pursue his studies. Rothmann was popular among the city's guilds, and they secretly funded his study in Wittenberg. When he returned to Münster in 1531, Rothmann's sermons were condemned by ecclesiastical authorities, but lauded by the popular masses and the guilds.

Rothmann preached his first fully Protestant sermon on February 18, 1532. By the beginning of 1533, the reformation was well under way in Münster. In May 1533, Rothmann voiced his opposition to infant baptism. That summer, he celebrated the Lord's Supper with common bread sprinkled with wine, an act which split the city's Protestants between the more conservative Lutherans, and the radicals led by Rothmann.

A theological debate was held, and civil authorities declared Rothmann and his followers victorious. However, a conservative councilman was opposed to Rothmann's authoritarian stance. With the support of the Catholic sector, he ordered the expulsion of Rothmann and his followers. He filled the city square with armed agents, but Rothmann's supporters were also prepared for battle. To prevent a blood bath, the order of expulsion was withdrawn on the condition that Rothmann stop preaching.

Despite the apparent success of the conservatives, there were many Sacramentists among the popular sector, and they were reinforced by the arrival of Melchiorites late in 1533. Bolstered by popular support, Rothmann resumed preaching in open defiance of city council. He was fully supported by the population, and by January 1534, Rothmann controlled religious life in Münster. He spoke of forming a Christian republic based on community of goods. His message was all the more appealing because crop failures threatened famine in the area surrounding Münster.

Jan Mathijs in Münster

Meanwhile, Jan Beukels, a Melchiorite from Leiden, had visited Münster in the fall of 1533. Beukels found that Rothmann's teachings echoed the Melchiorite beliefs. He returned to Holland, where the Melchiorites were victims of extreme persecution, with news of Münster's favorable conditions. Beukels interpreted these conditions as a sign of the coming of the new kingdom, predicted by Melchior Hofmann. Beukels's news inflamed Jan Mathijs's imagination. Mathijs revised Hofmann's prediction to suit these new parameters. The New Jerusalem would no longer be Strassburg, but Münster.

Two of Mathijs's apostles arrived in Münster on January 5, 1534. They rebaptized Rothmann and Henry Rol, an ex-Carmelite friar. During the following week, Rothmann and his helpers went from home to home, baptizing approximately 1,400 citizens. Anabaptists from the Low Countries continued to arrive, including Jan Mathijs and Jan Beukels. Mathijs and Beukels began preaching that the time had come to break from the old order. They argued that true believers had the right to destroy anyone who rejected their message.

The Catholic bishop, alarmed by these events, ordered his troops to take up positions around the city of Münster. The citizens of Münster sent emissaries to enlist a militia to defend their New Jerusalem. City council continued to govern, but Mathijs became Münster's *de facto* ruler. Mathijs ordered the expulsion of conservative Catholic and Lutheran burghers, and announced his intention to execute those who refused rebaptism. On February 25, 1534, there was a skirmish between the Münsterites and the mercenary troops serving the bishop. The entire population, including women and children, was organized to defend the city. All Anabaptists were invited to join the "holy city of Münster."[14]

One of the great ironies of this tragedy was that the popular masses, whose Sacramentist-Melchiorite origins were non-violent, willingly joined the militant theocracy in Münster. Dutch Melchiorites responded to the Mathijs's invitation *en masse*. Authorities intercepted five ships from Haarlem, and six ships from Amsterdam as they were setting sail for Münster. However, another thirty boats crossed the Zuyder Zee carrying some 3,000 persons, all armed for Münster's defense. Two groups were detained and forced to return home, but only a few were executed.

During his reign of four or five months, Mathijs introduced community of goods: partly to provide for the influx of people arriving from the Low Countries; partly in response to the situation created by the military siege against the city; and partly to restore the Anabaptist ideal of the primitive church.

The Reign of Jan of Leiden

After Mathijs's death in April of 1534, Jan of Leiden assumed leadership and disbanded city council. He replaced council with twelve "elders or judges of the tribes of Israel," whom he named personally.[15] Leiden organized a theocratic kingdom, inspired by the patriarchs and the monarchy of ancient Israel. Polygamy was permitted, and defended theologically by Rothmann. Rothmann used the demographic disequilibrium in Münster – there were three women for every man – to justify polygamy and male domination. Jan of Leiden's introduction of polygamy did not go unchallenged. Concerned townspeople protested by taking Leiden hostage, but Leiden's followers prevailed, and the protesters were executed.

Münster's inhabitants, women as well as men, fanatically defended the city. With the blessing of Münsterite authorities, a young woman named Hille Feyken attempted to kill the bishop, whose troops were besieging the city. Feyken unsuccessfully used the strategy once employed by Judith against Holofernes. She was mercilessly executed for her attempt.

Rothmann interpreted the violent events as part of God's "restoration of all things" (Acts 3:21). The community was suffering the birth pangs of the coming of a new order. Rothmann's theological interpretations freely connected images and institutions in the Old and New Testaments. Rothmann declared that the reign of David was the necessary violent prelude to Solomon's peaceful reign, and the biblical paradigm for Münster's situation. Thus, practicing polygamy, and restoring civil authority into "the hands of the saints" would precede the coming of a new order.[16] This was holy warfare: society's outcasts acting as instruments of divine wrath against God's enemies.

By the end of 1534, the armed conflict had entered its most critical stage. A series of desperate attempts to enlist reinforcements from the Low Countries had failed. Subversive elements in city council were attempting to betray Münster to the enemy. The final months of Jan of Leiden's reign were marked by indecision, cruelty, religious fanaticism, and the malicious acts of a madman. The besieged city lacked a food supply, and its population was going hungry. In April 1535, an estimated 1,500 starving women, children, and elderly people fled Münster. They fell into enemy hands, and many were slaughtered.

A month before the tragic end, Münster had an estimated population of 9,500 people: approximately 900 able-bodied men, 5,500 women, and 3,100 children.[17] During the night of June 24, 1535, two deserters opened one of the city's gates to the mercenaries waiting outside. The massacre lasted for two days. The city was taken and its inhabitants executed. The bishop's forces showed mercy only to pregnant women and priests.

Menno Simons

Menno Simons, 1496-1561, did not join the Anabaptist movement until early in 1536, in the wake of the Münster debacle. Shortly thereafter, he was called to shepherd the Sacramentist-Anabaptist conventicles scattered throughout the Low Countries and Northwest Germany. Simons would become a principal pastor, apologist, and spokesman for the movement.

Early Experiences

In 1524, at the age of 28, Simons was ordained into the Catholic priesthood and named vicar of the parish at Pinjum in West Frisia, near his native village of Witmarsum. Simons served in this capacity for seven years, and, according to his own testimony, did so in a careless manner. (2) Early in his career, Simons expressed doubts about the Catholic doctrine of transubstantiation, and soon began to question the practice of infant baptism. Both questions had been raised by the Sacramentarian movement which had spread throughout the Low Countries. Simons found justification for his doubts in the New Testament.

> *(2) Menno Simons,* **Reply to Gellius Faber**
> *The two young men ... and I spent our time emptily in playing [cards] together, drinking, and in diversions as, alas, is the fashion and usage of such useless people.*[18]

Wanting to better himself, Simons accepted a transfer to his native village of Witmarsum. He had begun to use the Bible in his ministry, but was still motivated by ambition, arrogance, and vanity. Around this time, Melchiorite emissaries began coming to his parish, attempting to persuade people to join the movement in support of the Anabaptists in Münster. Simons energetically opposed the Melchiorite doctrines, but within he was deeply disturbed. He could not comfortably conform to the old order, a thing he had come to detest, without contradicting the new directions toward which he had been moving.

Then an event occurred that would radically change the direction of Simons's life. On their way to Münster, a group of Melchiorite supporters under the leadership of Jan van Geelen occupied a Cistercian monastery near Witmarsum. On April 7, 1535, they were attacked by imperial troops and three hundred people were massacred. Among the dead was Peter Simons, possibly a brother of Menno Simons.

During the following nine months, Menno Simons preached fervently against the dangerous excesses of Münster, but his conscience could stand it no longer. On January 30, 1536, Simons abandoned the priesthood to live as a simple believer among the common people. He dedicated himself to reading and reflecting on the Scriptures. According to his own confession, Simons had experienced a "spiritual resurrection."[19] Faithful to his convictions, Simons was rebaptized by Obbe Philips.

Menno Simons' Ministry

About a year later, a small group of pacifist Sacramentist-Anabaptists asked Simons to shepherd the disoriented survivors of the movement. Although he was unsure of his abilities to take on this task, Simons recognized that the movement desperately needed leadership in the wake of the tragedy at Münster.[20] Like other Anabaptists, Simons also believed in reordination, and early in 1537, he was ordained by Obbe Philips. When Simons joined the Anabaptist movement, he went into hiding, and lived the rest of his life as an outlaw. He married around this time, but would never have a fixed residence.

Some of Simons' writings reflected on this difficult lifestyle. Simons believed that faith must be expressed even if it was "contrary to the emperor's decree, tyranny, persecution and permission."[21] He was critical of those Anabaptists, such as Gellius Faber, a Lutheran pastor, who preached under the protection of civil authorities. Simons demanded of himself an exacting practice of faith. He ministered to his followers despite the constant threat of persecution, and admitted that this life had taken a toll on him and on his family. Simons compared his own anxious existence to that of authorized preachers, who lived a life of material ease. (3)

---

(3) Menno Simons, Reply to Gellius Faber
[God] knows that I seek not wealth, nor possessions, nor luxury, nor ease, but only the praise of the Lord, my salvation, and the salvation of many souls. Because of this, I with my poor, weak wife and children have for eighteen years endured excessive anxiety, oppression, affliction, misery and persecution. ... to drag out an existence in fear. ... When [other preachers] are greeted as doctors, lords, and teachers by everyone, we have to hear that we are Anabaptists, bootleg preachers, deceivers, and heretics ... In short, while they are gloriously rewarded for their services with large incomes and good times, our recompense and portion must be fire, sword, and death.[22]

Over the course of twenty-five years, Simons practiced his clandestine ministry, writing tracts and offering pastoral care. Simons contributed to the restoration and consolidation of the movement, which stretched from Belgium, in the southwest, to Poland, in the northeast. By 1542, Simons had become notorious as the leader of a heretical sect. East Frisian authorities placed a bounty of 500 florins of gold on his head. Despite this reward, authorities were never able to apprehend Simons. Believers were willing to die rather than betray their pastor.

Merely receiving Simons into one's home was sufficient cause for the death sentence. Jan Claez was decapitated because he ordered the printing of 600 copies of one of Simons's writings. A Dutch Anabaptist, Elizabeth Dirks, was arrested when a Latin New Testament was discovered in her house. She was suspected of being a teacher in the Anabaptist movement, and authorities pressed her to betray Simons. Dirks responded that she hoped God's grace would keep her from becoming a traitoress. She endured torture, but resisted throughout twelve days of interrogation. Dirks was condemned to death and "drowned in a bag."[23]

Simons and his family spent the last years of his life in relative peace. They lived in the province of Holstein on the lands of a noble, Bartholomew von Ahlefeldt, who was sympathetic toward the Anabaptists. There, Simons was able to write and publish without persecution. He died on March 31, 1561.

Evangelical Anabaptism in the Low Countries

(4) Menno Simons, **Reply to False Accusations**
No one among them is allowed to beg. They take to heart the need of the saints. They entertain those in distress. They take the stranger into their houses. They comfort the afflicted; assist the needy; clothe the naked; feed the hungry; do not turn their face from the poor.[24]

In 1530, during the early years of the Melchiorite movement in the Low Countries, evangelists had reached Flanders in the south, where they discovered that Sacramentarian conventicles had already been established. Between 1535 and 1541, there were more Anabaptist martyrs in Flanders than all Lutheran and Calvinist martyrs combined. Leonard Bouwens, who had been baptized by Menno Simons, was the most effective Anabaptist evangelist in Flanders. According to Bouwens' list, he baptized 10,251 persons during his ministry. For the last twenty-five years of his life, Bouwens had a bounty on his head of 300 florins of gold, offered by Antwerp authorities.

The Anabaptists in southern Flanders were mainly weavers and small merchants, while in the north they were mainly peasants, fishermen, sailors, and women. Anabaptists were severely persecuted in Flanders. They were not permitted to meet together. Itinerant preachers would speak to small groups in clandestine locations. They even preached along the roads and in the markets. In time, many Anabaptists fled northward where there was less persecution.

Simons defended the Evangelical Anabaptists against accusations that they perpetuated the excesses of Münster. In their defense, he praised their economic practices. They shared with those in need, and served their neighbor with both material and spiritual goods. (4) Simons adamantly advocated compassion for the poor, and harshly criticized his accusers who lived in wealth, and let the needy beg at their door. Generous words and sentiments were meaningless unless they were acted upon. (5)

> **(5) *Menno Simons,*** Reply to False Accusations
> *O preachers ... where is the power of the Gospel you preach? Where is the thing signified in the Supper you administer? ... Where is the righteousness of your faith which you dress up so beautifully before the poor, ignorant people?*[25]

When Menno Simons abandoned the priesthood, and with it his security, comfort, and good name, he chose to live in solidarity with his country's outcast. Simons wrote powerfully about the meaning of true evangelical faith, which "cannot lie dormant, but manifests itself in all righteousness and works of love."[26] Simons' faith was not theoretical, but practical. Faith must be acted out, and made manifest.

Conclusion

The Sacramentist-Anabaptist movement sought to reclaim the means of grace for the common people. Their intention was to do so without resorting to coercion or violence. After the disaster at Münster, they were able to work toward this goal under the leadership of Menno Simons.

Because the movement suffered severe repression at the hands of civil authorities, it became a form of social protest. Simons argued that a true church proved its faithfulness during times of duress.[27] The Anabaptists became witnesses to and martyrs for their beliefs. All those who committed themselves to the movement were willing to die for it, despite threats of torture and death.[28] They shared their faith with their persecutors, withholding only the names of their fellow believers.

Despite severe persecution, Anabaptists had a solid sense of their collective identity. They were God's people. They stood in contrast to the world. They suffered the birth pangs of the new order which was being born. They anticipated the advent of the God's Kingdom. They thought of themselves as a people living in solidarity with the Messianic community of the first century. A century later, they would begin their martyrology with Jesus himself, identifying Christ's suffering with their own history of persecution. (6)

---

(6) **Martyrs Mirror:** *An Account of the Pious Martyrs and Witnesses of Jesus Christ who suffered during the first century*
[Christ's] entrance into this world, as well as His progress and end, was full of misery, distress and affliction, indeed it may be said: He was born under a cross; brought up under a cross! He walked under a cross, and finally died on the cross. ... This, then, was the end, not of a [mere] martyr, but of the Head of all the holy martyrs, through whom they and we all must be saved.[29]

	Notes

[1] George H. Williams, ed., *Spiritual and Anabaptist Writers* (Philadelphia: The Westminster Press, 1957), 203.

[2] Williams, *Spiritual and Anabaptist Writers*, 209-210.

[3] John C. Wenger, ed., *The Complete Writings of Menno Simons* (Scottdale, PA: Herald Press, 1956), 671.

[4] This section relies largely on the following source. George H. Williams, *The Radical Reformation* (Philadelphia: The Westminster Press, 1962), 27-37.

[5] Williams, *The Radical Reformation*, 50.

[6] Williams, *The Radical Reformation*, 35.

[7] Williams, *The Radical Reformation*, 36.

[8] Thieleman J. van Braght, *The Bloody Theater of Martyr's Mirror* (Scottdale, PA: Herald Press, 1950), 422-424.

[9] This section relies largely on the following source. George H. Williams, *The Radical Reformation* (Philadelphia: The Westminster Press, 1962), 259-264.

[10] Klaus Deppermann, *Melchior Hoffman: Social Unrest and Apocalyptic Visions in the Age of Reformation*, trans. Malcolm Wren (Edinburgh: T. & T. Clark, 1987), 217.

[11] George H. Williams, ed., *Spiritual and Anabaptist Writers* (Philadelphia: The Westminster Press, 1957), 207.

[12] George H. Williams, ed. *The Radical Reformation* (Philadelphia: The Westminster Press, 1962), 358.

[13] This section relies largely on the following source. George H. Williams, *The Radical Reformation* (Philadelphia: The Westminster Press, 1962), 362-381.

[14] Williams, *The Radical Reformation*, 370.

[15] Williams, *The Radical Reformation*, 371.

[16] Williams, *The Radical Reformation*, 379.

[17] Cornelius Krahn, *Dutch Anabaptism* (Scottdale, PA: Herald Press, 1981), 159.

[18] John C. Wenger, ed., *The Complete Writings of Menno Simons* (Scottdale, PA: Herald Press, 1956), 668.

[19] George H. Williams, *The Radical Reformation* (Philadelphia: The Westminster Press, 1962), 393.

[20] John C. Wenger, ed., *The Complete Writings of Menno Simons* (Scottdale, PA: Herald Press, 1956), 672. "When the persons before mentioned did not desist from their supplications and my own conscience made me somewhat uneasy even in my weakness, because I saw the great hunger and need referred to, then I surrendered myself soul and body to the Lord, and committed myself to His grace and commenced in due time, according to the contents of His holy Word, to teach and to baptize, to till the vineyard of the Lord with my little talent."

[21] Wenger, 675.

[22] Wenger, 674.

[23] Thieleman J. van Braght, *The Bloody Theater of Martyr's Mirror* (Scottdale, PA: Herald Press, 1950), 482-483.

[24] John C. Wenger, ed., *The Complete Writings of Menno Simons* (Scottdale, PA: Herald Press, 1956), 558.

[25] Wenger, 559.

[26] Wenger, 307.

[27] Wenger, 741. "That the name, will, Word, and ordinance of Christ are confidently confessed in the face of all cruelty, tyranny, tumult, fire, sword, and violence of the world, and sustained unto the end."

[28] Wenger, 633. "We preach ... both day and night, in houses and in fields, in forests and wastes, ... in prisons and in dungeons, ... on the scaffold and on the wheel, before lords and princes, ... with possessions and blood, with life and death." (Menno Simons, *Reply to Gellius Faber*).

[29] Thieleman J. van Braght, *The Bloody Theater of Martyr's Mirror* (Scottdale, PA: Herald Press, 1950), 67-69.

Chapter 15

Seventeenth-Century Movements: George Fox and the Quakers

As I travelled through markets, fairs, and divers places, I saw death and darkness in all people, where the power of the Lord had not shaken them. ... I was moved of the Lord to go to [the excise men] and warn them to take heed of oppressing the poor .... (George Fox, *Journal, III*).[1]

[I] was moved to write to the judges concerning their putting men to death for cattle and for money and small things ... how contrary to the law of God it was. ... And there was a young woman to be put to death for robbing her master; and judgement was given and a grave made for her and she carried to execution. I was made to write to the judge and to the jury about her, and when she came there ... they had no power to hang her ... but she was brought back again. ... Afterwards in the prison this young woman came to be convinced of God's everlasting Truth. (George Fox, *Journal, III*).[2]

Our practices have always been to seek peace ... The spirit of Christ ... will never lead us to fight and war against any man with outward weapons, neither for the kingdom of Christ, nor for the kingdoms of this world. (George Fox, *Journal, XVIII*).[3]

Introduction: George Fox and the Quaker Movement

Williston Walker described George Fox as "one of the few religious geniuses of English history."[4] George Fox, 1624-1691, grew up far from the centers of political, economic, and religious power and influence. His academic preparation was minimal and largely informal. The relationships he had with influential people, were of his own initiation. Fox was a man of spiritual strength, a good man in every sense of the term, whose message had a powerful effect on the poor and uneducated, and on those belonging to the more privileged sectors of society.

William Penn, son of the renowned Admiral Penn, wrote a description of George Fox. Penn was a personal friend of Fox's for many years, and said that he "lived nearer to the Lord than other men."[5] Penn was laudatory in his praise, and stated that Fox knew exactly how to approach each individual soul, to fathom its depths, and reveal the truth of scripture to that individual. (1) According to Penn, no matter where he traveled, Fox was never out of his element, but spoke his message with moderation and quiet authority.

> *(1) William Penn,* Preface to the Original Edition of George Fox's Journal, 1694
> *In his testimony or ministry, he much laboured to open Truth to the people's understandings, and to bottom them upon the principle, and principal, Christ Jesus, the Light of the world, and that by bringing them to something that was of God in themselves, they might the better know and judge of him and themselves.*[6]

A Sense of Mission

George Fox was born into a pious home in a village near Leicestershire, in northern England. His mother was a gifted woman descended from a family which had known martyrdom. His father, Christopher Fox, was a poor but honest weaver who was called "Righteous Christer" by his neighbors.[7] During his youth, Fox experienced spiritual insights, and had concerns about the practices of established religion which he could neither explain nor deny. In 1647, after a long search in both established and separatist churches, Fox, aged 23, would have a life-changing spiritual experience.

For the five previous years, Fox had wandered throughout England, sharing his vision, but without convincing his hearers. He had been imprisoned several times for disturbing the peace. Finally, Fox received a vision on a mountain in northwest England called Pendle Hill. The vision transformed him into an effective instrument for communicating his radical and prophetic message. Fox now had a sense of mission. In the vision, he looked northward and saw "a great people that should receive him and his message ...."[8]

After Fox had this vision, the Quaker movement began to grow by leaps and bounds. One Sunday afternoon, after the congregation had heard the regular sermon in the separatist chapel, Fox received "a word from the Lord."[9] He stood on a rock jutting from the hillside, and began to preach. Fox spoke for three hours to a crowd of nearly a thousand people. Fox recalled that many people found it strange to listen to "a man to preach on a hill or mountain and not in their church," but the message was nevertheless well-received.[10]

The Quaker Movement

Fox was no longer a solitary prophet. Many of his hearers became emissaries of the vision. Like the apostles, they traveled two by two, first throughout North England, then through the entire country, and eventually to the ends of the earth. The movement spread quickly between 1650 and 1690. At one time, it was the most rapidly growing movement in the western world. An estimated 20,000 people joined the movement during the first five years of its existence.

The Quaker movement was severely persecuted by religious and secular authorities. Thousands of Quakers, women and men, were incarcerated and tortured. During the movement's first twenty-five years of existence, some 15,000 Quakers were sent to prison. George Fox was imprisoned on eight separate occasions during his lifetime. The longest occasion lasted two years and eight months, and was because he refused to swear an oath of loyalty.

Almost all Quakers became emissaries of the Quaker vision. They witnessed to their jailors, to judges, to kings, but above all to the common people. They witnessed to Christians and pagans without distinction. They witnessed by any means available, even taking advantage of the judicial processes to which they were submitted. They published an estimated 25,000 printed pages between 1652 and 1665. Quaker men and women traveled to the Sultan of Egypt and the Ruler of China. They believed that the seed "planted by God in every human" would respond to their message.[11]

The counter-cultural lifestyle of the early Quakers was an integral part of their witness. Women and men were treated as equals. Quakers used the familiar forms of address, "thou" and "thee," to address everyone, regardless of rank or social convention. Quaker men refused to take off their hats to anyone, even the authorities, because they believed that all were equal.

The Social and Economic Roots of the Quakers [12]

The growth of the Quaker movement was dramatic, spreading rapidly throughout England, the European continent, and the colonies in the New World within the first fifty years of its existence. But the Quaker movement had its roots in rural North England. Feudalism was strong in this region, and the most productive lands were controlled by a few wealthy families. The abbeys had been part of the feudal power structure, controlling large tracts of land dedicated to the production of wool. When the abbeys were closed in the 1530s, control of their lands passed to aristocratic families without benefitting the peasants.

The Pennine Region

In the Pennine region, where there were many Quakers, the villagers were mainly of Nordic origin. Following their ancestral customs, they tilled their own plots of land and lived in their own cottages. They had always resisted the feudal system, which had been imposed on them from the twelfth century onward. A traditional Nordic custom was the practice of assembling in open fields around a protruding rock or sepulcher on a hillside. It was no coincidence that early Quakers preached to assemblies gathered in such a fashion. Early Quaker preachers were largely of peasant origin.

In the Pennine region, during the sixteenth century, there had been a peasant rebellion protesting injustices perpetrated by the established powers. A century later, this region became the center of Quaker influence. Both movements were inspired by similar causes: the peasants were oppressed by the heavy tax burdens inflicted on them by powerful noblemen and the clergy. The region was extremely poor. During the English civil war, which began in 1649, thousands of families were without bread, or seeds for planting, with no market for their artisans' products. Adding to their misery, a plague was sweeping through the land.

Answering a Spiritual Need

Although sixteenth-century England had experienced the Anglican version of the Protestant reformation, vestiges of medieval Catholicism persisted in the rural areas. People continued to observe the saints' days, to offer money at burials, and to pray the rosary. Most people did not know the Apostles' Creed or the Ten Commandments. By the Puritan period in the seventeenth century, many people in rural parishes had never heard of Jesus. Clergymen were accused of intemperance, drunkenness, and immorality. Many vestiges of paganism remained. The sacrament of marriage had been all but abandoned. Following ancient common-law customs, a man and woman simply consented in the presence of their friends to co-habit, a practice which anticipated the Quaker protest against marriage being made sacramental.

The Quakers' opposition to the clergy, the "steeplehouses," the sacraments, and other symbols of established Christianity arose out of this context. Many who heard the Quaker message had never before been presented with evidence of a vital and transforming faith. The peasants and shepherds of northern England resented their oppressed situations. Abstract doctrines of equality, socialism, and class struggle were unknown to them. But though they were poor, they possessed an innate sense of dignity. The Quaker message gave a voice and purpose to their struggle against social injustices. It affirmed their human dignity, and offered an alternative to the prevailing structures of oppression.

Many Quakers in the rural areas of northern England came from a separatist background, or from Puritan parishes weakened by a lack of spiritual leadership and paganism among members. The Quaker faith answered the deepest needs of these peasants and artisans. Early on, the Quaker faith spread throughout the southwestern part of England, along the Welsh border. In this region, Baptists and Puritans had been active, and the Quakers attracted people from the artisan class. The Quakers also attracted followers in the urban centers of London and Bristol, particularly from those in the working classes, the artisans, and the small shopkeepers. The Quakers sided with radical protest groups on the fringes of Puritanism, although they rejected all acts of violence. They often suffered official repression because they were identified with these radical movements.

Leadership among the Quakers was charismatic. Quaker leaders generally came from the working and peasant classes. In contrast, Baptist members also came from the underprivileged sectors of society, but Baptist pastors were army officers, prominent merchants, and ex-Anglican clergymen, educated in the universities. Many Quaker women who became preachers had been domestic servants. The prominence of women in the Quaker movement is evidence of how radically it confronted the values and social conventions of the period.

The Quaker Vision [13]

What did it mean to be a Christian?

Early in his spiritual search, at the age of twenty-one, George Fox glimpsed what it meant to be a Christian. As he entered Coventry on his pilgrimage, he reflected that true believers were "born of God and passed from death to life.."[11] Anyone who claimed to be a believer, yet had not experienced this passage, was not a true believer. It was that simple.

Fox's observation may appear superficial, but it gave him profound insight into what it meant to be a Christian. The Catholic answer to the question was essentially sacramental, and the Protestant response was essentially doctrinal. Neither had satisfied Fox. His simple observation in Coventry overcame the difference between appearance and reality, which the established churches had come to accept. The sure sign that one had become a true Christian was a changed life. The role of the sacraments and of sound doctrine did not determine a believer's faith. What mattered was the actual experience of a new life. If this was lacking, all else was in vain. Fox's observation was fundamental to the Quaker vision.

What did it mean to be a minister?

George Fox wrote in his journal about having a moment of revelation while walking in a field one day. It occurred to him that a university education "was not enough to fit and qualify men to be ministers of Christ ...."[15] Common belief held that ministry was a profession requiring a theological education, but Fox suddenly saw it in a different light. Ministry was about fundamental service to others and to God, not about right doctrine.

Fox believed that ministry should be functional and charismatic, an opinion shared by other English dissidents.[16] Questions of apostolic succession, ordination, and the laying-on of hands had nothing to do with ministering to the people of God. Only God's spirit could prepare one for ministry. Fox's vision allowed women, as well as men, to answer the ministerial call, extraordinary during a time when the English still seriously debated whether or not women had souls.

What was the Church?

Fox refused to identify the church with a material structure or an ecclesiastical hierarchy. (2) Instead, he identified the church as a community of the faithful. The church was a living community, not a steeplehouse. The Quakers sought to avoid false distinctions between places which were secular and those which were sacred, calling their places of worship "meeting-houses."

> *(2) George Fox,* **Journal I**
> *But the Lord showed me, so that I did see clearly, that he did not dwell in these temples which men had commanded and set up, but in people's hearts.*[17]

What was the source of spiritual authority?

George Fox received little human help in his spiritual search. Clergymen and laymen alike warned against using the Book of Revelation, a text which inspired Fox. Fox studied the Bible almost constantly. Gradually, his "openings" took on a coherence, and became a consistent philosophy.[18]

Fox received his most important opening when he was twenty-three years old. At this time, he realized that a university education did not make a man a minister. However, he soon discovered that not all separate

(3) George Fox, **Journal, I**

But I had forsaken all priests, so I left the separate preachers also, and those called the most experienced people; for I saw that there was none among them all that could speak to my condition. And when all my hopes in them and in all men were gone, ... I heard a voice which said, "There is one, even Christ Jesus, that can speak to thy condition" ... Jesus Christ ... enlightens, and gives grace, and faith, and power. Thus, when God doth work who shall let it? And this I knew experimentally.[19]

preachers were ministers either. Only Jesus Christ had the power to enlighten and minister. (3)

Fox came to know Christ by following Him, more than by reflection or rational thought. The Quaker movement was not a body of doctrines to be confessed, but a path to be walked. Spiritual experiences guided their use of the Bible, and their attitude toward the sacraments, Christian traditions, and daily life. After his revelation, Fox no longer felt a need to consult the clergy. He had experienced the Source of life.

What was the goal of the evangelizing mission?

The Quaker goal was fearless witness to the presence of the living Christ, and his kingdom in the world. In 1652, five years after his moment of revelation, George Fox received an opening that would prove decisive for the Quaker movement. In his travels, Fox had come upon a hill called Pendle Hill, and he climbed to its peak. As he stood overlooking the land, he had a vision of the multitudes who would respond to his vision. (4) Fox's vision changed the Quaker movement into a community of mission.

Fox believed that Christ could be found in the present. The Christian life was not a memory of what once was, or a hope for a better future, but

(4) George Fox, **Journal, V**

I spied a great high hill called Pendle Hill, and I went on the top of it with much ado, it was so steep ... and there atop of the hill I was moved to sound the day of the Lord; and the Lord let me see ... in what places he had a great people to be gathered.[20]

a present experience of the living Christ. Shortly after climbing Pendle Hill, Fox went into the town of Sedbergh, which was having a fair. He climbed a tree in the steeplehouse yard and proclaimed, to a large audience, that Christ could teach his people in the *present.*[21] The following Sunday, Fox again proclaimed Christ's presence, and asked his audience to know Christ as "their teacher, their counsellor, their shepherd to feed them ... and to know their bodies to be the temples of God and Christ for them to dwell in."[22]

The most fundamental element of Quakerism was the vision of Christ as present in His community. For example, George Fox looked at the period's apocalyptic expectations from a radically different angle. He believed that the new kingdom would not be outwardly visible, but that change would occur within individuals, whose hearts were open to Christ. In fact, Fox argued that God's kingdom was already on earth, if only one was willing to see it. (5)

> *(5) George Fox,* **Journal, VII**
> *While I was in prison here the Baptist and Fifth-Monarchy-Men prophesied that this year Christ should come and reign upon earth a thousand years. And they looked upon this reign to be outward. ... But Christ is come and doth dwell in the hearts of his people and reigns there.*[23]

However, Fox did not believe that God's kingdom was limited to an invisible expression in the individual heart. Rather, he argued that God's kingdom might not resemble the political kingdoms of human experience. Fox believed that God's kingdom was present and visible, and profoundly affected the life experiences of its participants.

The Quaker vision of the present Christ determined the theory and practice of the movement's evangelizing mission. From his prison cell, Fox wrote to his followers, advising them to "Walk cheerfully over the world, answering that of God in every one."[24] Fox reminded his fellow ministers that God's presence was in both adversaries and friends.

The Quaker community did not remain dependent on its prophet's charisma. Instead, the vision of the present Christ created a vital and dynamic community. Most Quakers were from the lower sectors of English society, but upper-class people, such as William Penn and Robert Barclay, were also drawn to the community. Quakers shared each other's burdens. When someone in the group was incarcerated, others assumed the family's support without any prompting or discussion. When the adults in a group were imprisoned, their children took on all responsibilities, because the authorities would not arrest them. Being a Quaker was a serious choice, undertaken with joy.

The Lamb's War

The metaphor of the Lamb's War most clearly expresses the Quaker sense of vocation. James Nayler, an early "public friend," or itinerant minister, first used the metaphor. Nayler described the Lamb's War as an intensely personal inner struggle, fought with weapons of the Spirit, against one's own selfish desires to possess, to dominate, and to stand out. Nayler believed that one must fight the Lamb's War, and form "a new Man, a new Heart, new Thoughts, and a new Obedience" before one could share the kingdom message.[25]

Fighting the Lamb's War, and coming out victorious, gave Quakers the inner peace and assurance which enabled them to face the world with serenity and hope. Within themselves, they fought against anything that wasn't of God.[26] The Quakers' sense of serenity came from the constant presence and direction of God's spirit in their lives.

Establishing a Kingdom

By 1649, the Quaker movement was spreading throughout England. That year, the Puritans assassinated the English monarch and imprisoned the nobility, all in the name of God and of His kingdom on earth. Deeply troubled by these events, George Fox wrote that violence had no place in God's kingdom. He charged his followers to "seek the peace of all men, and no man's hurt."[27]

The Quakers fought with different weapons. God was establishing a different kingdom through His people. From 1652 to 1657, the Quaker movement spread like wildfire. Nayler believed that Christ had come, and was present "with ten thousand of his saints."[28] Before 1652, there were about 500 Quakers; in 1654, there were 5,000; and in 1657, there were at least 20,000. If the movement had continued to grow at this rate, the world would have become Quaker within a generation.[29]

From the beginning, Quakers accepted the name given them by their disdainful adversaries. George Fox recalled how Justice Bennet had called them "Quakers" in the year 1650, when Fox and his friends "bid them tremble at the word of God."[30] After being beaten by a mob which had been incited by a clergyman, Fox and his friends returned to the meeting where they were insulted and called "Quakers." There, they spoke with such power that "the priest fell a-trembling himself so that one said unto him, 'Look how the priest trembles and shakes, he is turned a Quaker also.'"[31]

> **(6) Wenlock Christison responding to the judge**
> *Do not think to weary out the living God by taking away the lives of His servants. What do you gain by it? For the last man you put to death, here five come in his room. And if you have power to take my life from me, God can raise up the same principle of life in ten of His servants and send them among you in my room.*[33]

The Quakers did not assume their vocation without understanding the cost. Convinced that they were the chosen objects of God's grace, they accepted their outsider status.[32] In Massachusetts, four Quakers were hanged. During one of these trials, Wenlock Christison revealed the secret of Quaker tenacity. For every person put to death, another five would come to take his place. The living God would continue to live through His servants. (6)

Lives of Prophetic Protest

The Lamb's War was a spiritual vision grounded in real human experience. Quakers spoke continually of the Day of the Lord, the goal toward which salvation history pointed. Quakers awaited victory in the War of the Lamb. They anticipated corporate salvation for those who worked together in God's name.[34] Already having experienced a restoring power present and active in the world, the Quakers' apocalyptic expectations were full of wonder and joy, not desperation. They fought against the "principalities and powers" of evil, both in themselves and in the world.[35] They shared a message of good news and a judgement that would ultimately be redemptive.

The Quakers looked forward to the coming of the kingdom, in which peace, justice, and equality would prevail. However, they also believed that this same kingdom was already present in their midst. They fought for this kingdom at all times, leading counter-cultural lives of prophetic protest. From the beginning, the Quakers wore the clothes of the ordinary working class, to show their solidarity with the poor. The simplicity of their lives was a direct protest against injustice. Quakers took a stand against exploitation, admonishing landlords who "grind the faces of the poor, who rack and stretch out their Rents."[36] At a time when prices were based on supply and demand rather than on the real costs of manufacturing, Quakers initiated fixed pricing in an effort to bring justice into the marketplace.

> *(7) George Fox,* **Journal, II**
> *Though "thou" to a single person was according to their own learning, their accidence and grammar rules, and according to the Bible, yet they could not bear it, and the hat-honour, because I could not put off my hat to them, it set them all into a rage. But the Lord showed me that ... it was an honour invented by men in the Fall, and in the alienation from God.*[37]

Quakers used the familiar forms of address, "thou" and "thee," and refused to take off their hats to the authorities. These protests might seem insignificant, but allowed the Quakers to put the values of God's kingdom into practice. (7) Quakers believed that all people were equal, and should be treated as such. They refused to swear oaths of loyalty required by the authorities because they were committed to a higher authority. When a Quaker gave his or her word, yes meant yes, and no meant no. In these ways, Quakers expressed their adherence to the kingdom of God, and criticized the kingdoms of this world.

Conclusion

Quakers led lives of integrity and action. Evangelical preaching and social protest were aspects of the same spiritual vocation. George Fox wrote in his journal about a demon-possessed woman who had suffered her affliction for thirty-two years. She had sought help from the priests, but to no avail. Finally, she approached Fox, who was in prison, saying that the Lord had told her to seek redemption among the Quakers. At Fox's bidding, the woman went to live with the Quakers. There, in Elizabeth Hooten's home, she was freed.[38] After spending several more weeks among the Friends, the woman returned home to her family.

Practicing another aspect of his vocation, George Fox went to the courts, approaching judges and exhorting them to do justice. He went to the public houses, to fairs and markets, and spoke against all manner of

---

(8) George Fox, **Journal, II**

When I was in Mansfield, there was a sitting of the justices about hiring of servants; and it was upon me from the Lord to go and speak to the justices that they should not oppress the servants in their wages. ... I was moved to go to several courts and steeplehouses at Mansfield and other places to warn them to leave off oppression and oaths, and to turn from deceit and to turn to the Lord, and do justly.[40]

---

deceitful behaviour, "forewarning them of the great and terrible day of the Lord."[39] Quakers also witnessed against slave trafficking, and were pioneers in jail reform. They struggled against the exploitation of workers, and denounced inhuman labor conditions. These activities were all aspects of the Lamb's War. (8)

Quakers saw themselves as "the seed of Abraham ... in which all nations are blessed."[41] They also believed that they were primitive Christianity revived. They spoke of themselves as "the true Church," which was not part of Protestant or Catholic Christendom. The church, they believed, was characterized by the presence of God's power within it. Quakers saw themselves as heirs of the heretics of an earlier period, including the Waldensians, the Lollards, the Hussites, and their own martyrs.[42]

In the Lamb's War, the humblest Quakers joined Christ in the struggle against the powers of evil. They fought the evils hidden deep within their own hearts, and those embodied in society's oppressive structures.

Notes

[1] John L. Nickalls, ed., *The Journal of George Fox* (Cambridge: University Press, 1952), 49.

[2] Nickalls, 65-66.

[3] Nickalls, 399-400.

[4] Williston Walker, *A History of the Christian Church* (New York: Charles Scribner's Sons, 1959), 420.

[5] John L. Nickalls, ed., *The Journal of George Fox* (Cambridge: University Press, 1952), xliv.

[6] Nickalls, xlii-xlvii.

[7] Donald F. Durnbaugh, *The Believers' Church* (Scottdale: Herald Press, 1985), 110.

[8] John L. Nickalls, ed., *The Journal of George Fox* (Cambridge: University Press, 1952), xl.

[9] Nickalls, 108.

[10] Nickalls, 108-109. "In the afternoon the people gathered around me with several Separate teachers, where it was judged there were above a thousand people; and all those several Separate teachers were convinced of God's everlasting Truth that day; amongst whom I declared freely and largely God's everlasting Truth and word of life about three hours; and there were many old people that went into the Chapel, and looked out of the windows and thought it a strange thing to see a man to preach on a hill or mountain and not in their church (as they called it)."

[11] Donald F. Durnbaugh, *The Believers' Church* (Scottdale: Herald Press, 1985), 112-113. They walked "'cheerfully over the world' confidently expecting that the 'seed' or 'innerlight' planted by God in every human would respond to a witness unafraid."

[12] This section relies largely on the following source. Hugh Barbour, *The Quakers in Puritan England* (New Haven, CN: Yale University Press, 1964), 72-93.

[13] This section relies largely on the following source. D. Elton Trueblood, *The People Called Quakers* (New York: Harper and Row Publishers, 1966), 30-39.

[14] John L. Nickalls, ed., *The Journal of George Fox* (Cambridge: University Press, 1952), 7.

[15] Nickalls, 7.

[16] D. Elton Trueblood, *The People Called Quakers* (New York: Harper and Row Publishers, 1966), 31 n. 8. John Milton wrote: "It is a fond error, though too much believed among us, to think that the university makes a minister of the Gospel: what it may conduce to other arts or sciences I dispute not now, but that which makes fit a minister the Scripture can but inform us to be only from above."

[17] John L. Nickalls, ed., *The Journal of George Fox* (Cambridge: University Press, 1952), 8.

[18] Nickalls, 9.

[19] Nickalls, 11.

[20] Nickalls, 103-104.

[21] Nickalls, 107. "In the week there was a great fair at Sedbergh. ... I went to the fair and declared through the fair the day of the Lord, and after I had done I went into the steeplehouse yard and got up by a tree, and most of the people of the fair came to me, and abundance of priests and professors. There I declared the everlasting Truth of the Lord and the word of life for several hours, and the Lord Christ Jesus was come to teach his people himself and bring them off all the world's ways and teachers to Christ, their way to God; and I laid open all their teachers and set up the true teacher, Christ Jesus."

[22] Nickalls, 109.

[23] Nickalls, 261.

[24] Nickalls, 263.

[25] Hugh Barbour, *The Quakers in Puritan England* (New Haven, CN: Yale University Press, 1964), 40-41.

[26] Barbour, 94. "God ... doth nothing but by his Son, the Lamb. ... His appearance in the Lamb ... is to make War with the God of this World, and to plead with his Subjects concerning their revolt from him their Creator ... The Manner of this War is, first ... he gives his Light into their Hearts, even of Men and Women, thereby he lets all see ... what he owns and what he disowns ... so he may save ... all that are not willfully disobedient. ... They are to War against ... whatever is not of God."

[27] John L. Nickalls, ed., *The Journal of George Fox* (Cambridge: University Press, 1964), 357.

[28] Hugh Barbour, *The Quakers in Puritan England* (New Haven, CN: Yale University Press, 1964), 181.

[29] Barbour, 181-182.

[30] John L. Nickalls, ed., *The Journal of George Fox* (Cambridge: University Press, 1952), 58.

[31] Nickalls, 99.

[32] D. Elton Trueblood, *The People Called Quakers* (New York: Harper and Row Publishers, 1966), 21.

[33] Trueblood, 15.

[34] Hugh Barbour, *The Quakers in Puritan England* (New Haven, CN: Yale University Press, 1964), 184.

[35] Barbour, 185.

[36] Barbour, 170-171.

[37] John L. Nickalls, ed., *The Journal of George Fox* (Cambridge: University Press, 1952), 36.

[38] Nickalls, 42-44. Elizabeth Hooten was the first Friend and preacher to join the Quaker movement through the testimony of George Fox.

[39] Nickalls, 37-38.

[40] Nickalls, 26.

[41] Lewis Benson, *Catholic Quakerism: A Vision for all Men* (Philadelphia: Book and Publication Committee Philadelphia Yearly Meeting of the Religious Society of Friends, 1968), 12. "Quakers are the seed of Abraham, of that seed in which all nations are blessed, and of the faith of Abraham and never from the several Protestants nor Papists neither from their evil root nor stock ..."

[42] Hugh Barbour, *The Quakers in Puritan England* (New Haven, CN: Yale University Press, 1964), 189-190.

Chapter 16

Eighteenth Century-Movements: Pietism and the Church of the Brethren

We must be baptized according to Jesus and the apostles....

The apostles remained single-mindedly obedient and did not lay any emphasis on whether the Holy Spirit came to the persons before or after baptism; rather, they remained firmly by the commandment of their Father and baptized those who had shown themselves repentant. (Open Letter of the First Eight Brethren to the Pietists in the Palatinate).[1]

Finally, in the year 1708, eight persons agreed together to establish a covenant of a good conscience with God, to accept all ordinances of Jesus Christ as an easy yoke, and thus to follow after their Lord Jesus ...

After they were thus prepared, the said eight went out to the water called the Eder in the solitude of the morning. The brother upon whom the lot had fallen, first baptized that brother who wished to be baptized by the church of Christ. When the latter was baptized, he baptized him who had first baptized, and then the other three brethren and the three sisters. Thus all eight were baptized in an early morning hour. ... They were all immediately clothed inwardly with great joyfulness.

(Alexander Mack, Jr., *The First Baptism*)[2]

Introduction: Pietism

The Lutheran Reformation had been primarily concerned with reforming doctrine. The unfortunate legacy of this concern was an insistence that agreement upon "sound doctrine" would provide the basis for unity among Lutheranism's various factions. As a result, honest differences in interpretation were seen as obstacles to Christian communion. Faith, which

Luther had first conceived of as a personal relationship with God, became instead an "assent by which you accept all articles of the faith."[3] The Formula of Concord (1580), adopted fifty years after the Confession of Augsburg, was a stricter Lutheran interpretation than the earlier confession, and resulted in a new Protestant scholasticism.[4] A century later, the Pietist movement would emerge in protest to this.

Spener and Francke

The earliest Pietists were more interested in reforming daily life than in reforming doctrine. Pietism was a reformation which arose within the Lutheran church. The principal proponents of the movement were Philipp Jakob Spener, 1635-1705, and August Hermann Francke, 1663-1727. Pietism reacted against Protestant scholasticism, which had become increasingly sterile, concerned with the church's official confessions of faith and with theological debates. The Pietist movement encouraged personal spiritual experience and moral seriousness. Lutheranism had forgotten Luther's dictum that "the heart of religion lies in its personal pronouns."[5]

Philipp Jakob Spener was a Lutheran pastor in the city of Frankfurt. In 1670, Spener began to organize circles for prayer and Bible study in his parish. These were essentially cell groups organized to encourage spiritual renewal within the established congregation (*ecclesiolae in ecclesia*). In his book, *Pia Desideria*, or *Pious Desires*, Spener laid out six steps for spiritual renewal within the church: the laity should study the Bible; church members must care for one another; works of Christian charity should be encouraged; differences created by theological controversy must be overcome; pastors needed better spiritual formation; and preaching should be more fervent.

Spener believed that Luther had foreseen conventicles of committed Christians existing within the shelter of an established church. But Spener may have misread Luther's preface to his German Mass. In this preface, Luther described a third order, which would keep its own membership, exercise its discipline, administer its own economy, and celebrate the sacraments. Luther later dismissed this possibility when he couldn't find

Christians who were interested in participating.[6] Spener did not want to organize new congregations with the authority to celebrate the sacraments. He simply believed that cell groups would encourage the spiritual renewal of an established congregation.

August Hermann Francke was an eminent professor of Oriental studies at the University of Halle. He shared Spener's vision. Concerned about the lack of missionary commitment in the contemporary Lutheran church, Francke dedicated his energies to creating agencies of social service and evangelization. He instituted orphanages, asylums, Bible societies, and mission societies. Members of the established church could now give tangible expression to their desire to serve in Christ's name. Although the church hierarchy did not officially involve itself in Francke's projects, such forms of service have persisted within established churches to the present.

The Principal Characteristics of Pietism

Pietism emphasized an individual's emotional and volitional response to the biblical message. Originally, a Pietist was a person who studied the Bible, and attempted to lead the life of holiness described in its pages. While the Protestant was concerned about sound doctrine, the Pietist was interested in his inner assurance of salvation. Pietists did not perceive God to be working out salvation through political, doctrinal, or historical courses, or through a human community which fulfilled divine purposes. Instead, Pietists believed that God was at work primarily in one's subjective experience, in the heart of the individual.

More a spirit than an institution, Pietism manifested itself in many subsequent movements of spiritual renewal, and in other expressions of evangelical spirituality in western Protestantism. In some cases, it produced para-church institutions of evangelization and service, independent of official ecclesial structures. In other cases, Pietism became a new evangelical denomination despite its initiators' intentions otherwise.

By the beginning of the eighteenth century, a more radical expression of Pietism emerged. After searching for ways to channel its spiritual vitality, this new movement created communities in which a highly emotional spirituality was coupled with radical obedience to the teachings of Christ and the apostles. In 1708, in southwestern Germany, the radical Pietists, or the Brethren, as they called themselves, formed a "believers' church." They committed themselves through water baptism, thereby adding Pietist content to the radical ecclesial forms of Anabaptism.

The Thirty Years War

The Peace of Augsburg (1555) recognized the existence of Catholics and Lutherans – but not Calvinists – in German lands, and proclaimed that the inhabitants of each territory must take the religion espoused by their ruler (*cuius regio, eius religio*). However, tensions arose over changes in government, and the Calvinists' lack of recognition. These tensions eventually led to the outbreak of the Thirty Years War, which lasted from 1618 until 1648. All of Europe, from Scandinavia to the Iberian Peninsula, and from France to Bohemia, was affected by this upheaval.

The inhabitants of the Palatinate in southwestern Germany were among those who suffered most. Monetary depreciation contributed to the country's impoverishment. During a period of 150 years, the territory's official religion had changed no less than eight times, alternating between the established confessions: Catholic, Lutheran, and Calvinist. The forcible imposition of faiths upon the Palatinate inhabitants added to their frustration. In the ensuing spiritual vacuum, witchcraft was widely practiced. The clergy spent their time fighting amongst themselves over the rights to church properties, while the secular authorities of the Palatinate led lives of ostentatious luxury, burdening the common people with exorbitant taxes and forced labor.

The Thirty Years War was terrible. For decades, the agricultural lands of the Palatinate were ravaged and pillaged by foreign armies. The German population fell from sixteen million to less than six million. Commerce and industry were destroyed. In 1648, the Peace of Westphalia officially ended the war, but it took the people more than a century to recover from the devastation.[7]

The Peace of Westphalia once again imposed on the people the formula of *cuius regio, eius religio*. This time, the Calvinists were included in the agreement. But for the people of the Palatinate, the latter half of the seventeenth century continued to be turbulent. Armies still ravaged the countryside, stealing the peasants' meager harvests. In 1688, the army of Louis XIV of France marched through the Palatinate. Dissident radical Pietists, who by this time were meeting in their own houses, were subjected to the ravages of invading armies, and to persecution by their own country's authorities.

The Price of Religious Dissidence

The Pietist Brethren movement arose in a environment marked by increasing dissidence. Early in the eighteenth century, in Lambsheim in the Palatinate, the established church was being openly criticized. In 1705, four local men refused to swear the oath of allegiance required by the authorities, saying that the Bible forbade it. They were incarcerated until they were able to prove that they were members of one of the officially established churches. Two of the four men later joined the Brethren movement, which began three years later.[8]

In 1706, the consistory of the Reformed church in Heidelburg reported to the civil authorities that certain citizens were taking part in unauthorized evangelistic activities. The consistory accused citizens of meeting in their own homes, preaching in the streets, and upsetting the established congregation. (1) Authorities discovered and dispersed the conventicle of

---

(1) A report from the Reformed church council at Heidelburg to the Palatine government
For some time the so-called Pietists have been getting the upper hand here in the city as well as in various places in the country, especially in Schriesheim. They meet from time to time in their homes and hold conventicles. They also preach in the streets, sing, and distribute books in order to attract the inhabitants when the latter return from the fields to their homes. Through this, the congregation might become upset and led astray by their errors.[9]

fifty men and women, but the accused were able to escape before the orders for their arrest could be carried out.[10]

Three weeks later, authorities surprised a group meeting in the house of a shoemaker in Mannheim. All were arrested, incarcerated, and interrogated. The authorities described the group as "a very dangerous sect" which was willing to commit civil disobedience in matters pertaining to their faith.[11] The prisoners were sentenced to forced labor and "a bread-and-water diet."[12] To the authorities' dismay, many of the townspeople went out to the place where the prisoners were engaged in forced labor, and spent the day listening to their preaching. Finally, under pressure from these sympathizers, the authorities released their prisoners.

The Formation of a Radical Pietist Community [13]

Early Brethren Leaders

In this hostile environment of official repression, eight radicals wrote an open letter to their Pietist brothers and sisters. Several months later, the eight were baptized in the Eder River, in open defiance of the authorities.

Ernst Christoph Hochmann von Hochenau, 1670-1721, was a radical Pietist leader who was largely responsible for organizing this Pietist community. Of noble birth, Hochmann had met Francke while studying law at the University of Halle, and had experienced a radical conversion. Hochmann refused military service, and turned down other attractive vocational opportunities. He spent his life as an itinerant evangelist. Hochmann became convinced that salvation depended on separation from "Babylon," as he called the established churches.

The German mystic, Jacob Boehme, 1575-1624, was the ideological father of many of the radicals. Boehme believed that the institutional church was Babel. He insisted that faith should not be regulated by the state, nor was it the duty of Christians to participate in the wars of Babel.

The well-known historian, Gottfried Arnold, 1666-1714, was also influential among the radical Pietists. Arnold believed that the Christian church should model itself after the Christians of the first three centuries.

He believed that the church had fallen because of its alliance with the Constantinian empire. Arnold was the first historian to treat the Anabaptist movement favorably. In his *Impartial History of the Church and the Heretics*, Arnold made the novel argument that no one should be called a heretic simply because some of his contemporaries described him as such.

In 1706, Hochmann was invited to Schriesheim to attend a meeting in a mill owned by Alexander Mack, a member of a prominent Reformed family. After this meeting, Mack joined Hochmann in his evangelistic efforts, preaching to the peasants when they returned from their work in the fields. Both men were persecuted and arrested by civil authorities for their activities. Persecution forced Mack to sell his mill and move away.

Dissidents in Wittgenstein

Hochmann had lived earlier in Wittgenstein, near the Eder river, where residents enjoyed a degree of religious liberty. The area soon became a refuge for dissidents. In the Schwarzenau-Eder region, a landholding family was sympathetic toward the movement, and opened their lands to the refugees. Soon, hundreds of refugees began to arrive, turning the area into a center of radical Pietism.

Here, the refugees held intense discussions on the nature of true faith. Some lost heart and returned to their own lands and churches of origin. Others were dissatisfied with the extreme individualism of Pietism, and sought a corporate alternative. The eight radicals were of this latter persuasion. They were baptized in the region, and committed themselves to forming a community of believers, separate from the established church.

The baptism of the eight radicals was a relatively private event, but news of it spread rapidly throughout the region. Secular authorities interpreted it as an act of open rebellion against established authority. They feared that it was a new manifestation of the infamous Anabaptist kingdom of Münster. Hochmann and other Pietists were also displeased, although for very different reasons. They saw the baptisms as a step toward another institutionalization of the faith, the very thing they denounced in the established churches.

The Brethren immediately began to witness their faith publicly, and found that many people in the Schwarzenau region were sympathetic to the movement. The Brethren meetings became so large that groups could no longer meet in private homes, so they held open air meetings. Emissaries scattered throughout southwestern Germany, forming new congregations.

Testimony in Heidelburg

Testimony given in a judicial trail held in Heidelburg, in April 1709, described these congregational meetings.[14] The service would begin with hymn singing. Then they would open the Bible and read and explicate a passage together. Finally, they would pray for protection and offer their thanks to God. Questioned about the frequency of these meetings, a witness answered that they had no appointed days, "but come together ... as God moves them."[15] The same witness stated that the Brethren could meet freely in the county of Wittgenstein, where as many as sixty people would gather together at one time.

Under the interrogation of officials, the witness described how the Brethren read the Bible together. They would explain the meaning of biblical passages to one another, and if they disagreed about an interpretation, they did not let this stand in the way of their mutual respect and love. The Brethren did not need clergymen, but taught each other, like the early disciples. (2) Nevertheless, they did recognize those in their midst who were gifted with the charisma of teaching, stating that such skill was a grace given by God.[17]

Further interrogated about their doctrines, the witnesses explained that the Brethren had no new doctrines, but tried to live as Christ lived. They loved God and neighbor as themselves. They shared with those in need, even their enemies. They obeyed God before worldly authorities. To defend their beliefs, the Brethren were "ready to sacrifice everything they have, their bodies and their lives, for they are only dust and ashes."[18]

> **(2) Heidelberg court records, April 30, 1709**
> *They explain the Bible to one another, according to their grace from God. ... When they differ they pray to God until He grants them His grace, through which they remain in love and thus can agree. ... [T]he clergyman cannot explain it better to them than they do themselves, because the first teachers were also common people like fishermen and rug weavers.*[16]

As shown by their testimony, the Brethren were radical dissidents who openly confronted the religious and civil authorities. Theirs was a church of the poor, which did not use force to defend itself against persecutors. This was another attempt, on the part of outsiders and common people, to participate in God's plan of salvation.

Persecution and Migration

The movement was severely repressed by civil authorities. Among other punishments, itinerant evangelists and their converts suffered imprisonments, fines, confiscation of goods, forced labor, and exile. Count Heinrich Albrecht of Wittgenstein, who had shown favor toward refugees in his territories, received a threatening letter from the Landgrave of Hesse. Count Heinrich Albrecht was accused of bringing disgrace on himself and on the territory by protecting the dissidents. He was warned that he must expel the "vicious and most scandalous pack" from his lands, and never allow them to return.[19] To his credit, Count Heinrich Albrecht defended his right to tolerate the Brethren, describing them as devout people who "led quiet lives ... out of a pure desire to lead lives pleasing to God."[20]

Among those who experienced official repression were six men of Reformed origin from Solingen, who had been baptized in the Wupper River. They were arrested and imprisoned, and several theological faculties were consulted about appropriate sentences. The most lenient opinion called for life imprisonment and forced labor. The six were sentenced to imprisonment in the border fortress at Julich. Finally, through the intercession of a Dutch gentleman, their sentence was commuted. Another brother, Christian Liebe, was sentenced to the galleys of the king of Sicily for unauthorized preaching in Bern. Liebe was also later released, again through Dutch intervention.[21]

An estimated 500 people joined the Brethren movement during its first ten years of existence.[22] However, severe repression prompted the group to migrate out of Europe, to the Pennsylvania colony in the New World. In 1719, the first contingent from the Krefeld congregation left. Like dissident Germans before them, the Brethren sought religious liberty and economic opportunity in the colony established by the Quakers in

America. In 1720, Brethren from Schwarzenau migrated to Pennsylvania. In 1729, Alexander Mack led a large group there. Others left during the following decade. By 1740, virtually no Brethren remained in Europe. The movement had emigrated *en masse* to the New World, leaving behind their European oppressors.

The Church of the Brethren in Colonial America

The Brethren settled near Philadelphia and worked principally as weavers and farmers, as the land was fertile. In the fall of 1722, Peter Becker and others began to visit the scattered Brethren, and organized worship services in their homes. Before long, new believers were requesting baptism. Since there was no ordained minister in their midst, they wrote to the Brethren in Europe seeking counsel. On their advice, the group chose Peter Becker to serve as minister.

On December 25, 1723, the Brethren held their first baptism by immersion, followed by a love feast in the home of the Becker family. On that winter afternoon, a group of twenty-three people kneeled by an icy stream and prayed. Then six followers were baptized in the stream by immersion, and the group returned to Germantown. (3) Back at the Becker home, they celebrated the love feast in the traditional way, washing one another's feet, partaking of a simple meal, greeting one another with the outstretched hand and a holy kiss, breaking the bread and drinking from the cup, and ending with a hymn.

The new beginning in Pennsylvania occasioned spiritual renewal, especially among the youth. Waves of revival spread among the German-speaking population. The following year, all men in the Germantown congregation set out to evangelize in the frontier areas of Pennsylvania. Their campaign saw the organization of two new congregations.

(3) Based on the contemporary record in the Ephrata Chronicle
[T]hese twenty-three souls walk out in the winter afternoon, in single file, headed by Peter Becker. ... The group kneels. ... The icebound stream utters strangely solemn music. ... The prayer is ended. The six candidates for membership in God's family are led one by one into the water and are baptized in trine immersion.[23]

During the years that followed, differences of opinion and practice caused painful divisions among the Brethren. But despite these difficulties, the movement grew rapidly. In their first fifty years in the New World, the Brethren established fifteen congregations in Pennsylvania, and eighteen more in Maryland, Virginia, the Carolinas, New Jersey, and possibly Georgia.[24]

A Pacifist Stance

An important characteristic of the German Baptist Brethren, as they came to be called in Pennsylvania, was their pacifism. In this conviction, they were supported by their Quaker and Mennonite neighbors. During the French and Indian Wars, and the American Revolution, the Brethren suffered terribly. They were victims of barbarous massacres, but remained faithful to the word of Jesus: "Do not resist an evildoer." (Matt. 5:39). They literally trusted in God for their survival.

In 1777, in an attempt to achieve absolute patriotism among its citizens, the Revolutionary Assembly passed a law requiring every male citizen, over the age of fifteen, to swear an oath of allegiance. At their annual meeting, the Brethren concluded that their members must refuse to take such an oath.[25] Elder Christopher Sauer, Jr. was proprietor of an important printing press in the colony. He refused to the swear the oath and was arrested, accused of treason, and tortured by the revolutionary army. All his goods were confiscated.

The Church of the Brethren maintained its conscientious objection to military service, refusing to serve during the war with England, 1812-1815, and with Mexico, in 1845. During the war with England, some of the poorer families were reduced to poverty by fines levied against them. The annual assembly agreed to share these burdens among the brotherhood.[26]

Ever since the movement had come to America, the Brethren had expressed opposition to slavery. They refused to receive slave owners into their congregations as members. Due to their position against slavery, and their pacifism, the Brethren suffered severe persecution during the Civil War.

The story of John Kline, who was an Elder in the Church of the Brethren in Virginia, illustrates the difficulties faced by the Brethren during

*(4) Benjamin Funk, **Life of John Kline**, 1900*
My highest conception of patriotism is found in the man who loves the Lord his God with all his heart and his neighbor as himself. Out of these affections spring the subordinate love of one's country; love truly virtuous ... in its most comprehensive sense takes in the whole human family. Were this love universal, the word patriotism, in its specific sense, meaning such a love for one's country as makes its possessors ready and willing to take up arms in its defense, might be appropriately expunged from every national vocabulary.[27]

the Civil War. Kline was accused of anti-military activities for his efforts to free Brethren and Mennonite men from military service. He was incarcerated and mistreated. Concerned about the unity of the church, Kline took great risks, crossing the battle lines between North and South to pastor to his people. Suspected of subversive activities, he was assassinated in 1864 by an anonymous patriot.

In John Kline's diary, he shared his conception of patriotism, which he believed was found in one's love of God above all else. If this love were practiced, then love for one's country would not be considered more valuable than love for one's neighbor. (4) Kline's faithfulness helped maintain the communion between Brethren in the South and in the North. In 1865, by the end of the war, there were nearly 200 congregations in America, with a total membership of some 20,000 people.[28]

Conclusion

It has been over 250 years since the Church of the Brethren first came to North America, and the church has spread from coast to coast. Itinerant elders and the annual assembly greatly contributed to the church's unity. Through their teaching and service, traveling ministers built up congregations, and helped develop a common vision. The Brethren's annual assemblies, held at Pentecost, continue to provide opportunities for communion, so essential to the Brethren understanding of the church.

The Church of the Brethren has become another denomination in North America's evangelical family. However, characteristics of its radical heritage persist: simplicity of life; the importance of fraternal relationships; a resistance to doctrinal definitions; a vision of evangelization; and the vital promotion of peace and social justice.

Notes

[1] Donald F. Durnbaugh, ed., *European Origins of the Brethren* (Elgin, IL: The Brethren Press, 1958), 116, 118.

[2] Durnbaugh, *European Origins of the Brethren*, 121, 122.

[3] Williston Walker, *A History of the Christian Church* (New York: Charles Scribner's Sons, 1959), 389. Attributed to Melanchthon.

[4] Walker, 389-391.

[5] Donald F. Durnbaugh, *The Believers' Church: The History and Character of Radical Protestantism* (Scottdale: Herald Press, 1985), 119.

[6] Ulrich S. Leupold, ed., *Luther's Works: Liturgy and Hymns*, vol. 53 (Philadelphia: Fortress Press, 1965), 63-64.

[7] Williston Walker, *A History of the Christian Church* (New York: Charles Scribner's Sons, 1959), 392-396.

[8] Donald F. Durnbaugh, ed., *European Origins of the Brethren* (Elgin, IL: The Brethren Press, 1958), 38.

[9] Durnbaugh, *European Origins of the Brethren*, 40.

[10] Durnbaugh, *European Origins of the Brethren*, 41. According to the report of the authorities, the accused "cited some texts from Dr. Martin Luther's Bible which speak of spirit, brethren and sisters in Christ, and similar things. This they interpret according to their own caprice and supposed benefit, and delude the poor rabble with it."

[11] Durnbaugh, *European Origins of the Brethren*, 42.

[12] Durnbaugh, *European Origins of the Brethren*, 42.

[13] This section relies largely on the following source. Donald F. Durnbaugh, *The Church of the Brethren Past and Present* (Elgin, IL: The Brethren Press, 1971), 12-14.

[14] Donald F. Durnbaugh, ed., *European Origins of the Brethren* (Elgin, IL: The Brethren Press, 1958), 73. "When they come together they sing two or three hymns, as God moves them; then they open the Bible and whatever they find they read and explain it according to the understanding given to them by God, for the edification of their brethren. After they read, they fall to their knees, raise their hands to God and pray for the authorities, that God might

move them to punish the evil and protect the good; then they praise God that He has created them for this purpose."

[15] Durnbaugh, *European Origins of the Brethren*, 75.

[16] Durnbaugh, *European Origins of the Brethren*, 75-76.

[17] Durnbaugh, *European Origins of the Brethren*, 76. "God gives the present craftsmen today the same grace [to teach the Scriptures] as He did to His apostles."

[18] Durnbaugh, *European Origins of the Brethren*, 76-77.

[19] Durnbaugh, *European Origins of the Brethren*, 143.

[20] Durnbaugh, *European Origins of the Brethren*, 145.

[21] Donald F. Durnbaugh, *The Church of the Brethren Past and Present* (Elgin, IL: The Brethren Press, 1971), 13-14.

[22] Donald F. Durnbaugh, *The Believers' Church: The History and Character of Radical Protestantism* (Scottdale: Herald Press, 1985), 127.

[23] Donald F. Durnbaugh, ed., *The Brethren in Colonial America* (Elgin, IL: The Brethren Press, 1967), 62.

[24] Donald F. Durnbaugh, *The Church of the Brethren Past and Present* (Elgin, IL: The Brethren Press, 1971), 15-16.

[25] Dale W. Brown, *Brethren and Pacifism* (Elgin, IL: The Brethren Press, 1970), 28-29. "The first record of a decision of an annual meeting [of the Church of the Brethren] was one which forbade Brethren to take an oath of allegiance to the new country."

[26] Brown, 31.

[27] Brown, 35-36.

[28] Donald F. Durnbaugh, *The Church of the Brethren Past and Present* (Elgin, IL: The Brethren Press, 1971), 22.

Chapter 17

Eighteenth-Century Movements: John Wesley and the Methodist Movement

Persecution never did ... give any lasting wound to genuine Christianity. ... [T]he grand blow which was struck at the very root of that humble, gentle, patient love, which is the ... essence of true religion, was struck in the fourth century by Constantine the Great, when he called himself a Christian, and poured in a flood of riches, honours, and power, upon the Christians .... (John Wesley, *On the Mystery of Iniquity*). [1]

From the time that the Church and State, the kingdoms of Christ and of the world were ... unnaturally blended together, Christianity and Heathenism were so thoroughly incorporated with each other, that they will hardly ever be divided till Christ comes to reign upon earth. (John Wesley, *Of Former Times*). [2]

I am distressed. I know not what to do. I see what I might have done once. I might have said peremptorily and expressly, "Here I am; I and my Bible. I will not ... vary from this book, either in great things or small. I have no power to dispense with one jot or tittle of what is contained therein. I am determined to be a Bible Christian ...." But, alas! the time is now past; and what I can do now, I cannot tell. (John Wesley, *The Causes of the Inefficacy of Christianity*). [3]

Introduction: John Wesley

John Wesley, 1703-1791, was born into a pious Anglican home. His father, Samuel, was a parish priest and ardent defender of the Anglican High Church tradition, and of the English monarch. Wesley's mother, Susannah, was the daughter of a renowned dissident preacher. Susannah Wesley's ecclesiastical and political views were decidedly nonconformist. By all accounts, she was a matriarch, a teacher, and a saint, dedicated to the Christian nurture of her children. John Wesley was the fifteenth child of nineteen. When he was only six years old, the parsonage burned to the ground. John was rescued from a window in the upper story at the last moment. Wesley would remember himself as a "brand plucked from the burning."[4]

Wesley began his studies at Oxford in 1720, where he received an excellent education. At Oxford, in 1725, Wesley experienced the first in a series of conversions.[5] These moments of revelation greatly affected Wesley, and he would later recount them on several occasions. The experiences arose out of a number of influences, including his nurtured Christian childhood, conversations with a spiritual friend, and his reading of Jeremy Taylor, Thomas a Kempis, and William Law. Wesley resolved to fully commit himself to God and to his fellows, in life and in death.

Wesley was particularly attracted to the Desert Fathers' concept of perfection as the *goal* of Christian life. He interpreted perfection as a dynamic process, not a stable condition, an idea which would remain fundamental to him throughout his life.

The Beginnings of Methodism

After being ordained, first as deacon in 1725, and later as presbyter in 1728, John Wesley served for several years in Anglican parishes. Returning to Oxford, he joined a semi-monastic group which was dedicated to Bible study, mutual discipline, frequent communion, and works of charity. Members shared a keen interest in ancient liturgies and monastic piety. They were given a series of nicknames: The Holy Club, Supererogation Men, Bible Moths, Enthusiasts, and Methodists. The last name stuck.

At the invitation of the Society for the Propagation of the Gospel, Wesley and two Holy Club colleagues left England for Georgia. There, they planned to work among the indigenous peoples and the English colonists. However, despite Wesley's idealistic intentions, he was barely able to establish contact with the indigenous population.[6] After three years, Wesley's relations with the colonists reached their nadir and he was forced to return to England.

Wesley's humbling experience in Georgia also gave him time for personal and theological growth through reading and meditation. His contacts with Moravian missionaries proved especially inspiring. They taught him that true faith freed one from anxiety, and that authentic spirituality led to happiness.

Back in London, Wesley found himself in a deep spiritual depression. During this time, he was moved by a reading of one of Luther's texts at a meeting in Aldersgate Street. (1) Some Protestant historians treat this experience as a key event in John Wesley's life. However, Wesley himself saw it as merely one climactic moment among many. In fact, the moment was referred to only twice in Wesley's writings.[7]

Wesley began attending the Moravian society that met on Fetter Lane, while continuing to preach in Anglican congregations. Wesley observed closely the Moravian life and faith, which he admired. However, close observation also awakened some concerns. Wesley was not comfortable with the Protestant emphasis on salvation by faith alone. He believed that the goal of Christian life was holiness, which demanded faith, but also justification through acts of love. "'Faith,'" Wesley wrote, "... is only the handmaid of love.'"[9]

> *(1) John Wesley,* **Journal, I**
> *Wednesday, May 24, ... in the evening, I went very unwillingly to a society in Aldersgate Street, where one was reading Luther's Preface to the Epistle to the Romans. About a quarter before nine, while he was describing the change which God works in the heart through faith in Christ, I felt my heart strangely warmed. I felt I did trust in Christ ... and an assurance was given me that he had taken away my sins .... I then testified openly to all there what I now first felt in my heart.*[8]

Wesley was filled with zeal, but he still lacked inner assurance. On October 9, 1738, as he walked from London to Oxford, he read a report about the hundreds of conversions resulting from Jonathon Edwards' powerful preaching in New England. Wesley was moved by a sudden sense of spiritual power. He was being inwardly prepared for a new stage of his life and ministry, in which he would preach to the poor in open fields, outside the structures of established Christendom.

Evangelizing the Poor

Since the end of the seventeenth century, English dissidents had been evangelizing in Wales. The Welsh people were nominal Catholics or Protestants, but in reality still clung to pagan practices. The Anglican clergy preached in English, and Anglicanism, being rather cold and dogmatic, had had little impact on the Welsh, who were a warm and expressive people. But the dissident evangelists preached in Welsh and won the people's hearts, succeeding where established Christianity had failed. People responded to this gospel preaching with deep emotion and visible signs of excitement.

Preaching to the People

The Anglican evangelist, Griffith Jones, inspired by the dissidents' success in Wales, imitated their methods. Jones preached in Welsh, distributed copies of the scriptures in the vernacular, opened schools for children, and adapted his doctrinal expositions to the spiritual needs of the people. His methods were rejected by the Anglican church, so he preached instead in people's homes and outdoors in the church yards. In 1735, Jones' disciple, Howell Harris, assumed the leadership of the Welsh movement. Harris evangelized in Wales, and in the mining and industrial region around Bristol. He convinced the Holy Club member, George Whitefield, to preach to miners in the open fields at Kingswood.

George Whitefield, Wesley's colleague at Oxford, was a man of humble birth. During his youth, Whitefield, the son of an innkeeper, had experienced the struggles of the common people. Late in 1738, he had returned from the American colonies, where his participation in the revival had been well-received. Whitefield's experiences in the colonies had shown him that evangelistic efforts could bypass the structures of official Anglicanism, and directly respond to people's needs.

In Bristol, Whitefield preached to coal miners in the open fields near the mines. His efforts were very successful. When Whitefield left

Bristol, he called on John Wesley to continue the task of evangelization. Wesley, and other members of the Oxford group, were scandalized by the idea of preaching outside of the parish structures. Wesley went to Bristol unwillingly, as if he were going to his own martyrdom.

John Wesley's True Vocation

But in Bristol, John Wesley finally found his true vocation: evangelizing the poor. On April 2, 1739 , Wesley "submitted to be more vile" and preached in the open air near Bristol to about 3,000 people.[10] The next day, he preached in a field outside a nearby village. On the following Sunday, he spoke at Hannam Mount to the impoverished miners of Kingswood. The people's reaction was astonishing, and no one was more surprised than Wesley himself. Multitudes of listeners were moved by his message. Many miners were converted, and their lives visibly changed. The conversions were as dramatic as those described in the report on Jonathon Edwards' preaching in America.

The evangelist had been evangelized. Wesley noted with amazement that some of his listeners would cry out sharply, tremble violently, and even faint. These visible signs helped Wesley overcome his prejudices. The idea of preaching in the open had once so scandalized him that he had "thought the saving of souls almost a sin if it had not been done in church."[11]

Wesley remained a loyal Anglican all his life, but his experiences in Bristol gave him the courage to break away from the parochial system. His life before this experience had been a series of spiritual crises marked by anxiety, insecurity, and futility. After preaching in Bristol, Wesley's spiritual crises all but disappeared.

Solidarity With the Poor

Perhaps the best evidence of the evangelization of the evangelist could be seen in John Wesley's new and profound solidarity with the poor. He reached the conclusion that the poor were both the objects and the subjects of

> **(2) John Wesley, Journal, III, *May 21, 1764***
> *Religion must not go from the greatest to the least, or the power would appear to be of men.*[12]

evangelization. Religion did not favor the greatest over the least, because it did not reside in the territory of man, but of God. (2) Wesley's evangelizing mission sent the poor to preach to the poor.

Wesley felt more comfortable among the poor than he did among the affluent. He criticized the love of money possessed by many wealthy English people, including the Methodists, writing: "The poor are the Christians."[13] Wesley stood up to his harshest critics in the established church, stating that he would allow them to minister to the rich and honorable, provided he could care for the outcast. (3) Clearly, Wesley believed that worldly values were poor markers of spiritual worth.

> **(3) John Wesley, A Farther Appeal to Men of Reason and Religion**
> *The rich, the honourable, the great, we are thoroughly willing (if it the will of our Lord) to leave to you. Only let us alone with the poor, the vulgar, the base, the outcasts of men.*[14]

Wesley shared the physical suffering of those whose labors bore little fruit. He knew that such miseries could be understood by experience alone. No mere description could capture the degradation of a day's hard labor followed by a cold and hungry night. His passionate words on the subject speak for themselves: "O want of bread! want of bread! Who can tell what this means, unless he hath felt it himself?"[15]

Out of solidarity, Wesley visited the poor, the sick, and the imprisoned. By doing so he sought to console the disconsolate and bring hope to the hopeless. But he also wanted to share in their suffering, so that he might show them true compassion. Wesley believed if the rich would visit the poor they would understand their plight.[16] Writing to a woman of the upper class, Wesley exhorted her to: "Take up your cross, woman! ... I want you to converse more, abundantly more, with the poorest of the people. ... Creep in among these, in spite of dirt, and a hundred disgusting circumstances; and thus put off the gentlewoman."[17]

An Economics of Sharing

Common interpretation of the parsonage fire from which John Wesley was rescued in early childhood concentrated on the providential preservation of little John. However, Wesley offered another interpretation of the event. On the day after the fire, his father was raking through the smoking ruins when he found a page from the Bible with the legible line, "Go, sell all that thou hast; and take up thy cross, and follow me."[18] In effect, this passage would reflect the guiding principle of Wesley's life. He would be determined to live a life free from the tyranny of possessions, sharing with the poor, and following the biblical precepts as he understood them.

Wesley's critique of the established church's Constantinian posture – its rich purse and political connections masked by the thin rhetoric of poverty – was not entirely consistent. His conservative political views prevented him from taking a truly radical stance against the use of coercive force in socio-political relationships.[19] However, he recognized that many Christians were misusing their social privilege and economic power. Wesley argued that true Christian stewardship should alter the economics of private property and ultimately lead to a redistribution of wealth.[20]

Through his lifestyle and his writings, Wesley exposed the shabby deceit of the church's pseudo-gospel of prosperity and power. More than once, Wesley observed that "it is easier for a camel to go through the eye of a needle, than for those that have riches not to trust in them."[21] Wesley intended to restore "the simplicity and the purity of the gospel" to the Methodist societies.[22] He never tired of warning the societies of the dangers of wealth, pointing to the fall of the established church as a potent example of this. (4) The fruits of the earth belonged to God and not to man, and man bore the responsibility of sharing that portion of goods with which he had been charged.[24]

Wesley believed that Christians owed *all* of their surplus wealth to the poor.[25] He did not conceive of riches as a satisfying abundance of goods, but simply as the surplus remaining after one had met one's essential needs. (5) Further, ostentatious consumption was not simply foolish and selfish, but was outright theft. "Every shilling

> **(4) John Wesley**, Journal, **III**, *July 7, 1764*
> *I gave all our brethren a solemn warning not to love the world, or the things of the world. This is one way whereby Satan will surely endeavour to overthrow the present work of God.*[23]

> **(5) John Wesley**, The Danger of Riches *and* On God's Vineyard
> *Whoever has sufficient food to eat, and raiment to put on, and a place where to lay his head, and something over, is rich. ... Are you not increasing in goods, laying up treasures on earth; instead of restoring to God in the poor, not so much, or so much, but all that you can spare?*[26]

which you needlessly spend on your apparel is, in effect, stolen from the poor!" wrote Wesley.[27] Earthly goods were not private property, to be squandered according to individual desires, but belonged to God and therefore to all.

Wesley was bent on restoring holiness to the church, and this led him to oppose worldliness. Instead of echoing the Protestant belief in justification by faith, Wesley sought out a faith that would sanctify. Worldliness was most threatening to the church when it entered into economic relationships.

The Methodist Societies

Within the first decade of the movement's existence, Wesley organized followers into societies, bands, and classes. These small groups provided the corporate context for teaching, spiritual growth, mutual discipline, and pastoral care. Charles Wesley was a counselor and companion to his brother, John, and the hymns he wrote helped to build a sense of community among the Methodist societies.

Ministry in this network of Christian communities was carried out by lay leaders, who were called helpers. Wesley's Anglican loyalties did not permit him to call them ministers, nor were they allowed to administer the sacraments. However, in 1744, Wesley organized an annual conference to unify the movement and provide encouragement to its leaders. For all practical purposes, the Methodist movement was an evangelistic order within the Anglican church, which sought to restore holiness to the church.

Methodist societies lacked official recognition, and were often persecuted by mobs incited by Anglican authorities. Methodists were accused by Anglican officials of enthusiasm, a word whose Greek roots literally mean possessed by a god. In defending his cause, Wesley distinguished among varying definitions of enthusiasm, arguing that authentic faith was an intensely personal experience, and therefore possessed of a positive enthusiasm.

The Methodist societies were the corporate context in which John Wesley's vision of holiness could be realized. The groups were intended to encourage members to grow toward Christ's perfection. They were places where the gifts of the Spirit could be exercised and encouraged. Within these communities individuals cared for one another with love, and practiced mutual discipline.

In these societies, holiness was often expressed through the members' economic practices. The gospel was not merely a beautiful ideal, but became a transforming reality. Each society organized itself according to biblical principles. Wesley noted with pleasure that one society of young men lived communally, giving away all their surplus earnings.[28] Another society met once a week to determine the community's needs and promptly meet them with goods contributed for that purpose.[29] The principles were John Wesley's, but the societies seemed relatively free to pursue that course best suited to their organizational capacities.

Parallel Social Influences

Methodism and the Poor

The open air preaching of George Whitefield, John Wesley, and others gave rise to Methodism. The evangelists traveled in the southwestern part of England, speaking to those who were victims of the earliest stages of the industrial revolution. Between 1738 and 1739, the workers and miners in the region staged an uprising to protest escalating food prices. People could no longer afford to buy wheat. In their desperation, mobs attacked wheat storage warehouses, stealing food and burning factories. Whitefield wrote of these needy people as sheep without a shepherd.[30] The despair of the working class provided the raw material to which Methodist doctrine and discipline gave shape.

Methodism was successful because it was willing to become a popular movement. Breaking from the parochial system of the established church, it proclaimed a gospel of grace and holiness that would save the masses from their misery. Methodism placed salvation directly within the reach of the common people. It gave dignity to the needy, and made them protagonists in their destiny, and participants in their community.

Wesley's solidarity with the poor was key to the movement's success. Wesley confronted the adversaries of the outcast. He denounced the practices of merchants, and condemned capitalism's fundamental strategy of buying cheap and selling dear. He denounced physicians who were motivated by profit rather than compassion, and lawyers who participated in a corrupt justice system. Wesley also took a prophetic stance against colonialism, slave trafficking, and warfare.[31]

Within the Methodist societies, Wesley introduced innovations which alleviated human suffering by converting victims into protagonists active in their own liberation. The argument has been made that John Wesley's revolutionary innovations helped to save England from suffering the violent revolution experienced in France.[32]

Methodism and the Middle Class

Even during Wesley's lifetime, a parallel current of influence existed within Methodism. As the eighteenth century progressed, a growing number of Methodists came from the more affluent middle classes. In defending his movement against the establishment's charges of political and economic subversion, Wesley had tended to minimize the differences between the movement's radical evangelical values and those which prevailed in society.

An example of this is found in Wesley's sermon, *On the Use of Money*, written only five years after the movement's explosive beginnings in Bristol. In the sermon, he espoused the idea that "The fault does not lie in the money but in them that use it."[33] Wesley then laid out three rules for using money well: "*Gain all you can ... Save all you can* [and] ... *Give all you can.*"[34] It was one thing to encourage factory workers and miners to follow these economic principles, but when the message was appropriated by the middle class its meaning shifted ominously.

In Wesley's defense, each time he referred to these rules, he focused on the importance of the third.[35] Wesley spent some energy clarifying the meaning of the rules, stating, for example, that "save all you can" meant "Don't spend on yourself what God gives you to aid the poor."[36] But Wesley's evangelical vision had fallen victim to his rhetorical fervor, for "gain all you can," did not mean "gain all you need." He continued to lament the movement's increasing materialism, as Methodism attracted a growing proportion of its members from the middle and upper classes.[37] However, the social changes within the movement meant that Wesley's sermon, *On the Use of Money*, could be used to confirm the values of the English middle class.

Conclusion: John Wesley's Legacy

Contrary to his intentions, John Wesley left behind a Methodist church. The War of Independence in the American colonies created an urgent need for leadership within the Methodist movement, inducing Wesley finally to ordain ministers for the American communities. However, only after his death would English Methodism become an independent denomination.

Present-day Methodism bears the stamp of John Wesley's legacy, but so do many social institutions in the contemporary Western world. Faithful to their lower class roots, Methodists organized schools for working class children, who were victims of industrialization with its attendant need for cheap labor. The revolutionary initiative created a popular alternative outside of the official education system, which did not serve the needs of the poor. These schools later became Sunday school, now an institution in almost all Protestant denominations.

Another Methodist legacy was the rise of the labor movement, as workers struggled to obtain more humane labor conditions. Many early protagonists in this movement came from Methodist societies, and in some cases the societies provided models for the new labor organizations.

Efforts to reform penal institutions, notorious for their inhumane conditions, were also a part of the Methodist legacy. Methodist criticism of the colonial system helped to raise the consciousness of the English people and mobilize them against this commercial and social exploitation. Wesley's opposition to slave trafficking played a principal role in the successful struggle to have this practice banned by the British parliament.

When John Wesley died, in 1791, there were approximately 80,000 members in the organized Methodist societies and classes under his pastoral care. The classes had proven especially attractive to the common people. In small group meetings, where all were active participants, they found communion and mutual support. These classes were both a spiritual and a social alternative to the violent uncertainties of eighteenth century English life. By their mere existence, these communities constituted the greatest legacy of the Methodist movement.

Notes

[1] Theodore W. Jennings, Jr., *Good News to the Poor: John Wesley's Evangelical Economics* (Nashville: Abingdon Press, 1990), 40.

[2] Jennings, 41.

[3] Jennings, 177.

[4] Donald F. Durnbaugh, *The Believers' Church* (Scottdale: Herald Press, 1985), 133. John Wesley, *Journal, IV*, 90.

[5] Albert J. Outler, ed., *John Wesley* (New York: Oxford University Press, 1964), 7. "Being in the twenty-third year of my age, I met with Bishop Taylor's *Rules and Exercises of Holy Living and Dying.* In reading several parts of this book I was exceedingly affected. ... Instantly, I resolved to dedicate all my life to God, all my thoughts and words and actions. ... In the year 1726 I met with Kempis' *Christian's Pattern.* ... I saw that giving even all my life to God ... would profit me nothing unless I gave my heart, yea, all my heart to him. ... A year or two after, Mr. Law's *Christian Perfection* and *Serious Call* were put into my hands. These convinced me more than ever of the absolute impossibility of being half a Christian, and I determined through his grace (the absolute necessity of which I was deeply sensible) to be all-devoted to God: to give him all my soul, my body and my substance."

[6] Theodore W. Jennings, Jr., *Good News to the Poor: John Wesley's Evangelical Economics* (Nashville: Abingdon Press, 1990), 53. Reflecting later on his unfortunate experiences in Georgia, Wesley wrote, "In the afternoon I visited many of the sick; but such scenes, who could see unmoved? There are none such to be found in a Pagan country. If any of the Indians in Georgia were sick, (which indeed exceedingly rarely happened, till they learned gluttony and drunkenness from the Christians) those who were near him gave him whatever he wanted. O who will convert the English into honest heathens!" (*Journal*, Feb. 8, 1753).

[7] Albert J. Outler, ed., *John Wesley* (New York: Oxford University Press, 1964), 14.

[8] Outler, 66.

[9] Outler, 28, 27.

[10] Outler, 17.

[11] Elie Halevy, *The Birth of Methodism in England* (Chicago: University

of Chicago Press, 1971), 61.

[12] Theodore W. Jennings, Jr., *Good News to the Poor: John Wesley's Evangelical Economics* (Nashville: Abingdon Press, 1990), 49.

[13] Jennings, 49.

[14] Jennings, 49.

[15] Jennings, 51.

[16] Jennings, 55. "... one great reason why the rich, in general, have so little sympathy for the poor, is, because they so seldom visit them."

[17] Jennings, 57.

[18] Jennings, 119.

[19] Wesley was not entirely consistent in his rejection of Constantinianism. His attitude toward the Christian use of coercive force was ambiguous at best. On the one hand, Wesley lamented Christian bellicosity, if not for clearly evangelical reasons, at least for humanitarian ones: "There is a still more horrid reproach to the Christian name, yea, to the name of man, to all reason and humanity. There is war in the world! war between men! war between Christians! ... Now, who can reconcile war, I will not say to religion, but to any degree of reason or common sense?" (Jennings, 79). On the other hand, Wesley's allegiance to the monarchy led him to support the policies of the English Crown against the American colonies during the Revolutionary War. In 1782, Wesley wrote: "Two or three years ago, when the kingdom was in imminent danger, I made an offer to the Government of raising some men. The Secretary of War (by the King's order) wrote me word, that 'it was not necessary; but if it ever should be necessary, His Majesty would let me know.'" (Jennings, 212-213).

[20] Jennings, 24-25.

[21] Jennings, 33.

[22] Jennings, 39.

[23] Jennings, 39.

[24] Jennings, 99, 104. "Thou no longer talkest of thy goods, or thy fruits, knowing they are not thine, but God's. The earth is the Lord's, and the fulness thereof; He is the Proprietor of heaven and earth. He cannot divest himself of his glory; he must be the Lord, the possessor, of all that is. Only he hath left a portion of his goods in thy hands, for such uses as he has specified. ... What shalt thou do? Why, are not those at the door whom God hath appointed to receive what thou canst spare? What shalt thou do? Why, disperse abroad, and give to the poor. Feed the hungry. Clothe the naked. Be a father to the fatherless,

and a husband to the widow."

[25] Jennings, 226 n. 4. In this evangelical conception of economic relationships, giving to the poor is not merely a matter of charity, but of justice. Gregory the Great enunciated this principle in his *Pastoral Rule* some 1,000 years earlier: "For when we administer necessaries to the indigent, we do not bestow our own on them, but render to them what is theirs; we rather pay a debt of justice than accomplish works of mercy."

[26] Jennings, 107-108.

[27] Jennings, 109-110.

[28] Jennings, 125. "Here I found twelve young men, whom I could almost envy. They lived together in one house, and continually gave away whatever they earned above the necessities of life."

[29] Jennings, 125. "They met together at six every Thursday morning; consulted on the business which came before them; sent relief to the sick, as everyone had need; and gave the remainder of what had been contributed each week to those who appeared to be in the most pressing want. So that all was concluded within the week; what was brought on Tuesday being constantly expended on Thursday."

[30] Elie Halevy, *The Birth of Methodism in England* (Chicago: University of Chicago Press, 1971), 69.

[31] Theodore W. Jennings, Jr., *Good News to the Poor: John Wesley's Evangelical Economics* (Nashville: Abingdon Press, 1990), 71-88.

[32] Bernard Semmel, *The Methodist Revolution* (New York: Basic Books, Inc., 1973), 3.

[33] Albert J. Outler, ed., *John Wesley* (New York: Oxford University Press, 1964), 240.

[34] Outler, 241-249. Emphasis in original.

[35] Theodore W. Jennings, Jr., *Good News to the Poor: John Wesley's Evangelical Economics* (Nashville: Abingdon Press, 1990), 230 n. 5.

[36] Jennings, 167.

[37] Albert J. Outler, ed., *John Wesley* (New York: Oxford University Press, 1964), 238.

Chapter 18

Nineteenth-Century Movements: The Christian Church (Disciples of Christ)

As the first Disciples came together on the first day of the week for the breaking of bread; and they agreed that in this, as in everything else, they ought to be followers of the first churches, being guided and directed by the Scriptures alone. The introduction of this was a remarkable approximation to the primitive church order and discipline. (*Memoir of John Glas*, xli)[1]

Our desire, therefore, for ourselves and our brethren would be, that rejecting human opinions and inventions of men, as of any authority, or as having any place in the church of God, we might forever cease from farther contentions about such things; returning to, and holding fast by, the original standard; taking the divine word alone for our rule ... (Thomas Campbell, *Declaration and Address*)[2]

The Bible alone is the Bible only, in word and deed, in profession and practice; and this alone can reform the world and save the church. (Alexander Campbell, *The Christian System*)[3]

Introduction

Early in the nineteenth century, movement known as the Christian Church (Disciples of Christ) arose in the United States when two restorationist movements converged. One tributary of the movement had British roots, and the other originated in North America. Thomas and Alexander Campbell, of Scottish-Irish background, were instrumental in the development of the British restorationist movement. The American restorationist movement originated in Baptist and Methodist groups. After a series of camp meetings on the frontier between Kentucky and Ohio, the two tributaries eventually consolidated, organizing a new group of Christian congregations. The church's forms of worship and congregational structures were suited to frontier life. The church would succeed in adapting the gospel to the needs of those living on the frontier in precarious economic and social conditions.

The British Restorationist Movement [4]

Around the turn of the nineteenth century, a number of minor restorationist movements arose in Great Britain. These movements espoused the ideal of restoring the practices of early apostolic communities to contemporary forms of worship. The restorationist ideal was reflected in the names adopted by these groups: Brethren, Church of Christ, Disciples, and Christians. At this time, Christian authority was embedded in complicated traditions and creeds, with limited focus on scriptural imperatives. Theology was more speculative than practical. Worship was formal, and the clergy seemed more interested in prestige and power, than in service. In this environment, the restorationist perspective held particular appeal.

Glas and Sandeman

One of these movements was initiated by John Glas, 1695-1773, a minister in the Church of Scotland. Glas concluded that the New Testament church had been a purely spiritual community. In 1728, he resigned his position in the established church and formed an independent congregation, where he intended to restore primitive New Testament practices.

Robert Sandeman, 1718-1771, Glas's son-in-law, carried on the movement begun by his father-in-law. Adherents observed a weekly celebration of the Lord's Supper. They shared communal agape meals and the holy kiss among Christians, took weekly offerings for the needy, and practiced fraternal admonition and the community of goods. Congregations placed ministerial responsibilities in the hands of bishops, elders, and teachers. Some of Sandeman's colleagues in the Scottish movement arrived at the conviction that believers should be baptized by immersion. This group called itself the "Old Scotch Baptists."

The influential movement begun by Glas and Sandeman would grow to about twenty or thirty congregations spread throughout Great Britain and North America.

The Haldane Brothers

A similar restorationist movement was begun by the Haldane brothers, James Alexander, 1768-1851, and Robert, 1764-1842. The brothers were influential laymen in the Church of Scotland, and shared concerns about the church's rationalistic theology and spiritual sterility. Inspired by a deep spiritual experience, they broke with the established church in 1799, and formed an independent congregation in Edinburgh. There, they encouraged evangelistic preaching as a means of renewing the church's life. This led them to organize a bible school in Glasgow where young men of modest means could prepare themselves for the ministry. They also invited Roland Hill, 1744-1833, a renowned English evangelist, to preach in Scotland.

In their congregation in Edinburgh, the Haldane brothers instituted measures that would restore apostolic ideals to the church. They believed that the congregation should act on its own convictions, guided by scripture. They began a weekly celebration of the Lord's Supper. Shortly thereafter, they discontinued the practice of child baptism. The Haldane brothers were convinced that authentic renewal called for exact conformity to apostolic teachings and practices. Many nineteenth-century renewal movements in Great Britain and North America would emphasize the restoration of primitive church order. Among these was the movement known as the Christian Church (Disciples of Christ).

Sectarian Conflict in Northern Ireland

The turn of the nineteenth century was a time of social and religious turbulence in Northern Ireland. Militant Protestants organized secret militias with the goal of expelling Roman Catholics from Ulster. The militants searched houses under cover of night, looking for hidden weapons, and attacked Catholic villages. To defend themselves, Roman Catholics organized their own paramilitary units. This culminated in an Irish rebellion against the English in 1798. In 1801, peace was partially restored, but a climate of mutual suspicion and social unrest persisted.

Thomas Campbell in Ireland

Thomas Campbell, 1763-1854, and his son Alexander, 1788-1866, were instrumental in bringing the restorationist vision to the United States. In his youth, Thomas Campbell's father had been a Roman Catholic, but joined the Church of Ireland because he felt its practices were closer to biblical teachings. In his own youth, Thomas Campbell felt that his father's church lacked evangelistic zeal, and joined the seceder Presbyterians. By 1798, Campbell was serving as pastor in one of these congregations.

Thomas Campbell was opposed to the secret militias, and their use of violence against people of different religious convictions. He declared his opposition to all forms of intolerance and sectarian violence. Several influences contributed to Campbell's social and religious convictions.

Firstly, his congregation was tolerant toward other spiritual currents, including the new restorationist movements led by Glas and the Haldane brothers.

Secondly, the evangelical open air preaching of Roland Hill, and others, invited renewed interest in a popular style of evangelization. Campbell began to consider the scriptures as an adequate basis for the organization and unity of the church.

Thirdly, Campbell was deeply affected by the sectarian spirit of contemporary Irish society. He was moved by the writings of John Locke, the English philosopher, who encouraged authorities to tolerate dissident religious groups. Locke called on religious groups to tolerate a variety of practices and opinions within their own membership. Locke argued that individuals had the right to choose freely their religious affiliations. However, profound differences continued to produce bitterness and divisions among denominations within the Presbyterian church of Campbell's time.

On several occasions, Campbell attempted to mediate conflicts between different groups, but without success.

Thomas Campbell in America

In 1807, discouraged by his fruitless efforts at mediation, and facing health problems, Thomas Campbell decided to emigrate to America. Once he had settled, he planned to send for his family. Due to political turbulence, religious dissension, and economic oppression, many Scottish and Irish families were emigrating at that time.

Upon his arrival in the New World, Thomas Campbell traveled directly to Washington County in western Pennsylvania. The region had been colonized largely by Scottish and Irish immigrants of Presbyterian faith. A majority belonged to the Church of Scotland, although some, like Campbell, came from seceder congregations. Presbyterian ministers were scarce on the American frontier, and Campbell was frequently invited to preach to congregations of both groups.

Campbell had lamented the divisions within the Presbyterian church in Ireland. However, he soon discovered that Presbyterian congregations on the frontier were even more intolerant and mutually exclusive. Invited by one of the congregations to serve communion, Campbell included people from other branches of Presbyterianism in the eucharistic celebration. For this dissenting act, the presbytery accused him of heresy and indefinitely suspended his right to preach in Presbyterian congregations. All attempts to appeal the decision proved fruitless, and Campbell's relationship with the Associate Synod of North America was severed.

Campbell continued to preach and serve communion in sympathetic circles. His sermons often explored the theme of Christian unity based on scripture. (1) In August 1809, Campbell proposed the formation of The Christian Association of Washington, to encourage unity among churches of the region. Sponsors of the Association erected a meeting-house, inviting Campbell to share his vision. On this occasion, Campbell gave his *Declaration and Address*, which presented his guiding principles. He believed that

> *(1) Attributed to Thomas Campbell,* **Memoirs of Alexander Campbell**
> *That rule, my highly respected hearers, is this, that where the Scriptures speak, we speak; and where the Scriptures are silent, we are silent.*[5]

individuals had the right to form their own opinions guided by the exclusive authority of the scriptures. He opposed sectarianism. Finally, he believed that Christian unity could be achieved through scriptural conformity.[6]

Alexander Campbell's Parallel Journey

Meanwhile, Thomas Campbell's family had remained in Ireland. After a year in America, Campbell sent for them. In October 1808, Alexander Campbell, along with his mother and six younger brothers and sisters, set sail for their new home. However, they suffered shipwreck off the Scottish coast, and spent the following year in Scotland.

Taking advantage of being in Glasgow, Alexander Campbell studied at the university. He also came into contact with the movement begun by the Haldane brothers, something which would shape his spiritual vision. Grenville Ewing, director of the school founded by the Haldane brothers, became Alexander Campbell's intimate friend. Ewing's ideal of an evangelical Christianity, in which sectarian divisions could be overcome, proved attractive to Alexander. Increasingly, Alexander was interested in the restoration of early apostolic practices and organizational forms.

Influenced by the writings of Glas and Sandeman, and by discussions with Ewing and the Haldane brothers, Alexander envisioned a radical renewal for the church, based strictly on the Bible. This restored church would be governed by the congregation, and have a ministry untarnished by the privileges traditionally given the clergy. There would be a plurality of congregational ministries, and a weekly celebration of the Lord's Supper.

Alexander Campbell began to feel more comfortable in independent circles than in the Presbyterian Church. His uneasiness about established Christianity was confirmed by his reading of John Locke. Locke wrote that the key to salvation was in the scriptures, not in traditional church structures.[7] When the Campbell family finally journeyed to America, Alexander was no longer committed to the seceder Presbyterianism in which he had been raised. It was with great joy that he discovered his father had made a similar spiritual pilgrimage. Remarkably, both had arrived at a restorationist vision of church renewal.

The Christian Association of Washington

The Christian Association of Washington had been unsuccessful in its efforts to encourage unity among Christians. In May 1811, the Association moved to constitute itself as a group of churches of congregational government. Thomas and Alexander Campbell were called to minister to these churches. Following restorationist principles, they introduced the practices of the early church into congregational life, including baptizing new believers by immersion.

Both father and son were themselves baptized by immersion by a Baptist preacher. Their first priority was the restoration of the church, and on the basis of this, unity among Christians. Seeking to realize their ideal of Christian unity, the Campbellite congregations joined an association of Baptist congregations.

Late in 1821, Alexander Campbell met a young Presbyterian in Pittsburgh named Walter Scott. Born in 1796 in Scotland, Scott had made a spiritual pilgrimage which paralleled that of the Campbells'. Scott had immigrated to America in 1818. In Pittsburgh, he found employment at a Bible school similar to the one instituted by the Haldane brothers in Scotland. There, Scott discovered the writings of Glas, Sandeman, the Haldane brothers, and John Locke. After study and reflection, he concluded that Christians only needed one confession of faith: "Jesus is the Christ."[8]

Scott was a gifted preacher. He was invited to serve as an itinerant evangelist among the Baptist congregations, and the Disciples associated with them, in western Pennsylvania and eastern Ohio. He enumerated the five points of his message on the five fingers of his hand: faith, repentance, baptism, forgiveness of sins, and the gift of the Holy Spirit. Scott's preaching style was clear and persuasive, and tailored to his frontier audiences. Hundreds of new believers joined the church, although many had little appreciation for Baptist traditions.

Unfortunately, the diverse nature of these new converts caused tensions between the Baptists and the Disciples. Finally, orthodox Baptists terminated their fifteen-year relationship with the Association. Baptist congregations separated from Campbellite congregations. Bitter divisions also occurred within local congregations. In 1830, the Disciples congregations were limited to the frontier region of western Pennsylvania and eastern Ohio.

The North American Restorationist Movement [9]

Despite its European tributary, the movement known as the Christian Church (Disciples of Christ) was characteristically North American in its spirit and structures. Inspired by the evangelism of Jonathon Edwards and George Whitefield, a renewal of faith, called The Great Awakening, had swept through the American colonies. Whitefield's preaching, in particular, had induced nominal Christians to confess their faith and repent. Through the latter half of the eighteenth century, pioneer evangelists preached on the frontier. Early in the nineteenth century, the revival movement crossed the mountains into Kentucky and Tennessee where a Second Great Awakening began.

During the decades following the American War of Independence, the influence of established churches was notably reduced. It is estimated that during this period, less than ten per cent of the total population was affiliated with a church.[10] Lacking the coercive support of civil authorities, churches had to find new methods of evangelization. Church growth depended on the power of persuasion. In this setting, evangelistic revival preaching attracted multitudes from the lower classes and frontier settlers. In this new environment, Christianity was no longer dominated by dogma and a hierarchical structure, but became a more democratic institution.

Three North American tributaries, with their roots in the revival movement, would eventually come together, in 1968, under the name of the Christian Church (Disciples of Christ). The three tributaries were a Methodist movement in the southern colonies of Virginia and North Carolina; a Baptist movement, congregational in structure; and a movement that arose out of a camp meeting revival at Cane Ridge, Kentucky, on the western frontier.

The Methodist Tributary

Since its beginnings, American Methodism had been episcopally structured. However, some frontier preachers began to question the way in which Francis Asbury, the first bishop, exercised his power. They wished to apply the ideals of local self-determination to church government. A group of Methodists, headed by preachers James O'Kelly and Rice Haggard, spent several years attempting, unsuccessfully, to democratize the church's episcopal structures. In 1744, they formed a new group called the Christian Church.

The movement was founded on five defining principles. Members advocated equality among all preachers. They dismantled the hierarchy of bishop, superintendent, and governing elders. They believed that ministers and laymen should have the freedom to interpret the scriptures. Congregations were governed independently. The Christian Church conference would give counsel, but congregations had the right to call their own pastors.

The Baptist Tributary

Five years later, a similar movement arose in New England. Two dissident Baptist pastors, Elias Smith and Abner Jones, protested the Calvinist doctrine of predestination, which was held in Baptist circles. According to this doctrine, some are destined by God to salvation and others to condemnation, and Christ's atonement benefits only the elect. Smith and Jones were also dissatisfied with the creedal nature of Calvinist orthodoxy, preferring a more direct style of evangelization. They wanted to restore the practices of the early church to contemporary forms of worship.

In 1801, Jones organized an independent congregation in Lyndon, Vermont, calling it simply a Christian Church. Smith and Jones continued their ministries for nearly forty years. During this period, the movement spread throughout New England, into New York, New Jersey, Ohio, Pennsylvania, and Canada.

The Cane Ridge, Kentucky Tributary

Barton Stone was the primary leader of the movement which emerged out of an explosive camp meeting held in Cane Ridge, Kentucky, in 1801. Stone came from a politically prominent family living in the southern frontier region of Virginia. As a young man, Stone was confronted with the Calvinist doctrine of predestination, and despaired of being saved. While studying law, he experienced a vision of a loving God, and abandoned his studies to become a minister in the Reformed Presbyterian Church. To pay off debts accrued, Stone found employment at a school in Georgia. There, he met dissident Methodist leaders who envisioned a congregational church structure.

After several years, the presbytery commissioned Stone to preach in two frontier congregations in Kentucky, at Cane Ridge and Concord. He proved popular among the mountaineers of the region, and was offered a permanent pastorate. However, Stone found the Calvinist system of doctrine unconvincing. He believed in the authenticity of an evangelical spirituality practiced in daily life. Despite his doubts, Stone was ordained into the Presbyterian ministry in 1798.

Life on the American frontier was hard. After the War of Independence, the population began moving westward in droves. Most frontier people had individualistic ideals, which were manifested in a lack of respect for the law, and an indifference toward institutions like the church. The struggle for survival in this hostile environment desensitized people, and alcoholism and violence were endemic.

Several revivalist preachers began organizing camp meetings on the western frontier. Hundreds of people attended the open air meetings, camping out for the duration. In July 1800, the first such meeting took place, establishing a precedent for what was to become an American institution. In 1801, Barton Stone attended a meeting in a nearby county, and was convinced that a new day had arrived for the frontier church. He decided to sow the seeds of revival in his own congregations.

The Second Great Awakening reached its zenith in Stone's Cane Ridge congregation, August 7-12, 1801. The Cane Ridge Camp Meeting was both a spiritual and social event. An estimated 30,000 people–or ten per cent of Kentucky's population–attended the revival. The vast majority were not church members, drawn instead by curiosity or loneliness. The meeting was organized by Presbyterians, but Baptist and Methodist preachers also mounted stumps to proclaim their messages.

An historian described the event as "in all probability, the most disorderly, the most hysterical, and the largest revival ever held in early-day America."[11] The meeting was charged with emotion. Skeptics repented. Listeners fell down and rolled on the ground. Some grunted or barked, their heads moving violently. Others laughed with a strange solemnity, and sang "not from the mouth but entirely from the breast."[12] People danced, shouting with joy. Indeed, revival meetings were characterized by this spontaneous freedom from inhibitions.

> *(2) Barton Stone,* **The Christian Messenger**
> *I saw the religion of Jesus more clearly exhibited in the lives of Christians then than I had ever seen before or since to the same extent.*[13]

Barton Stone had reservations about the hysteria, but never doubted that God was present at the event. (2) He had witnessed God's grace touching hardened, rustic men. He had seen the sectarian spirit overcome by the power of a unified cause: "We all engaged in singing the same songs of praise–all united in prayer–all preached the same things–free salvation urged upon all by faith and repentance."[14]

The Christian Church

Reactions against the camp meetings were not long in coming. The Presbyterian ministers resented the absence of traditional distinctions between ordained and unordained ministers. The Calvinist doctrine of double predestination was not being taught, and they were offended by the lack of decorum shown at the revival meetings. Their opposition reflected the established church's hierarchical concept of worship

The revival was more curse than blessing for the presbytery. Ministers who had participated in the meetings were accused of excesses, and of deviating from doctrinal orthodoxy and ecclesiastical order. All five Presbyterian ministers who had participated in the revival, including Stone, withdrew from the presbytery in protest.

Although the ministers had rejected the authority of the synod, they continued to consider themselves Presbyterians. In autumn of 1803, they organized a new presbytery composed of six ministers and fifteen congregations in northern Kentucky and southern Ohio. They believed that scripture alone provided an adequate basis for the faith and unity of the church. In contrast to traditional synods, relationships within the new synod would be fraternal and informal. The new synod would not exert control over participating congregations.

Ten days later, the new presbytery unanimously resolved to dissolve the synod, and declared the fifteen congregations independent, within an association called the Christian Church. In an important document of the movement's history, titled "The Last Will and Testament of the Springfield Presbytery," the writers stated that each congregation had the right to self-government, and declared that the Bible was "the only standard of Christian faith and life."[15]

In line with this vision, Barton Stone refused to confess that Christ died only for the salvation of the predestined. He also resisted the Anselmian tradition which held that Christ died to satisfy the wrath of a vindictive Father. As a frontier minister, Stone had experienced God's unfailing love for humanity. Stone always contended that human salvation did not depend on one's doctrinal knowledge, but on God's grace.

Over the next twenty-five years, the movement grew to 12,000 members. The spread of the movement depended largely on lay preachers. Frontier preachers supported themselves by tilling the land, and served a number of congregations as circuit riders. Within the Christian Church, congregational polity gave ordinary Christians the authority to make decisions and to serve their church. Simple believers became protagonists in the Christian mission.

The Rise of the Christian-Disciples Movement

In 1823, Alexander Campbell met Barton Stone on a visit to Kentucky. If the union of the two groups had depended on their leaders' ability to agree, it may never have occurred. But in spite of their differences, both men held to their visions for the restoration and reunification of the church on the basis of the New Testament.

The Christians and the Disciples were active in the same region on the American frontier. They held in common a concern for church unity, a vision for restoring apostolic ideals to the church, a refusal to grant authority to creeds, similar baptismal and eucharistic practices, and a preference for congregational government.

The union of the two movements was made possible by congregational support. Christian and Disciple congregations began relating to one another on a local level as early as 1828, and merged by 1831. The union of the groups in Kentucky was largely due to Stone's initiative, although Campbell later lent his support. Itinerant evangelists played a key role in the process by bringing in new believers who were, strictly speaking, neither Disciples nor Christians. Between 1830 and 1833, approximately 10,000 Christians and 12,000 Campbellites joined together. Twenty-five years later, membership had grown to 190,000, largely due to the church's success in adapting methods of evangelization to frontier conditions.

Pursuit of Wealth

In the decades that followed, the movement became increasingly composed of the emerging middle class. Historian David Edwin Harrell, Jr. observed that like their fellow Americans, Disciples were preoccupied by the pursuit of wealth. Their church paper contained many aphorisms on the Christian legitimacy of earning money: "'It is your solemn duty to make money.'"[16] Many Disciples came to associate righteousness of life with the acquisition of wealth.[17] The overwhelming majority of Disciples fully supported North American capitalism, and had nothing but admiration for the wealthy.

Only a minority of Disciples protested that the church was abandoning its poor, frontier roots. Some preachers reminded their congregations that the poor were God's people: "The poor, rather than the rich, have been the world's benefactors. Jesus our Lord was poor, very poor, and so were all his apostles."[18] But these voices were few and far between, and came mainly from rural states in the South and the Midwest.

As a consequence of social, regional, and theological differences, the movement divided into three principal denominations. In addition to the General Assembly of the Christian Church (Disciples of Christ), the Churches of Christ came into being in 1906, and the Conference of the Christian Churches was created in 1955.

Shifting Views on Pacifism

The restorationist movement opposed violence as a means of establishing social peace. Alexander Campbell was a pacifist, and expressed his opposition to warfare in all of his writings. He emphasized the New Testament stance on warfare, dismissing the Old Testament wars of Israel as irrelevant to Christians.[19] Barton Stone was also a pacifist. In 1827, he wrote in *The Christian Messenger* that "war and slavery [are the] greatest evils in the world."[20]

But the movement was not unified in its pacifist stance. In 1846, the War with Mexico created a crisis in the church, revealing a growing lack of unanimity among the movement's leaders, and even greater divergence among the membership. The erosion of pacifist convictions became even more clear during the Civil War in 1860, and the Spanish-American War of 1898. In the final decades of the nineteenth century, leaders in the movement strongly supported capital punishment. The movement known as the Christian Church (Disciples of Christ) had adopted middle-class American values, and sought to protect its interests, even by violent means.[21]

Conclusion

From its inception, the Christian-Disciple movement confronted established Christianity, questioning the traditional creeds by which it sought to conserve its doctrinal hegemony. The movement was dedicated to restoring New Testament ideals to contemporary forms of worship. On the rugged North American frontier, the Disciples and Christians entered into solidarity with social outsiders. Their democratic message, and their popular methods of evangelization, were well-suited to the demands of the frontier.

However, around 1860, the movement got caught in a current of upward social mobility, accompanied by a growing sense of patriotism. In the process of acculturation, the Christian Church (Disciples of Christ) became an important part of the established church in North America. The movement's family of denominations currently include some five to six million members. Along with the Baptist and Methodist churches, the Christian Church (Disciples of Christ) has become a *de facto* establishment, despite the very different visions which inspired its founders.

Notes

[1] Winfred Ernst Garrison and Alfred T. DeGroot, *The Disciples of Christ: A History* (St. Louis, MO: The Bethany Press, 1948), 47.

[2] Garrison and DeGroot, 146.

[3] Alexander Campbell, *The Christian System* (New York: Arno Press, 1969), 6.

[4] This section relies largely on the following source. Lester G. McAllister and William E. Tucker, *Journey in Faith: A History of the Christian Church (Disciples of Christ)* (St. Louis, MO: The Bethany Press, 1975), 89-119.

[5] McAllister and Tucker, 110.

[6] McAllister and Tucker, 112.

[7] Winfred Ernst Garrison and Alfred T. DeGroot, *The Disciples of Christ: A History* (St. Louis, MO: The Bethany Press, 1948), 143. "... the Church of Christ to make the conditions of her communion consist in such things, and such things only, as the Holy Spirit has in the Holy Scriptures declared, in express words, to be necessary to salvation ..."

[8] Garrison and DeGroot, 182.

[9] This section relies largely on the following source. Lester G. McAllister and William E. Tucker, *Journey in Faith: A History of the Christian Church (Disciples of Christ)* (St. Louis, MO: The Bethany Press, 1975), 61-88.

[10] McAllister and Tucker, 43.

[11] McAllister and Tucker, 72.

[12] McAllister and Tucker, 72.

[13] McAllister and Tucker, 61-62.

[14] McAllister and Tucker, 73.

[15] McAllister and Tucker, 79.

[16] David Edwin Harrell, Jr., *The Social Sources of Division in the Disciples of Christ (1865-1900)* (Atlanta, GA: Publishing Systems, Inc., 1973), 33. "Most Disciples shared their fellow Americans' preoccupation with the pursuit of wealth. Adoration of wealth and power could be found in any church paper. ... 'The Lord never said to you, Ye shall not make money. It is your solemn duty to make money.' ... 'Wealth in itself considered is an individual and national blessing. It is not essentially evil.' ... 'Make all you can honestly; save all you

can prudently; give all you can possibly.'"

[17] Harrell, *The Social Sources of Division*, 40.

[18] Harrell, *The Social Sources of Division*, 49.

[19] David Edwin Harrell, Jr., *Quest for a Christian America: The Disciples of Christ and American Society to 1886* (Nashville, TN: The Disciples of Christ Historical Society, 1966), 141. "My kingdom is not of this world. If my kingdom were of this world, my servants would have fought."

[20] Harrell, *Quest for a Christian America*, 140.

[21] David Edwin Harrell, Jr., *The Social Sources of Division in the Disciples of Christ (1865-1900)* (Atlanta, GA: Publishing Systems, Inc., 1973), 252-253.

Chapter 19

Nineteenth-Century Movements: The Plymouth Brethren

I was a lawyer; but feeling that, if the Son of God gave Himself for me I owed myself entirely to Him. ... my chief thought was to get around amongst the poor Catholics of Ireland. I was induced to be ordained. ... As soon as I was ordained, I went amongst the poor Irish mountaineers ... where I remained two years and three months, working as best I could. I felt, however, that the style of work was not in agreement with what I read in the Bible concerning the Church and Christianity ... Working day and night amongst the people, who were almost as wild as the mountains they inhabited, much exercise of soul had the effect of causing the Scriptures to gain complete ascendancy over me. (John Nelson Darby, *Letter to Professor Tholuck*)[1]

    Christ preferred the poor; ever since I have been converted so have I. Let those who like society better have it. If I ever get into it, and it has crossed my path in London, I return sick at heart. I go to the poor; I find the same evil nature as in the rich, but I find this difference: the rich, and those who keep their comforts and their society, judge and measure how much of Christ they can take and keep without committing themselves; the poor, how much of Christ they can have to comfort them in their sorrows. (John Nelson Darby, *Letters I*, 205)[2]

Introduction

The Brethren movement began in Dublin in 1827. Brothers and sisters met in their homes to break the bread of communion together. In 1831, in Plymouth, England, the movement was organized into an Assembly of

Brethren. The Brethren formed themselves into an alternative movement, by separating from the established churches, which the Brethren believed to be in ruins. The movement must be explored in its historical context, in order to gain a thorough understanding of the influences which contributed to its rise, and to the rise of similar movements.

Historical Background

In the early decades of the nineteenth century, Great Britain was shaken by political and economic turbulence. The shifting relationship between Anglicans and Roman Catholics effected political and social change. In 1672, the government's Test Act had decreed that all military and civil personnel, living within a thirty-mile radius of London, must receive the Eucharist according to Anglican ritual, or revoke their posts. In 1828, British parliament repealed this statute. A year later, Catholics were granted the right to run for the House of Commons, and occupy other official positions. In 1832, the system of parliamentary representation was reformed to transfer power from the Anglican nobility to the middle classes.

These radical changes increased the influence of religious nonconformists. Conservative church authorities feared that the relationship between church and state was being irrevocably altered. In this context, many, both Catholics and Protestants, began rethinking the nature of the church. They looked to the patterns and forms of worship practiced by the early church. A series of new religious movements arose, all interested in renewing the contemporary church by returning to Christianity's roots.

Tractarianism

The Oxford Movement was begun by a group of young aristocratic intellectuals associated with Oriel College at Oxford University. The group soon formed the Anglo-Catholic party within the Church of England. Their approach to church reformation looked to the church's roots in ancient Catholicism, rather than in the New Testament community. They advocated a return to ancient traditions, including the apostolic succession of clergy, a sacramental understanding of salvation, an emphasis on the sacrificial character of the Eucharist, and the reinstatement of auricular confession, clerical celibacy, and veneration of the saints. The group also questioned the state's right to intervene in the life of the church.

Members of the Anglo-Catholic party included Richard Froude, John Keble, Edward Pusey, John Henry Newman, and Henry Manning, among others. In 1833, they publicized their ideas in a series of tracts, which accounted for the name by which the movement came to be known: "Tractarianism." They published ninety tracts, twenty-three of which were written by John Henry Newman. The group believed that Anglo-Catholicism represented the restoration of early Christianity. In his last tract, Newman proposed that the Thirty-Nine Articles of the Anglican Faith be reinterpreted in their Catholic sense.[3]

In 1845, at the height of his influence, John Henry Newman converted to Roman Catholicism. Several hundred prominent Anglican clerics and laymen followed his lead. Later, Manning and Newman became cardinals in the Roman Catholic curia. The attempt at renewal was not limited to doctrinal and liturgical aspects of faith, but was accompanied by a dedication and commitment to those who lived on the fringes of the church. The movement sought to renew the church's relationship with those in the lower social classes, who had been alienated by the hierarchical imperatives of the Church of England.

The Apostolic Catholic Church

Another primitivist movement brought about the formation of the Apostolic Catholic Church in 1832. The movement arose under the leadership of Henry Drummond, 1786-1860, and Edward Irving, 1792-1834.

Drummond came from an aristocratic family, and from 1810 onward was a prominent member of the English parliament. Drummond hosted a gathering in his country home in Surrey at which participants studied apocalyptic writings found in both Testaments. Participants "reaffirmed their conviction that the imminent return of Christ would be heralded by the restoration of the lost spiritual gifts of tongues and of prophesying."[4]

Irving was of Scottish origin, and in 1819 began serving as an assistant to Thomas Chalmers, a prominent pastor in the Church of Scotland in Glasgow. Irving became known for his ministry among the poor and outcast. In 1822, he was named to a pastorate in London. His eloquent preaching, his incessant attacks on the establishment, and his personal magnetism all contributed to the extraordinary growth of the congregation. Later, the Apostolic Catholic Church would also be known as the "Irvingite Church," in honor of its principal protaganist.

The Apostolic Catholic Church restored elements from ancient Catholic tradition to contemporary forms of worship. The Tractarian movement was disseminating such ideas throughout Great Britain, inclining people toward Catholic doctrines and practices. Catholicism was particularly evident in the Apostolic Church's liturgy. They used priestly vestments, incense, and holy water. They anointed the sick and celebrated the feast days on the church calendar. Their liturgical forms appealed to both the Latin and Greek fathers.

On the other hand, their charismatic vision for ecclesial life and ministry appealed to the New Testament. The Apostolic Catholic Church set out to restore the New Testament order of charismatic ministry: apostles, prophets, evangelists, pastors and teachers, and later, angels–or bishops–and deacons. By 1835, the church had named twelve apostles who would be sent on an evangelizing mission to the European continent and to North America. The church encouraged the gifts of tongues and prophecy in their public worship. They believed that the second coming of Christ was imminent. In 1827, inspired by apocalyptic ideas, Irving translated the Spanish work of the Jesuit Lacunza under the title, *The Coming of the Messiah in Glory and Majesty*.

In 1850, at the height of its popularity, the movement had thirty congregations in Great Britain, and approximately 6,000 active members. However, it soon became caught up in its own life and worship, and was no longer interested in attracting or assisting the poor victims of industrialization. The church became composed of only one social group, the upper middle class, and in the process "it hugged itself to death."[5]

The Primitive Methodist Church

The Primitive Methodist Church arose in 1812, inspired by the open air preaching of George Whitefield and John Wesley of an earlier century. The immediate roots of this renewed evangelistic activity were in the North American revival meetings, brought back to England by Lorenzo Dow. Indeed, the movement was originally called the "Camp-Meeting Methodists." The group sought to win back those sectors of society which had been alienated by traditional Christianity. British Methodists, who were beginning to show signs of domestication, were displeased by the new movement, and charged that their methods were "highly improper and likely to be of considerable mischief."[6]

Like the Quakers and Methodists, the movement was inspired by the New Testament, particularly the Sermon on the Mount. Meetings were marked by the physical and psychological phenomena often associated with charismatic movements. A group of preachers usually led the outdoor meetings, supported by the prayers of the entire group. Charismatic manifestations and the participation of women in ministry were radical features of the movement.

The Plymouth Brethren

The Plymouth Brethren movement shared the primitivist outlook. The movement sought to recover the simplicity of the New Testament church through biblical fidelity. The early Anglican leaders of the movement in Ireland soon cut off their relationship with the established church in Ireland. The Brethren recognized an unordained ministry, and restored the custom of weekly meetings at which Bible study and the breaking of the bread took place. They believed that the second coming of Christ was imminent, and chose to separate themselves from the established churches.

Origins of the Brethren Movement in Ireland

The Brethren movement arose out of several renewal initiatives which were undertaken independently throughout Great Britain: in Dublin, in 1825; in Plymouth, around 1831; and in Bristol and the surrounding region, in 1832. The movement, which came to be known as the Plymouth Brethren, would spread throughout Great Britain, into Switzerland, France, Italy, the Americas, Australia, Africa, and Asia.

The Influence of Anthony Norris Groves

The Brethren movement emerged out of one man's vision. Anthony Norris Groves, 1795-1853, was a successful dentist in Plymouth and Exeter who, from youth, had felt the call to foreign missionary service. His wife, Mary, did not share his vision, so he dedicated the early years of their marriage to the practice of his profession, and to serious Bible study. After immersing themselves in scripture, the couple decided to share a tenth of their considerable income with the poor in their neighborhood. Mary visited the needy and disbursed the funds. Later, in the midst of a health crisis which seriously reduced their means, the couple decided to share a quarter of their income with the needy.

Based on these experiences, Groves wrote a pamphlet entitled *Christian Commitment*, which expanded on his motto: "Labour hard, consume little, give much, and all to Christ."[7] Groves knew that wealth could corrupt those who possessed it. He believed that the deliberate accumulation of wealth was a barrier to true spirituality. He called on Christians to dedicate all their goods to the service of God. Christians should trust the providence of God and the generosity of their brothers and sisters. Groves's radical economic vision was at odds with the Christian ideals of the period. Established Christianity had accepted social and economic discrepancies with resignation, as if they were the will of God.

In 1825, with his wife's support, Groves abandoned his dental practice to study theology in Dublin under the auspices of the Anglican church. In Dublin, he found a group of like-minded people, "chiefly members of the establishment," who believed in Christian unity, and often met to discuss their beliefs.[8] Groves observed similarities between the primitive New Testament community, and the communion experienced among these sincere and open brothers and sisters.

Groves soon became a leader in the group. In 1827, he suggested that a group of believers should be free to break bread together in honor of the Lord's day, as Christ had admonished the apostles. (1) Until this point, the group had not expressed the least intention of separating from the Anglican church. Some members of the group were Anglican clergy, and they continued to serve their congregations. Groves himself certainly had no intention of transforming the group into a meeting of dissidents.

Nevertheless, Groves would abandon the idea of seeking ordination in the Anglican church. Instead, he offered his services to the Church Missionary Society as a layman. But when they told him he would not be able to administer the sacraments without ordination, he changed plans again. The experience led him to an insight which would become central to the Brethren movement. It occurred to Groves that the Bible did not make ordination a requirement for ministry. Anyone who was so moved could share the gospel and minister in Christ's name. (2)

In this way, Groves contributed two principles fundamental to the Brethren movement. Firstly, each Lord's Day should be set apart to take communion in memory of Christ's death, and in obedience to his teachings. Secondly, ministry should be based on the gifts of the risen Lord rather than on the church's ordination. In 1829, Groves, who had just been baptized as a believer, left with his family for mission

> *(1) Anthony Norris Groves,* **Memoir**
> *It appeared to him from Scripture, that believers, meeting together as disciples of Christ, were free to break bread together, as their Lord had admonished them; and that, in as far as the practice of the apostles could be a guide, every Lord's day should be set apart for thus remembering the Lord's death, and obeying his parting command.*[9]

> *(2) Anthony Norris Groves,* **Memoirs of Lord Congleton**
> *One day the thought was brought to my mind, that ordination of any kind to preach the gospel is no requirement of Scripture. ... This I doubt not is the mind of God concerning us—we should come together in all simplicity as disciples, not waiting on any pulpit or ministry, but trusting that the Lord would edify us together by ministering as He pleased and saw good from the midst of us.*[10]

service in Baghdad and India. The move essentially removed them from further personal participation in the emergence of the Brethren.

It was not easy for Groves to sever his ties with the Church of England. He found the idea of associating with dissident groups repugnant. According to his own testimony, Groves left the established church because it willingly justified Christian participation in warfare. The critical moment occurred when a friend asked whether Groves would subscribe to the following article: "'It is lawful for Christian men to take up arms at the command of the civil magistrate.'"[11] Groves, who had never contemplated the issue before, realized immediately that he could not support such an article. This ended his connection with the Church of England.

The Initiative of John Nelson Darby

John Nelson Darby, 1800-1882, was the person most responsible for the formation of the Brethren movement. Indeed, adherents to the movement are still known in Ireland and Europe as "Darbyites." Darby came from an aristocratic family: his uncle was Admiral Henry Darby, and his godfather was Lord Nelson of Trafalgar fame. John Darby had been a brilliant student of law in Dublin, where he had opened a legal practice. A profound spiritual awakening led him to abandon his legal career. He entered the service of the Anglican church, and was ordained deacon in 1825.

Darby was assigned to a difficult parish in a wild region of Ireland, where he dedicated himself to serving the poor mountaineers. In the course of his ministries, Darby traveled on foot through the mountainous country, often not reaching his bed before midnight. This dedication, combined with a sparse diet, gave him an ascetic emaciated appearance which greatly excited the Catholic peasants. They thought him "a genuine 'saint' of the ancient breed."[12] Darby utterly abandoned himself to his task.

A spiritual revival had begun among the Roman Catholics of the region. Darby calculated that as many as 700 or 800 people each week were converting to Anglicanism. However, the archbishop of Dublin stopped this revival in its tracks by decreeing that new converts must swear an oath of allegiance to the English monarch. Darby was devastated by the policy, which he felt compromised an individual's absolute loyalty to Christ. Having dedicated himself to reading only the Bible, he found this thinly-disguised attempt at political coercion unthinkable. Darby eventually left the established church, protesting its abuse of power.

During the period that followed, Darby studied the Bible, praying and reflecting on the relationship between the church and secular powers. During the winter of 1828, which he spent in Dublin, Darby began to meet with like-minded Christians, including Anthony Groves, J. G. Bellet, and Francis William Newman, the younger brother of John Henry Newman of the Tractarian movement. Under Darby's leadership, this group would become the Brethren movement in Ireland. In 1829, Darby produced a pamphlet entitled *On the Nature and Unity of the Church of Christ*, generally considered to be the movement's first publication.

The Brethren in Ireland

Meanwhile, another nonconformist group was emerging in Dublin. Among its participants were Dr. Edward Cronin, a recent convert from Roman Catholicism who had arrived in Dublin in 1826 as a medical student, and Edward Wilson, ex-secretary of the Bible Society. The two groups met independently for a time. Both groups espoused similar ideas, emphasizing Christian unity, and a mutual ministry shared among the brotherhood. Soon, they joined together and formed one group. The new group grew quickly, and they moved to a larger meeting place. Nevertheless, their relationship to the established church remained undefined, and some of their leaders, including Darby, continued to serve as clerics in the Church of England.

Six months later, the group had to find an even more spacious meeting place. This time they rented a hall and announced their meetings to the public. The change minimized economic disparities, allowing the poor to attend meetings freely and with dignity. From the beginning, the movement lessened the distinctions between rich and poor by dressing plainly and living simply.[13] Anyone who was guided by the spirit could exercise ministry. There was no official hierarchy in the group.

Darby's understanding of the church underwent a transformation. His highly sacramental view of the church was replaced by one that reflected his reading of the New Testament. Darby believed that the early church

(3) John Darby, Letter to Professor Tholuck

It then became clear to me that the church of God, as He considers it, was composed only of those who were so united to Christ, whereas Christendom, as seen externally, was really the world, and could not be considered as "the church."[14]

was composed of the active faithful, united together in Christ. He was saddened by the contrast between the early church, and the contemporary church. (3)

However, Darby was confronted with a dilemma. His reading of the Bible told him that no exclusive meeting could "find the fulness of blessing."[15] In other words, the true church would embrace all children of God. But Darby also believed that Christians had a duty to separate themselves from the evil reigning in the world without "pretending to set up churches."[16] They should meet as the two or three gathered in His name, awaiting the imminent coming of the Lord. It seemed to Darby that faithful Christians gathering together became, *de facto*, the church.[17]

In its early years, the Brethren movement carried the seal of Darby's character. He was a man with a singular love for Christ. In a society dominated by materialism, Darby's simple life and commitment to others was reminiscent of the saints of the early church. Not only did he give up a brilliant legal practice, but in his commitment to ministry he also freely assumed celibacy. In his humility, Darby expressed solidarity with the poor. This was the secret to his successful evangelization of the poor Roman Catholic mountaineers of Ireland, and of the peasants and workers of France and Switzerland.

Origins of the Brethren Movement in Plymouth

After fifteen months in Dublin, Francis Newman, one of the original members of the Irish movement, returned to Oxford. There, he shared his experiences with a friend, Benjamin Newton. When John Darby visited Oxford, Newman introduced him to his young friend. Newton, along with George Wigram and others, became enthusiastic disciples of Darby. When the young men returned home to Plymouth, England, they found that others were meeting in Bible study circles. In fact, one man, Percy Hall, shared almost the same the vision expressed by John Darby.

Percy Hall had been a naval commander, and, like Anthony Groves, had responded to a radical spiritual call. His reading of the New Testament had brought him to the conclusion that a Christian could not, in good conscience, serve even as a civil magistrate. Hall resigned his commission in the armed forces, gave away his possessions, and set out to follow Jesus. In Plymouth, the Bible study circle soon rented a meeting place, and began breaking the bread and studying the Bible together. Under Hall's inspired preaching, the group grew rapidly.

However, Benjamin Newton soon became recognized as the principle leader of the movement in Plymouth. Newton was a member of the Anglican church, although he had been born into a Quaker family, and was related through his mother to the prominent banking family, Lloyds. Newton had distinguished himself as a student at Oxford. There, he had been a classmate of the Newman brothers, Richard Froude, and other members of the Tractarian movement. Newton and his classmates had shared heated debates about the nature and role of the established church. When Newton returned home to Plymouth, his education and character brought him recognition as a principal leader in the Brethren movement.

The group in Plymouth attracted many followers from the city's prominent intellectual and ecclesiastical circles. Among these was Samuel Tregelles, a specialist in biblical languages and textual criticism, of Quaker heritage. When Tregelles joined the group in 1835, it had a membership of about eighty people. By 1840, approximately 800 people gathered regularly at the group's meetings. Despite its early leaders' original vision of Christian unity, the Brethren movement in Plymouth soon became a denomination.

The Influence of the Congregation in Plymouth

The congregation in Plymouth became a model for other groups in Great Britain. In the austere hall, seats were set in a semicircle facing a centrally located communion table. Everyone who participated in the ministry spoke from behind this table. The entire Sunday morning worship service focussed on the breaking of the bread.

The congregation in Plymouth became a center for evangelization, sending out its members and leaders to share their vision. Their methods were more aggressive than those of their Irish counterparts, and the tone of their message was more apocalyptic. Preaching imminent divine judgement, they invited members of the established church to join their apostolic communion.[18] The message proved attractive. Wealthy members of the congregation committed themselves to leading simple lives, in order to lessen economic disparities between members which could impede communion.

During the first fifteen years of existence, the congregation in Plymouth was remarkably vital, and grew quickly. However, from the beginning, the group was beset by a fundamental weakness. Much of their teachings were based on their interpretation of biblical prophecy, and were marked by apocalyptic speculation. Their message was based on John Darby's writings – which were of Irvingite origin – and called for separation from the apostasy of other groups. This sectarian spirit, which early leaders of the movement sought to avoid, eventually became a defining characteristic of the Plymouth Brethren.

George Muller and the Brethren in Bristol

George Muller, 1805-1898, received a university education with the intention of becoming a Lutheran pastor in his native Germany. Despite his pastoral vocation, Muller led a dissolute life, until, at the age of twenty, he had a profound spiritual experience. While studying at the University of Halle, Muller experienced a personal conversion in a Pietist prayer meeting. Soon thereafter, on a trip to England as a candidate for missionary service among the Jews, he met Henry Craik. Craik was a friend and colleague of Anthony Norris Groves in the Irish Brethren movement. Muller was drawn by Craik's warm and sincere spirituality, and soon began to question clerical ordination, and the relationship between the established church and civil powers.

Muller's convictions were similar to those held by the Brethren, and would change the course of his life. He was baptized as a believer, began breaking bread weekly, and opened up the congregational meetings to a mutual ministry. Muller refused to accept his pastoral salary, depending on freewill offerings for his support. He protested the practice of charging rental fees for church pews, a system which allowed the wealthy to enjoy the best seats. Muller detested these social distinctions. Eventually, he and his wife, who was Groves's sister, gave away all of their property.

Serving the Needy

Others in southwestern England shared a social vision rooted in the gospel. In 1832, Robert Chapman, a young lawyer of aristocratic heritage, began ministering to the poorest of the poor in the port city of Barnstable. Criticized for his lack of erudition as a preacher, Chapman responded that he wanted his life to speak louder than his words. (4)

Chapman's church in Barnstable was located in one of the city's slums. Out of solidarity with his congregation, Chapman established his residence there. He organized Sunday schools to teach reading and writing to child laborers. He fed the homeless. Chapman's simple lifestyle and personal integrity gave him the power to evangelize with extraordinary authenticity. Radical Christian communities arose throughout the southwestern region of England in what would later become a stronghold for English Brethren.

> *(4) W.H. Bennet,* **Robert Cleaver Chapman** *of Barnstable, 1902*
> *There are many who preach Christ, but not so many who live Christ: my great aim will be to live Christ.*[19]

In 1832, Henry Craik and George Muller accepted an invitation to serve a congregation in Bristol, under the condition that they be allowed to put into practice their primitivist vision for church renewal. Two months after their arrival in Bristol, there was a terrible outbreak of cholera. Both men served the sick with no thought for their personal safety. In the midst of this epidemic, they gathered together a group of believers. Within two years, their congregation had more than 200 members.

Despite his pastoral success, Muller's compassionate spirit was not satisfied. He had inherited the social concerns of the Pietists, and was led to respond to Bristol's urgent social needs. He fed hundreds of homeless children and adults. Within a year, he organized three schools which taught more than 400 children. As a student at Halle, Muller had visited orphanages founded by August Hermann Francke, the German Pietist. These had inspired Muller's dream, "not to imitate Franke [sic], but in reliance upon the Lord."[20] In 1836, Muller opened two houses for orphans, and in 1837, he opened another. The construction and operation of the orphanages relied on charitable donations.

By 1870, Muller's institutional complex had grown to include five large orphanages with the capacity to house 2,000 children. When Muller died in 1898, there were ten Brethren congregations in Bristol, in which thousands of people had been received into communion. George Muller's faith has become proverbial in the Protestant world. The biblical principle on which he based his faith was simple. Christians should joyfully repay God by sharing the material resources which they have earned by His grace alone.

Conclusion

The Brethren movement attempted to restore the spirit of the New Testament to the church. Specifically, the movement expressed its solidarity with ordinary Christians who had been disinherited by the established church in its recourse to secular power. Their resistance to the use of coercive force led Anthony Groves, Percy Hall, and John Darby to be conscientious objectors to the forms of violence used by the establishment of their time.

The anti-clericalism of the Brethren was another form of protest against the monopoly of church power. The movement rejected a system which supported the interests of the socially and ecclesiastically powerful. At the same time, the movement attempted to restore charismatic leadership to the church's ministry.

The Brethren protested British economic practices, in which the conservative social structure condemned large sectors of the population to being outcasts. Leaders among the early Brethren saw their spiritual communities as being social and economic alternatives.

However, concrete action in solidarity with the poor soon began to disappear from the Brethren movement. Despite having been born out of a vision of Christian unity, the movement would eventually become sectarian, defining itself in contrast to the churches of Christendom. In the process, sound doctrine would often take precedence over Christ-like living.

The movement defined the church as the community of brothers and sisters who break bread together and minister to one another. But a parallel vision of the church made this definition ambiguous. Another current in their midst, implicitly dispensationalism, defined the church as being purely spiritual, predestined to persevere, and known only to God. This contradicted the movement's radical vision of God's people and their mission in the world.

Apocalyptic expectations inspired the movement's life and mission in the world, while providing encouragement to its members. However, the dispensational system of biblical interpretation also diminished the importance of the church as an active human community, living in solidarity with the needy, and anticipating the advent of a kingdom on earth.

Notes

[1] H. A. Ironside, *A Historical Sketch of the Brethren Movement* (Grand Rapids, MI: Zondervan Publishing House, 1942), 181-182.

[2] F. Roy Coad, *A History of the Brethren Movement* (Exeter, Great Britain: The Paternoster Press, 1968), 107-108.

[3] Williston Walker, *A History of the Christian Church* (New York: Charles Scribner's Sons, 1959), 498.

[4] Horton Davies, *Worship and Theology in England: From Newman to Martineau, 1850-1900* (Princeton, NJ: Princeton University Press, 1962), 154.

[5] Davies, 162.

[6] F. L. Cross, ed., *The Oxford Dictionary of the Christian Church* (London: The Oxford University Press, 1958), 1106.

[7] F. Roy Coad, *A History of the Brethren Movement* (Exeter, Great Britain: The Paternoster Press, 1968), 17.

[8] Clarence B. Bass, *Backgrounds to Dispensationalism* (Grand Rapids, MI: Wm. B. Eerdmans Publishing Company, 1960), 65.

[9] F. Roy Coad, *A History of the Brethren Movement* (Exeter, Great Britain: The Paternoster Press, 1968), 20.

[10] Clarence B. Bass, *Backgrounds to Dispensationalism* (Grand Rapids, MI: Wm. B. Eerdmans Publishing Company, 1960), 66-67.

[11] F. Roy Coad, *A History of the Brethren Movement* (Exeter, Great Britain: The Paternoster Press, 1968), 22.

[12] Coad, 25-26. "He before long took Holy Orders, and became an indefatigable curate in the mountains of Wicklow. Every evening he sallied forth to teach in the cabins, and roving far and wide over mountain and amid bogs, was seldom home before midnight. ... He did not fast on purpose, but his long walks through wild country and indigent people inflicted on him much severe deprivation; moreover, as he ate whatever food offered itself–food unpalatable and often indigestible to him–his whole frame might have vied in emaciation with a monk of La Trappe. Such a phenomenon intensely excited the poor Romanists, who looked on him as a genuine 'saint' of the ancient breed. ... In no other way could he gain equal access to the lower and lowest orders. ... He was moved not by asceticism, nor by ostentation, but by a self-abandonment fruitful of consequences."

[13] Clarence B. Bass, *Backgrounds to Dispensationalism* (Grand Rapids, MI: Wm. B. Eerdmans Publishing Company, 1960), 71.

[14] F. Roy Coad, *A History of the Brethren Movement* (Exeter, Great Britain: The Paternoster Press, 1968), 28. "It then became clear to me that the church of God, as He considers it, was composed only of those who were so united to Christ, whereas Christendom, as seen externally, was really the world, and could not be considered as 'the church.' At the same time, I saw that the Christian, having his place in Christ in heaven, has nothing to wait for save the coming of the Saviour. ... The careful reading of the Acts afforded me a practical picture of the early church, which made me feel deeply the contrast with its actual present state, though still as ever, beloved by God."

[15] Coad, 32.

[16] Coad, 34.

[17] Coad, 34. "If schism be charged, schism from the world is always right, and is now above all, a duty to Christ, and the dishonour of His Church is the chief dishonour to Him."

[18] Coad, 67.

[19] Coad, 69.

[20] Coad, 48.

Chapter 20

Twentieth-Century Movements: Pentecostalism

They shouted three days and three nights. It was the Easter season. The people came from everywhere. By the next morning there was no way of getting near the house. As the people came in they would fall under God's Power; and the whole city was stirred. They shouted there until the foundation of the house gave way, but no one was hurt. (The Pentecostal Evangel, 1946)[1]

It was something very extraordinary, that white pastors from the South were eagerly prepared to go to Los Angeles to the Negroes, to have fellowship with them and to receive through their prayers and intercessions the blessings of the Spirit. And it was still more wonderful that these white pastors went back to the South and reported to the members of their congregations that they had been together with Negroes, that they had prayed in one Spirit and received the same blessings as they. (A. A. Boddy)[2]

Receiving the baptism of the Holy Spirit doesn't make you a Pentecostal. It's what you do after you receive the baptism that makes you Pentecostal. (W. I. Evans)[3]

Introduction

Pentecostalism has been an explosive, worldwide movement. Classic Pentecostalism arose in the United States at the turn of the twentieth century. It has since spread throughout the world. Neo-Pentecostalism, or the charismatic movement, began about half a century later, and has made its presence felt in all denominations. There are fundamental differences between these two expressions of Pentecostalism, as well as notable similarities. Although Neo-Pentecostalism is worthy of its own study, this chapter will treat only Classic Pentecostalism. The movement of outcasts has attempted to restore the primitive vision and dynamic of the apostolic community to contemporary forms of worship.

Origins of the Pentecostal Movement in the United States [4]

Charles Parham's Early Experiences

Charles F. Parham, 1873-1929, represented the quintessence of the Pentecostal personality. Parham was eccentric, restless in his spiritual pilgrimage, active, courageously prophetic, unbending in controversy, and motivated by a sense of divine destiny. He was born and raised in a modest pioneer family on the prairies of the old west, in Kansas. At the age of twelve, Parham had his first faith experience when an itinerant evangelist visited the region. Later, the family became friends with a pastor of a denomination that emphasized holiness and charismatic spiritual experiences.

After the death of Parham's mother, his father married the daughter of an itinerant Methodist preacher. She was a woman of spiritual depth, with a predilection for the powerful manifestations of old-time religion. By the time he was fifteen, Parham had begun to hold revival meetings. He enrolled in a two-year teaching program at the Methodist Academy in a nearby town, but found that his religious activities left little time for serious study. At the age of eighteen, Parham's health, which had never been robust, had seriously deteriorated. Parham prayed for healing, vowing to dedicate his life to the Christian ministry.

In 1893, Parham, armed with a ministerial license, took the first in a series of Methodist pastorates. After several restless years, Parham resigned his Methodist affiliation, and began an independent evangelical ministry. He questioned whether true biblical Christianity could be lived within a traditional denomination, and called his ministry "the apostolic faith."[5] In his travels, Parham discovered that many people were open to his ideas, and concerned about the holiness of the church. One of these people was David Baker, an English Quaker, with whom Parham studied the Bible. His friendship with Baker would affect the course of Parham's life. He gained an appreciation for Quaker spirituality, trusting in God's direct guidance, and separating himself from the institutions of established Christianity. Parham also married Baker's granddaughter.

Facing another health crisis, Parham again prayed for healing. Upon recovery, he began to integrate the concept of healing into his preaching. His doctrine emphasized salvation, healing, sanctification by faith, laying on of hands, the baptism of the Holy Spirit, and Christ's second coming. Parham taught that healing was integral to atonement, and as much a part of the gospel as the forgiveness of sins. He saw sanctification as a second work of grace. Parham's ideas were inspired by Wesleyan thought, to which he added the additional experience of baptism in the Holy Spirit.

Parham traveled through the northeastern United States and Canada, exploring "the latest truths restored by latter day movements."[6] In his travels, Parham was influenced by Frank Sandford, an ex-Free Baptist minister, who believed in "the restoration of all things," and the realization of the kingdom of God.[7] Sandford believed that an apostolic faith would be recovered in the last days, marked by intense spiritual revelations. Parham began to preach about the baptism of the Spirit, which would be experienced following sanctification.

The Baptism of the Spirit

When his travels were over, Parham opened a Bible School in Topeka, Kansas. On January 1, 1901, a student in Parham's Bible School asked for prayer and the laying on of hands, that she might receive the baptism of the Holy Spirit. She received the gift of tongues. Within several days, more than a dozen students had spoken in tongues. Parham concluded that the gift of tongues was biblical evidence of the baptism of the Holy Spirit, and another dimension of apostolic faith restored.

After this experience, Parham left the Bible School to travel throughout Kansas and Missouri, sharing his news. In January 1904, the Joplin, Missouri newspaper reported that nearly 8,000 people had experienced salvation, and approximately 1,000 had been healed.[8] Parham enjoyed an enthusiastic reception in this mining region, which had a largely uneducated population. During the following years, a number of apostolic faith congregations were organized in southeastern Kansas, southwestern Missouri, and northeastern Oklahoma. For the rest of his life, Parham's most loyal followers would come from this region.

The Roots of African American Pentecostalism

In 1905, Parham, and a large group of followers, traveled to Texas to share his message. Among those touched by his ministry in Houston were several African Americans: Lucy Farrow, William J. Seymour, and J. A. Warren. They would later play key roles in determining the movement's future in the southern United States. But Parham was not equal to the occasion. He was unable to overcome his racism. From then on, Parham continued his ministry under the shadow of suspicion.

Farrow and Seymour were active in African American mission churches in Houston. There, they met Neeley Terry, an African American woman who belonged to a Holiness congregation in Los Angeles. When she returned to Los Angeles, Terry asked her congregation to consider Seymour for an associate pastorate. In January 1906, Seymour left for Los Angeles, and was soon joined in his ministry by Lucy Farrow and J. A. Warren. In a poor section of the city, the three shared Parham's message of apostolic faith to people from independent missions. Their audience was eager to receive a new outpouring of the Holy Spirit, and to hear about the promise of the end times.

In his first sermon at the Holiness Church, Seymour told his audience about the gift of tongues, which was an initial sign of the baptism of the Spirit. The teaching proved too novel for the congregation to assimilate, and they dismissed Seymour. Later, a fundamental difference would distinguish African American Pentecostalism from the mainstream movement. Mainstream Pentecostals, led by William Durham, held a two-step understanding of salvation: conversion or regeneration, and baptism of the Holy Spirit, accompanied by tongues. African American Pentecostalism would teach a three-step method of salvation: conversion or regeneration; a crisis experience of sanctification, also called the "second blessing"; and the baptism of the Holy Spirit accompanied by tongues.[9]

The Azuza Street Movement

Seymour continued his ministry in the home of a sympathizer, preaching to a group of working class people. On April 9, 1906, Seymour and seven others received the baptism of the Spirit and spoke in tongues. News spread rapidly, and the street soon filled with people who came to hear Seymour preach from the porch. People of all races sought the baptism of the Holy Spirit. Interest grew, and Seymour secured an abandoned Methodist church building on Azuza Street in which to house his ministry. *The Los Angeles Times* alluded to these events with the following headlines: "Weird Babel of Tongues," "New Sect of Fanatics is Breaking Loose," and "Wild Scene Last Night on Azuza Street."[10]

At that time, Los Angeles had a population of around 250,000, and was growing rapidly due to an influx of people seeking employment. Many of these people were laborers from the midwestern and southern United States, with religious backgrounds in Holiness and Restorationist denominations. The developments on Azuza Street were of particular interest in these circles. *The Apostolic Faith*, a monthly periodical, described how meetings at Azuza Street would progress late into the night, to accommodate all the people seeking out the power of God. (1)

Some of the visitors to Azuza Street would later become leaders in the Pentecostal movement. All were deeply moved by the experience. Seymour was a charismatic leader whose humility and trust in the power of God impressed others. Healings occupied a prominent place at meetings. Seymour preached about repentance, restitution, sanctification, healing, the baptism of the Spirit, and the imminent return of Christ. No offerings were taken during meetings, consistent with Seymour's absolute trust in God.

The Azuza Street movement believed itself to be restoring New Testament practices

> *(1)* **The Apostolic Faith,** *Sept., 1906*
> *[M]eetings begin about ten o'clock in the morning and can hardly stop before ten or twelve at night, and sometimes two or three in the morning, because so many are seeking, and some are slain under the power of God.*[11]

to the church. Through the baptism of the Holy Spirit, "the faith once delivered to the saints" was being restored.[12] Members of the movement believed that they were living in the end times, recipients of the final evangelistic call of the Holy Spirit.[13]

Despite its ups and downs, and sometimes its excesses, the Apostolic Faith Movement in Los Angeles continued to grow. By the end of 1906, an estimated 13,000 people had received the gift of tongues. Seymour would take his congregation down to the beach, and baptize dozens of new members at a time in the Pacific Ocean. Many people came out of curiosity, and stayed until they had experienced the baptism of the Spirit. Some went on to share their experiences throughout the country.

In some ways, the movement was a new interpretation of salvation history. The people baptized at Azuza Street perceived themselves to be at the center of God's last salvation effort. Social and political outsiders found identity and meaning in the movement, and the experience was powerful. The movement was also enormously influential because it had deep roots in the Restorationist and Holiness movements, and therefore in the North American religious consciousness.

The Roots of North American Pentecostalism

The Holiness Movement

The Holiness movement, rooted principally in American Methodism, contributed to the rise of Pentecostalism. The Holiness movement was inspired by John Wesley's teachings on Christian perfection, and by his brother Charles's powerful hymns on spiritual experience. Methodist advocates of holiness referred to the possibility of "entire sanctification."[14] They believed in a second work of grace, by which the inclination to sin might be removed, leaving in its place a perfect love. This experience was also called the baptism of the Holy Spirit. Advocates of holiness thought of sanctification as being both a progressive work, and an instantaneous occurrence. (2)

During the last decades of the nineteenth century, the Holiness movement held popular revival meetings at which hymn singing and preaching encouraged the growth of personal holiness. The movement taught that there were two distinct spiritual experiences. The first of these was conversion or regeneration. The second experience was referred to as a "second delight of grace," which sanctified entirely.[16]

> *(2) J.W. Horne, from a sermon preached at a Holiness Camp Meeting, 1867*
> *Sanctification is a progressive work, while entire sanctification is the work of but a moment. There is a moment in which the darkness forever ceases; there is a moment in which the dying Adam is dead and the new Adam is alive; ... there is a moment in which sanctification passes into entire sanctification.[15]*

The Holiness movement was largely concentrated among the African American and white rural population in the southern and western United States. African Americans were going through a particularly difficult time, struggling to recover their sense of identity as a people, and their personal dignity as individuals, in the wake of their collective experience of enslavement.

The Restorationist Movement

The Restorationist movement was another tributary which fed into North American Pentecostalism. During the nineteenth century, the Disciples of Christ, the Christian Churches, and the Churches of Christ were the principal exponents of this tradition. They envisioned restoring New Testament values and practices to the life and worship of the contemporary church. They emphasized unity among Christ's followers. They believed that they were living in the end times, and that the restoration of the church was part of God's plan. Finally, they questioned authoritative claims to truth made by different denominations. They were suspicious of the traditions and creeds held by established churches.

The nineteenth century Restorationist movement helped form the separatist subculture in which Pentecostalism would flourish in the twentieth century. Its members lived on the fringes of mainstream society. Restorationists believed that they had found a new dynamic in the message and forms of primitive Christianity, and it fed their daily lives.

The Dispensational View of History

In the final decades of the nineteenth century, there was growing interest in the doctrine of a premillennial second coming of Christ. The dispensational view of history, articulated by John Nelson Darby, envisioned Christ's imminent return and a secret rapture of the church, followed by the thousand-year reign of Christ on earth. Darby's vision became widely influential in evangelical circles, including the Christian and Missionary Alliance, created in 1887 to promote the cause of evangelization in the United States and overseas. Several decades later, the millenarian expectations of evangelical circles would exercise a decisive doctrinal influence on emerging Pentecostalism.

Christ as Healer

Nineteenth-century American Protestantism envisioned Christ as a healer. Healing was seen as integral to Christ's saving work, and as one of the gifts of the Holy Spirit. In Southwestern Germany, the Reformed pastor Johann Christoph Blumhardt, 1805-1880, confronted a case of demon possession in his congregation. After a two-year struggle in prayer, the young woman was liberated with the cry, "Jesus is Victor."[17] News of the experience created a renewal of spiritual vitality, and the belief that the kingdom of God had become a present reality. Blumhardt's parish in Bad Boll became a center of ministry, attracting a variety of people who sought spiritual renewal and physical healing.

During the final decades of the nineteenth century, A. J. Gordon, a prominent Baptist pastor, and A. B. Simpson, the Presbyterian pastor who organized the Christian and Missionary Alliance, became influential advocates of healing. Gordon taught that Christ redeemed the soul from sin and the body from illness. Christ "endured vicariously our diseases," both physical and spiritual.[18]

Simpson emphasized holiness, the baptism of the Holy Spirit, divine healing, and the evangelizing mission of the church. He believed that physical healing was accompanied by an even richer healing of the soul, in the baptism of the Holy Spirit.[19] (3)

John Alexander Dowie, an Australian, brought a similar vision to Chicago when he built a city for his Christian Catholic Church in Zion City, Illinois. Dowie wanted to restore primitive Christianity to the church. He emphasized the unity of all Christians, entire sanctification, divine healing, and the exercise of apostolic gifts and ministries in anticipation of the end times. These elements would later be assimilated into Pentecostalism.

> *(3) A.B. Simpson,* **The Christian and Missionary Alliance,** *1907*
> *[W]e are to expect a great outpouring of the Holy Spirit in connection with the second coming of Christ and one as much greater than the Pentecostal effusion of the Spirit as the rains of autumn were greater than the showers of spring.*[20]

The Pentecostal movement would eventually be characterized by the doctrines of the four square gospel: salvation by faith, divine healing, the baptism of the Holy Spirit, and the imminent return of Christ. These doctrines were already being fervently preached in the Holiness movement, and widely disseminated among conservative Protestants in the United States.

Racial Segregation

The Pentecostal Movement generally attracted those on the fringes of society. In United States, it grew most rapidly in the southern and western states, among the rural population. These were regions where Methodists, Disciples of Christ, and Baptists had been dominant in the nineteenth century, and were becoming increasingly acculturated in the twentieth. By 1930, most Pentecostals in the United Sates came from the southern states. The economic level among Pentecostals was lower than the economic level in American churches in general.[21]

At the turn of the twentieth century, African Americans were at one of the lowest points in their collective existence. This period has been called the "nadir of the race" in the United States.[22] White mob violence was increasingly being directed against African Americans, and many lived in terror. Those who depended on the fragile agricultural economy of the southern United States suffered even more.

Many African Americans abandoned established churches for the Pentecostal movement, which offered them a socio-religious alternative compatible with their traditional forms of spirituality. It was the only church that gave African Americans the possibility of full participation. During the early years of the Pentecostal movement, racial segregation was overcome between members, who came largely from the same economic, if not racial, group. Frank Bartleman, one of the first leaders of the emerging movement, said that at Azuza Street "'the color line' was washed away in the blood [of Christ]."[23]

However, with a few remarkable exceptions, the new racial harmony would not survive. Gradually, American Pentecostalism became dominated by white members. African Americans had separate congregations and organized their own denominations. In 1948, the Pentecostal Fellowship of North America was organized to "demonstrate to the world the essential unity of Spirit-baptized believers ...."[24] Not one African American denomination was invited to join.

A Place for the Outcast

The Pentecostal movement quickly spread around the world, attracting the disinherited and outcast. In 1907, Chile experienced a Pentecostal renewal which began in Methodist circles but spread rapidly among peasants and workers. The movement soon became the largest single evangelical group in Chile, with fourteen per cent of the country's population. All other Protestant denominations combined added up to less than one per cent.[25]

Brazil's two principal Pentecostal denominations were founded around 1910. The first, the Assembleias de Deus en Brasil, was started by two Swedish men, Daniel Berg and Gunnar Vingren, who immigrated to Brazil from the United States. The second, the Congregacao Crista do Brasil, was started by Luigi Francescon, an Italian-American of Waldensian origin. Francescon had received the baptism of the Holy Spirit under the ministry of William Durham, a founder of the movement, in Chicago.

Both Brazilian denominations continue to depend on lay leadership. An overwhelming majority of their members come from the poor sectors of society. In Brazil, there are currently more than four million Pentecostals, the largest Protestant body in the Latin world.[26]

This story is repeated in country after country. The Pentecostal movement in Italy began when Luigi Francescon brought the "full gospel" to Giacomo Lombardi in Brazil.[27] Lombardi returned home to Italy to evangelize among his people. Despite severe repression by the authorities, the movement spread rapidly throughout Italy. The movement would gain particular popularity in impoverished southern Italy. Today, there are an estimated 250,000 Pentecostals in Italy. Elena Cassin, a sociologist, discussed the secret to the movement's success in Calabria, a poor province in southern Italy. Cassin argued that Pentecostal sects were popular amongst the poor because they created a real egalitarian society. The poor found pride in their poverty, because it brought them closer to Christ's message. (4)

> *(4) Elena Cassin,* **The "Proud Poor" will not remain poor**
> *The success of sects of Pentecostal type is largely explained by the real and egalitarian solidarity which they create amongst their members. ... Its adherents are drawn without exception from the most deprived classes .... They are the poor, but poor people proud of their poverty, proud of their ignorance, which permits them to be closer to the truth of the Gospel.*[28]

In Spain, the fastest growing evangelical denomination is the Iglesia de Filadefia, whose members are mainly Spanish gypsies. In the Pentecostal church, the gypsies have found a place where they can be recognized as a people. For the first time, some of them have been able to obtain an official document of Spanish identity.

Political Power and Military Service

Pentecostals have always perceived themselves to be "pilgrims and strangers" among the kingdoms of this world.[29] The first world war broke out barely eight years after the birth of Pentecostalism. The movement had to confront the question of warfare: should Pentecostals participate? Their response was not unanimous. Some members resisted out of deep Christian conviction. But patriotism was a powerful force in Britain and the United States, and many responded to their nation's call. In England, where Pentecostals first faced the test, Alexander Boddy, an ex-Anglican minister, proclaimed the justice of Britain's cause in the war.

Citizenship in the Kingdom of God

> **(5) Frank Bartleman, War and the Christian**
> *War is contrary to the whole Spirit and teaching of Christ. ... Christ's kingdom is "not of this world."*[31]

Younger British leaders like Donald Gee and Howard Carter objected to the call to arms. They believed that citizenship in the kingdom of God took precedence over earthly patriotic loyalties. Many members in the United States also held pacifist convictions. In 1915, William McCafferty wrote in *The Christian Evangel* that heavenly citizenship demanded pacifism. McCafferty wrote that all warfare, without exception, was evil. God's command for the church was this: "Ye followers of the Prince of Peace, disarm yourselves."[30] In a pamphlet on "War and the Christian," Frank Bartleman denounced warfare and called Pentecostals to an ethic of love. (5)

> **(6) Stanley Frodshom, Weekly Evangel, 1917**
> *From the very beginning, the [Pentecostal] movement has been characterized by Quaker principles. The laws of the Kingdom, laid down by our elder brother, Jesus Christ, in His Sermon on the Mount, have been unqualifiedly adopted, consequently the movement has found itself opposed to the spilling of blood of any man, or of offering resistance to any aggression. Every branch of the movement ... has held to this principle.*[33]

Pentecostal leaders emphasized that Christians had citizenship in an eternal kingdom, and were but pilgrims and strangers in their earthly nations. Samuel Booth-Clibborn, the grandson of the man who founded the Salvation Army, denounced patriotism in *The Christian Evangel*. The United States had entered the war, and Booth-Clibborn declared that patriotism was idolatry, and that young men were being sacrificed on its bloody altar.[32]

In April 1917, the general presbytery of the Assemblies of God adopted a pacifist position. The stance was particularly radical given that the United States had entered the war, and opposition to it appeared seditious. Despite a lack of unanimity on this question, the declaration of the presbytery adamantly opposed aggression in any form, based on principles laid down in the Sermon on the Mount. (6)

The Acculturation of the Pentecostals

However, with the passage of time, social acculturation began to occur among Pentecostals, especially those living in Texas. Perception shifted, and God was perceived to be supporting the American cause. In 1918, the war was coming to a close. E. N. Bell, a Texan and a Pentecostal, explained how he rationalized warfare: participation in warfare was not a sin, but hatred was. If a soldier kept hatred out of his heart, he had done no wrong in obeying his country's command, and "executing just punishment on the criminal Hun."[34]

North American Pentecostalism was undergoing a deep transformation, and the changing attitude toward warfare was just one symptom. Rather than offering a prophetic alternative to prevailing social attitudes, Pentecostals were beginning to support the mainstream system. The historian R. Lawrence Moore observed that at the same time that Pentecostals began suppressing their early "egalitarian innovations," Pentecostal journals began printing "reproductions of the American flag."[35]

The process of acculturation among the Assemblies of God culminated with their affiliation, in 1943, with the National Association of Evangelicals (NAE). In his presidential address to the NAE's constitutional convention that year, Harold Ockenga stated that the United States was destined to be favored by God. (7) The United States had just entered the Second World War. Evangelical rhetoric ran high, warning of the dangers of Catholicism, communism, and modernism. In one generation, white North American Pentecostalism had become part of the establishment. Even African American Pentecostals would bend under the pressure to conform, in order to earn the favor of national authorities.

> *(7) Harold Ockenga, speech to the NAE, 1943*
> *I believe that the United States of America has been assigned a destiny comparable to that of ancient Israel which was favored, preserved, endowed, guided and used by God.*[36]

African American Pentecostalism

The process of North American acculturation has not been as rapid nor as complete among African American Pentecostals. (8) The Church of God in Christ is the main African American Pentecostal denomination, and has twice as many members as the Assemblies of God. Unlike their white counterparts, African American Pentecostals have kept their faith in the power of non-violent resistance. They have done so despite the assassination of Martin Luther King which was, in part, an attack directed against African American Pentecostalism. They have not been moved by the campaigns of televangelists, which have received much support from white Pentecostals. George M. Perry, an African American evangelist, said: "We believe in the content of the Graham message, but we can't go along with its suburban, middle-class, white orientation that has nothing to say to the poor nor to the Black people."[38]

---

(8) Arthur Brazier, Pentecostal evangelist in Chicago
America cannot keep down thirty million people who are moving up, without destroying the entire nation in the process. ... America was built on the backs of the blacks. The blacks have planted cotton, but they have to walk around in rags. The blacks have built the railways, but they are not allowed to ride on them. A black doctor discovered blood plasma, but he died because nobody was ready to give him a blood transfusion. Changing this situation cannot be effected by the violence of arms, but only by the violence of non-violence.[37]

A Corporate Experience

For African American Pentecostals, holiness is not an individual, personal experience, but a corporate one. White Pentecostals tend to emphasize personal conversion, and the importance of individual ethical choice. African American Pentecostals emphasize a social understanding of holiness, pointing to the social consequence of loving one's neighbor.[39] African American Pentecostals are troubled by the alienation of peoples, from one another and from God. They believe that this separation must be healed before the Pentecostal message can move the world.

Worship forms used in African American Pentecostal churches reflect their members' social, economic, and political marginalization. In their songs, prayers, dances, instrumental music, testimonies, and preaching style members express their corporate consciousness, and their identity as a people crying out for liberation and salvation. Their worship is a spiritual expression of their experience.

Contrary to popular opinion, African American spirituals were not purely otherworldly, but had socio-political content. Thematically, spirituals were about the divine liberation of the oppressed. The songs expressed the slaves' resistance to the position imposed upon them. They sang to the God who, throughout history, came to free His people from servitude. For many African Americans, worship reaffirmed and celebrated their dignity as sons and daughters in God's family.[40]

Conclusion

Many early Pentecostals were socially and economically marginalized, and their spiritual needs were not being met by established churches. The lay nature of the Pentecostal movement placed the secrets to spiritual liberation within the reach of ordinary people. People who were otherwise powerless were drawn to the experience of a direct, immediate relationship with God and with the spiritual world.

The Pentecostal vision of an accessible supernatural world gave strength to the weak. Pentecostal language stresses the power of the Spirit of God, and the power of charismatic gifts, which may be given to anyone. The Pentecostal communication of grace was essentially oral, allowing uneducated people equal participation in ministry and worship.

The legacy of Pentecostalism lives on among poor and marginalized minorities in the industrialized world and in the third world.

Notes

[1] W. J. Hollenweger, *The Pentecostals: The Charismatic Movement in the Churches* (Minneapolis, MN: Augsburg Publishing House, 1972), 23.

[2] Hollenweger, *The Pentecostals*, 24.

[3] Edith L. Blumhofer, *The Assemblies of God: A Chapter in the Story of American Pentecostalism*, vol. 2 (Springfield, MO: Gospel Publishing House, 1989), 190.

[4] This section relies largely on the following source. Blumhofer, *The Assemblies of God*, vol. 1, 67-110.

[5] Blumhofer, *The Assemblies of God*, vol. 1, 71.

[6] Blumhofer, *The Assemblies of God*, vol. 1, 76.

[7] Blumhofer, *The Assemblies of God*, vol. 1, 77.

[8] Blumhofer, *The Assemblies of God*, vol. 1, 87.

[9] W.J. Hollenweger, *The Pentecostals: The Charismatic Movement in the Churches* (Minneapolis, MN: Augsburg Publishing House, 1972), 25.

[10] Edith L. Blumhofer, *The Assemblies of God: A Chapter in the Story of American Pentecostalism*, vol. 1 (Springfield, MO: Gospel Publishing House, 1989), 99.

[11] Blumhofer, *The Assemblies of God*, vol. 1, 103.

[12] Blumhofer, *The Assemblies of God*, vol. 1, 105.

[13] Blumhofer, *The Assemblies of God*, vol. 1, 105. "When the Holy Ghost fell on the one hundred and twenty, it was in the morning of the dispensation of the Holy Ghost. Today we are living down in the evening of the dispensation of the Holy Ghost. And as it was in the morning, so it shall be in the evening. This is the last evangelistic call of the day."

[14] Blumhofer, *The Assemblies of God*, vol. 1, 41-42.

[15] Blumhofer, *The Assemblies of God*, vol. 1, 42.

[16] Blumhofer, *The Assemblies of God*, vol. 1, 41-42.

[17] Vernard Eller, ed., *Thy Kingdom Come: A Blumhardt Reader* (Grand Rapids, MI: William B. Eerdmans Publishing Company, 1980), xviii.

[18] Edith L. Blumhofer, *The Assemblies of God: A Chapter in the Story of*

American Pentecostalism, vol. 1 (Springfield, MO: Gospel Publishing House, 1989), 28.

[19] Blumhofer, *The Assemblies of God*, vol. 1, 30-31. Simpson said that "the power which heals the body usually imparts a much richer baptism of the Holy Ghost to the heart."

[20] Blumhofer, *The Assemblies of God*, vol. 1, 151.

[21] W. J. Hollenweger, *The Pentecostals: The Charismatic Movement in the Churches* (Minneapolis, MN: Augsburg Publishing House, 1972), 26.

[22] Lawrence Neal Jones, "The Black Pentecostals," *The Charismatic Movement*, ed. Michael P. Hamilton (Grand Rapids, MI: William B. Eerdmans Publishing Company, 1975), 152.

[23] W. J. Hollenweger, *The Pentecostals: The Charismatic Movement in the Churches* (Minneapolis, MN: Augsburg Publishing House, 1972), 28 n. 33.

[24] Vinson Synan, *The Holiness-Pentecostal Movement in the United States* (Grand Rapids, MI: William B. Eerdmans Publishing Company, 1971), 179-180.

[25] W. J. Hollenweger, *The Pentecostals: The Charismatic Movement in the Churches* (Minneapolis, MN: Augsburg Publishing House, 1972), 64.

[26] Hollenweger, *The Pentecostals*, 65. Pentecostals in Brazil account for approximately seventy per cent of all evangelicals in the country.

[27] Hollenweger, *The Pentecostals*, 251.

[28] Hollenweger, *The Pentecostals*, 260-261.

[29] Edith L. Blumhofer, *The Assemblies of God: A Chapter in the Story of American Pentecostalism*, vol. 1 (Springfield, MO: Gospel Publishing House, 1989), 343.

[30] Blumhofer, *The Assemblies of God*, vol. 1, 349.

[31] Blumhofer, *The Assemblies of God*, vol. 1, 349-350.

[32] Blumhofer, *The Assemblies of God*, vol. 1, 350-351. Samuel Booth-Clibborn denounced "the wretched idolatry of nation-worship where parents sacrifice their young men on the bloody altars of the modern 'Moloch' of PATRIOTISM ...."

[33] Blumhofer, *The Assemblies of God*, vol. 1, 353.

[34] Blumhofer, *The Assemblies of God*, vol. 1, 354.

[35] Blumhofer, *The Assemblies of God*, vol. 1, 355.

[36] Blumhofer, *The Assemblies of God*, vol. 2, 30.

[37] Arthur M. Brazier, *Black Self-Determination: The Story of the Woodlawn Organization* (Grand Rapids, MI: Eerdmans, 1969), in Walter J. Hollenweger, "Pentecostalism and Black Power," *Theology Today*, 30.3 (1973): 228-229.

[38] W.J. Hollenweger, "Pentecostalism and Black Power," *Theology Today*, 30.3 (1973): 231.

[39] W. J. Hollenweger, *The Pentecostals: The Charismatic Movement in the Churches* (Minneapolis, MN: Augsburg Publishing House, 1972), 470. An African American pastor from a southern state said: "I feel that the greatest indictment against the church of the Lord Jesus in our century is our stand (or lack of one) on racial problems. We must search in our hearts to see if we have any type of racial misunderstanding in attitude or action."

[40] W.J. Hollenweger, "Pentecostalism and Black Power," *Theology Today*, 29.1 (1972): 232. See also James H. Cone, "Black Spirituals: A Theological Interpretation," *Theology Today*, 39.1 (1972): 54-69. "Contrary to popular opinion, the spirituals are not evidence that black people reconciled themselves with human slavery. On the contrary, they are black freedom songs which emphasize black liberation as consistent with divine revelation. For this reason it is most appropriate for black people to sing them in this 'new' age of Black Power. And if some people still regard the spirituals as inconsistent with Black Power and Black Theology, that is because they have been misguided and the songs misinterpreted. There is little evidence that black slaves accepted their servitude because they believed that God willed their slavery. The opposite is the case. The spirituals speak of God's liberation of black people, his will to set right the oppression of black slaves despite the overwhelming power of white masters. ... And if 'de God dat lived in Moses' time is jus de same today,' then that God will vindicate the suffering of the righteous black and punish the unrighteous whites for their wrongdoings." (54).

Chapter 21

Twentieth-Century Movements: Basic Ecclesial Communities

The Christian ought to find the living of the communion, to which he has been called, in his "base community" .... The members of these communities ... make of their community "a sign of the presence of God in the world." (Second General Conference of Latin American Bishops, Medellín, *Conclusions*, XV, 1968, 10-11)[1]

In particular we have found that small communities, especially the CEBs, create more personal inter-relations, acceptance of God's Word, re-examination of one's life, and reflection on reality in the light of the Gospel. They accentuate committed involvement in the family, one's work, the neighborhood, and the local community. (Third General Conference of the Latin American Episcopate, Puebla, *Final Document*, 1979, 629)[2]

United in a CEB ... Christians strive for a more evangelical way of life amid the people, work together to challenge the egotistical and consumeristic roots of society, and make explicit their vocation to communion with God and their fellow humans. ... The CEBs embody the Church's preferential love for common people. (Third General Conference of the Latin American Episcopate, Puebla, *Final Document*, 1979, 641-643)[3]

Introduction

Although analogous communities currently exist on other continents, Basic Ecclesial Communities originated in Latin American. In the fifties, "experiments" were going on in Brazil, Chile, and Panamá. In the sixties, the communities became popularly known as Basic Ecclesial Communities, or in Spanish as Comunidades Ecclesiales de Base, or CEBs. The name was drawn from the Basic Education Movement, a Brazilian organization which used radio in its teaching program. A desire for locally-based evangelization, and experiments in a lay apostolate, under the auspices of the pastoral program of the national church in Brazil, also contributed to the rise of the communities.[4]

Origins of Basic Ecclesial Communities

A Program for Evangelization

In 1956, the bishop of Barra do Pirai, in the district of Rio de Janeiro, initiated a program for evangelization in his diocese. The program was begun after an old woman complained that no priest would serve their neighborhood. (1) This challenge led to serious reflection within the Brazilian church. Did the life of a Christian community depend solely on the presence of a formally trained, ordained priest?

The church began preparing lay catechists who would serve, in the name of the bishop, as community coordinators. They would nurture fraternal communion at the local church level. On Sundays and other holidays, people from the neighborhood would meet together for a "'Sunday without mass' or the 'mass without a priest.'"[6] In this way, they could accompany, in spirit, the mass being celebrated in the distant mother parish.

Many of the lay catechists were public primary schoolteachers. The catechists, or community coordinators, assumed responsibilities for the group. They led daily prayer sessions, and weekly worship services. They served according to the community's needs, administering baptisms in urgent cases and ministering to the sick and dying. Instead of building chapels dedicated exclusively to worship, they built modest facilities that were used for primary education, sewing classes, religious instruction, and as community centers where neighbors could meet to share their concerns.[7]

(1) Woman speaking to the bishop of Barra do Pirai
Christmas Eve, all three Protestant churches were lit up and full of people. We could hear them singing. ... And the Catholic church, closed and dark! ... Because we can't get a priest.[5]

The Basic Education Movement

In the northeastern region of Brazil, the church made a special attempt to serve people in their struggle for survival. The church looked for viable solutions to the region's pressing social problems of malnutrition, endemic illness, illiteracy, and socio-economic exploitation.

The church raised the people's social consciousness, and encouraged the establishment of schools and centers of social welfare. In the process, the Basic Education Movement was born. "[R]adio schools" were vehicles for consciousness-raising, and seedbeds of the church.[8] By 1963, there were 1,410 radio schools in the archdiocese of Natal. The resource helped people learn to read, as well as offering religious instruction. In communities without a priest, people would meet around their radio to listen to a sermon and recite the prayers of the mass, which was being celebrated in the distant parish church.

The Basic Education Movement spread throughout the northeastern and western parts of the country, contributing to the formation of small ecclesial communities, which were more basic than traditional parishes. In this way, a network for education and evangelization was formed. In the process of being evangelized, these communities would also serve as agents of evangelization.[9]

The National Pastoral Program

With the approval of the Brazilian episcopate, a team of fifteen priests, nuns, and lay persons dedicated five years to a campaign called "A Better World." They visited parishes throughout the country, and offered 1,800 courses in spiritual formation and renewal. The initiative led to an atmosphere of spiritual awakening. People began questioning the social and religious status quo.

The National Bishop's Conference approved an "Emergency Plan" which would transform traditional parishes into a network of small communities of faith, worship, and charity. The plan was to develop basic communities within the parishes in which members would actively participate in the celebration of the Eucharist, and other sacraments.[10]

The church in Latin America was concerned about the numerous people who had been baptized, but had virtually no relationship with the church. For geographic and social reasons, many parishioners had little or no exposure to the sacramental expressions of salvation, or to the Bible, or to their spiritual brothers and sisters. These people could hardly be expected to evangelize others, or share the message of salvation.

The church's concern about evangelization was combined with a growing sense of responsibility for their poorest parishioners. For this reason, Basic Ecclesial Communities would flourish in those regions most affected by endemic social problems.[11]

Basic Ecclesial Communities have spread throughout Latin America. By 1975, there were 40,000 communities in Brazil, 4,000 in Honduras, and numerous others in Chile, Panamá, Ecuador, Bolivia, Colombia, Nicaragua, El Salvador, the Dominican Republic, and Paraguay. Basic Ecclesial Communities are now present in all Latin American countries.[12] Bishops met at the Second General Conference of the Latin American Episcopate in Medellín, in 1968, and at the Third in Puebla, in 1979, and discussed the development of Basic Ecclesial Communities. Both assemblies wholeheartedly approved of the movement.[13]

Characteristics of Basic Ecclesial Communities, José Maríns, 1975. [14]

1. *Church vitality is maximized, while its outer structures are minimized.*

2. *The evangelizing mission of the church and communal witness are focused upon.*

3. *They are open to other Christian groups through prayer, study, and fellowship.*

4. *The personal atmosphere calls all members to participate in the life of the church.*

5. *There is a charismatic understanding of ministry which is not hierarchical.*

6. *The spiritual focus is on Jesus, not the saints.*

7. *Catholics who have been baptized, but not evangelized, are participants.*

8. *Adults, as well as children, receive catechistic instruction.*

9. *The sacraments are celebrated communally.*

10. *The clergy are teachers, and lay people participate in the church's ministry.*

11. *The political dimensions of faith are recovered through service.*

Basic Ecclesial Communities are churches which challenge dominant ecclesiastical and secular structures. Committed to the welfare of humanity, the communities are part of the kingdom of God, and denounce the idolatry of sexism, power, and money that characterizes the kingdoms of this world. Their revolutionary stance is viewed with suspicion, but the movement is dedicated to building a new world based on New Testament values.[15] According to the principles that guide Basic Ecclesial Communitites, the church is not a powerful society, but a community of communities, committed to Christ and to one another.

Basic Ecclesial Communities

Leonardo and Clodovis Boff, Brazilian Franciscan brothers, are among the foremost advocates of Basic Ecclesial Communities. They have defended the movement against the ecclesiastical conservatism of traditional Catholicism.[16] The brothers summarized the principal ecclesiological characteristics of Basic Ecclesial Communities in their book, *Church: Charism and Power*, from which the following discussion is largely drawn.[17]

Concrete Expressions of Communion

Basic Ecclesial Communities are concrete expressions of communion. (2) In contrast to traditional Catholicism, the communities of faith do not depend on the ministry of ordained clergy. Lay people assume responsibility for evangelization and expression of faith. Interpersonal relationships are direct and fraternal.

Communities are usually made up of fifteen to twenty low-income families. They meet once or twice a week to share their problems and search for communal solutions based on their understanding of the gospel. Under the leadership of a coordinator, who is a member of the group, meetings are spent in Bible study, reflection, and prayer.

> **(2) Leonardo Boff, Church: Charism and Power, 1986**
> *After centuries of silence, the People of God are beginning to speak. ... It is true that the Church is Christ's gift which we gratefully receive. Yet the Church is also a human response to faith.[18]*

God's people are part of a community in mission that invites the participation of the poor and outcast. This active community is the real church of Jesus Christ. Admittedly, however, tensions do exist between those who believe that active service best expresses faith, and those who believe that faith is strictly sacramental and devotional.

The Gospel and the Communities

Basic Ecclesial Communities are born out of the Bible. People in these communities are guided by the gospel message. Scripture offers good news, and is the primary source of hope, promise, and joy. Communities are guided by the Bible through an extensive hermeneutical process. Listening to scripture leads people to take interest in the problems affecting others in their group. This awareness leads people to reflect on the problems affecting their neighborhood. Eventually, communal reflection urges them to question larger social and economic issues. By these means, the community's social commitment becomes strongly rooted in faith.

> *(3) Leonardo Boff,* Church: Charism and Power, *1986*
> *It is an exegesis that goes beyond the words and captures the living, spiritual meaning of the text. The gospel passage serves as inspiration for the group's reflection on life, where the word of God is actually heard.*[19]

The community becomes the primary place in which the Bible is read, heard, and interpreted. The entire community participates in this process. Leonardo Boff believes that popular exegesis in these communities is similar to the ancient exegesis of church fathers, because the text's message becomes a concrete way of life, a living expression of faith. (3) For many people in these communities, the gospel is a transforming force.

Successors of the Apostolic Community

Basic Ecclesial Communities represent both new and ancient ways of being a church. Lay people take on important roles in the mission of the church. The witness of these communities is expected to lead to the formation of new communities. In this way, they become true successors of the early apostolic church. The church is continually being renewed and reshaped through the activity of these communities. (4)

Further, the communities are family: all are brothers and sisters, and all are participants. Although they are all equals, not everyone participates in the same way. Each serves according to his or her best abilities. Paul called these abilities charisms, or gifts of the Spirit, and they include a wide variety of functions. Coordinators, often women, look out for the well-being of the community and preside over worship services. Other people care for the sick, or counsel the troubled, or teach the young and the old how to read and write.[21]

> **(4) Leonardo Boff, Church: Charism and Power, 1986**
> *The Church is not only the institution with its sacred scriptures, hierarchy, sacramental structures, canon law, liturgical norms, orthodoxy, and moral imperatives. ... The Church is also an event. It emerges, is born, and is continually reshaped .... This is what happens in the base ecclesial communities.*[20]

Signs of the Kingdom of God

Basic Ecclesial Communities are signs of the kingdom of God, and instruments of liberation. They are not sectarian, but are open to secular society. They are rooted in the message of the gospel, and reflect on the human problems of injustice and oppression from this perspective. They recognize all forms of violence as sin.

These communities practice a new way of being the church, and this determines their response to the problems of secular society. All members seek to share responsibility for their common life. They encourage and promote secular efforts to seek the common good, but do not claim these as their own.

Members of Basic Ecclesial Communities have sometimes been repressed and persecuted. Some have become witnesses and martyrs for their cause. But repression has not diminished the strength of the communities. As in the early church, suffering for conscience sake has served to consolidate these communities, and increase their courage. This has provided an opportunity for serious reflection on the meaning of innocent and vicarious suffering freely assumed on behalf of others, including the oppressor. (5)

> **(5) Leonardo Boff, Church: Charism and Power, 1986**
> *It is possible to accept the cross and death as an expression of love and communion with those who cause these injustices.*[22]

Popular Expressions of Faith

Basic Ecclesial Communities are, in the final analysis, made up of people who are experiencing and celebrating their own liberation. For this reason, the salvation of Jesus Christ occupies the center of each community's life. Overflowing joy is often one of their most visible characteristics, and is not diminished by the gravity of their struggles.

Popular expressions of faith, often frowned on by official Catholicism and orthodox Protestantism, abound in the communities. These are authentic expressions of faith made by people who value the symbolic logic of the spirit more than the rational logic of reason. Their faith is symbolized in processions, festivals, and veneration of the saints and martyrs. These celebrations have forced the church to reinterpret traditional pastoral practices, and to integrate popular expressions of spirituality into its forms of worship.

> *(6) Leonardo Boff, Church: Charism and Power, 1986*
> *A people that knows how to celebrate is a people with hope. They are no longer a wholly oppressed people but a people who march toward their liberation.*[23]

In Basic Ecclesial Communities, faith and life are seen to be one and the same. Members do not merely celebrate the sacraments, but the sacramental dimensions of all life. The lines between the sacred and the profane are muted, allowing worship to take on greater significance in the community. Their worship is marked by liturgical creativity. Long prayers relate the problems being faced by members, and celebrate victories and milestones. In their worship, they create new rituals, dramatize scripture, organize liturgical celebrations, and turn common meals into love feasts. (6)

Conclusion

Basic Ecclesial Communities have become concerned about reactionary tendencies in the church. At the Fourth General Conference of the Latin American Episcopate, held in Santa Domingo, in 1992, some members of the established church expressed their desire to place basic communities under firmer control. In his inaugural speech at the Conference, the Pope stated that Basic Ecclesial Communities should be "presided over by a priest ... in close union with their pastors and full harmony with the church's magisterium."[24] Basic Ecclesial Communities worry that their vital role among the common people will be severely restricted if the communities are controlled by church hierarchy.

For a number of years, Rome has put pressure on those Catholic theologians who encourage and defend the Basic Ecclesial Communities. Leonardo Boff, for example, chose to withdraw from the Franciscan Order in 1992, so that he could continue to teach and write without facing official censorship.[25] The future of Basic Ecclesial Communities is uncertain, but also filled with hope. These communities are at once humanly precarious and authentic signs of God's kingdom in our presence.

Notes

[1] Second General Conference of Latin American Bishops, *The Church in the Present-Day Transformation of Latin America in the Light of the Council, II Conclusions* (Washington, D.C: Division for Latin America - USCC, 1973), 201-202.

[2] John Eagleson and Philip Sharper, eds., *Puebla and Beyond: Documentation and Commentary* (Maryknoll, NY: Orbis Books, 1979), 211.

[3] Eagleson and Sharper, 212-213.

[4] José Maríns, "Basic Ecclesial Communities in Latin America," *International Review of Mission*, 68.271 (1979): 235.

[5] Leonardo Boff, *Ecclesiogenesis: The Base Communities Reinvent the Church* (Maryknoll, NY: Orbis Books, 1986), 3.

[6] José Maríns, "Basic Ecclesial Communities in Latin America," *International Review of Mission*, 68.271 (1979): 237.

[7] Maríns, 237-238.

[8] Maríns, 238.

[9] Maríns, 238-239.

[10] Maríns, 239. "Our present parishes are or should be composed of various local or basic communities, because of their extension, density of population and percentage of baptized who by rights belong to them. It will therefore be of great importance to undertake parochial renewal, by creating or promoting these basic communities. They should be developed in the parishes as far as possible ... The plan also proposes as a first goal of action 'to get the parishes to create and build up basic communities, ensuring their coordination. To create in the basic communities liturgical assemblies with the active participation of all their members, according to their function, especially in the celebration of the Eucharist and of the other sacraments.'"

[11] Maríns, 240.

[12] Leonardo Boff, *Church: Charism and Power* (New York: Crossroad, 1986), 126. In 1984, Leonardo Boff wrote about "a growing network of base ecclesial communities (especially in Latin America and Brazil in particular, where there are over 70,000 such communities), reaching countless Christians who live out their faith in these communities."

[13] José Maríns, "Basic Ecclesial Communities in Latin America," *International Review of Mission*, 68.271 (1979): 240.

[14] Maríns, 235-236.

[15] Maríns, 242.

[16] During the mid-eighties, disciplinary action was initiated by the Congregation on Faith and Doctrine against Leonardo and Clodovis Boff. This may have been an indirect Catholic response to their activity on behalf of Basic Ecclesial Communities.

[17] Leonardo Boff, *Church: Charism and Power* (New York: Crossroad, 1986), 125-130.

[18] Boff, *Church: Charism and Power*, 126.

[19] Boff, *Church: Charism and Power*, 127.

[20] Boff, *Church: Charism and Power*, 127-128.

[21] Boff, *Church: Charism and Power*, 128. "There are those who know how to visit and comfort the sick; they are given the task of gathering information and visitation. Others are educated and some teach about human rights and labor laws, some prepare the children for the sacraments, and still others deal with family problems and the like. All of these functions are respected and encouraged, and coordinated in order that everything tend toward service of the whole community. The Church, then, more than an organization, becomes a living organism that is recreated, nourished, and renewed from the base."

[22] Leonardo Boff, *Teologia desde el Lugar del Pobre* (Santander: Sal Terrae, 1986), 130-131. My translation. "It is possible to accept the cross and death as an expression of love and communion with those who cause these injustices. This ability to react in a reconciling way toward those who break relationships is not a refined form of escapism or the transfiguration of vengeance. ... This response is born out of a deep conviction and an absolute confidence in the power of love and forgiveness to restore harmony in a creation fractured by broken relationships. Meaning for all of life, including that of those who are filled with hatred and make crosses for others, is found in love. This uniquely loving response carries a reconciling power and is a powerful reminder that there is no sin in all of human history that cannot be fully healed. By forgiving and taking upon ourselves–by free decision and not as some kind of inner satisfaction (therefore opposing all sadism and masochism)–the cross and the death laid upon us, we redirect history toward its ultimate reconciliation which includes even enemies."

[23] Leonardo Boff, *Church: Charism and Power* (New York: Crossroad, 1986), 130.

[24] Marie Dennis, "Worldly Power and the Power of God: The Church of the Poor Meets the Church of Rome at the Latin American Bishop's Gathering," *Sojourners* (January, 1993): 31. The Pope's warning is reminiscent of the vision stated at the Council of Trent in 1546: "Let no one ... dare to interpret the Holy Scripture ... contrary to the sense in which the Holy Mother Church has understood and understands it." (Enrique Denzinger, *El Magisterio de la Iglesia* (Barcelona: Editorial Herder, 1955), 224. My translation.)

[25] The Spanish theologian, José María Castillo, has also experienced the inconveniences of ecclesiastical censorship. Castillo is the author of *Teologia para Comunidades* (Madrid: Ediciones Paulinas, 1990).

Epilogue

Lead on, O cloud of Presence, the exodus has come.
In wilderness and desert our tribe shall make its home.
Our slavery left behind us, new hopes within us grow.
We seek the land of promise where milk and honey flow.

Lead on, O fiery Pillar, we follow yet with fears,
but we shall come rejoicing though joy be born of tears.
We are not lost, though wand'ring, for by your light we come,
and we are still God's people. The journey is our home.

Lead on, O God of freedom, and guide us on our way,
and help us trust the promise through struggle and delay.
We pray our sons and daughters may journey to that land
where justice dwells with mercy, and love is law's demand.
(Ruth Duck, "Lead On, Oh Cloud of Presence," 1974)[1]

The Story of the Christian People

Radical faith has a long and uneven history in Western Christianity. The story of radical faith can be traced all the way back to the prophetic and priestly reform movements in ancient Israel, recorded in the Old Testament. However, its essential roots are found in the New Testament, in the community gathered around Jesus of Nazareth. Over the course of time, the remnants of this community became an established institution, irrevocably altering the dynamics of its original faith and life. The story of radical faith is therefore largely recorded as an alternative history of the Christian people, separate from the history of the established church.

The story of the Christian people told here is incomplete. Many other groups and movements share in this alternative history. However, it is my hope that the stories related here will give us a better sense of the characteristics common to radical faith, helping us to recognize its manifestations in our own time, and inspiring us to greater loyalty to Jesus Christ and his cause in our world.

Spiritual Authority

Members of radical faith movements frequently direct their lives according to the authority of scripture. They often attempt to translate scripture into living experience. Historically, this has contrasted with the established church's dependence on right doctrine, as defined in ecumenical councils, and on the church's institutional tradition, embodied in its clerical leadership and ecclesiastical polity.

Clearly, there exist notably different understandings of what constitutes a history of the Christian church. The history of established Christianity is traditionally told through church doctrines and institutions, with a focus on the influence of clerical leaders. Considerable attention is also given to the ongoing development of doctrine and tradition.

Radical movements tend to focus on the salvation story as it is told in the Old and New Testaments. The biblical history is central to the history told by radical movements because that story underpins their own life and mission. Radical movements generally bear a closer resemblance to the Messianic restoration movements of biblical history than do their established church counterparts.

Restored Community

A profound sense of peoplehood is embedded in the consciousness of radical movements. Salvation is seen as restoring communion, both with God and among humans. Across the broad range of radical movements represented here, we find, in one form or another, this sense of restored community. Following in the tradition of the New Testament church, those who "were not a people" become a people of God, through salvation. (1)

As God's people, members of radical movements often believe themselves to be the first-fruit of restored creation. Their role is as the vanguard of a new era, a people through whom the true meaning of salvation history again flows.

> *(1) But you are God's own people ... that you may proclaim the mighty acts of him who called you out of darkness into his marvelous light. Once you were not a people, but now you are God's people; once you had not received mercy, but now you have received mercy. (1 Pet. 2:9-10)*

Reflecting the story told in the New Testament, radical movements generally appeal to the poor and the marginalized, women, outsiders, the ceremonially unclean, outcasts and sinners. These are the people without access to the power, money, or prestige which is often at the service of established Christendom. They are the people who quite literally depend on God's providence and protection for their salvation. Among movements of radical faith, the doctrine of "salvation by grace" takes on a deeper significance.

A Community of the Spirit

All radical movements acknowledge the Spirit of the living Christ in their midst. This characteristic may be observed particularly in movements like the second-century Montanists, the twelfth-century Waldensians, the sixteenth-century Anabaptists, the seventeenth-century Quakers, and the Pentecostals of the twentieth century.

This frees the movements from the established church's apparent monopoly over the means to grace, both sacramental and clerical. The voice of the Spirit is accessible to all, not merely to an ecclesiastical elite. Within radical movements, common lay persons can become active protagonists in the life and mission of the church. For example, in all of the movements mentioned previously, women were full-fledged participants in the worship and mission of the church, despite prevailing social and ecclesiastical conventions dictating the contrary.

Many radical movements recognize the place of prophetic witness and apostolic evangelization in carrying out God's mission in the world. The monopoly of established Catholicism forbade the Waldensians to preach without authorization, and established Protestantism did the same to the Anabaptists and Quakers. But in the Spirit of the living Christ, all Christians are candidates for charismatic ministry.

Communities of Compassion

Radical movements show compassion to the outcasts of a Christendom which often seems callous to human suffering. The Montanist and Donatist movements responded compassionately to rural populations suffering the devastating effects of official policy. The early Franciscans and the Waldensians restored dignity to society's outcasts. Oppressed peasant populations found hope among the Czech Brethren and the Anabaptists. Christendom's unevangelized found new life among the Lollards in medieval England, and more recently among the Basic Ecclesial Communities of Latin America.

The established church traditionally offers only condescending charity to the poor and the outcast. Radical movements give these same people an opportunity to participate in a living church. Within radical movements, the poor are subjects of their own liberation. Movements like the Waldensians and Franciscans became agents for the re-evangelization of Christendom. These movements showed that hope for the oppressors' salvation lay in their openness to respond to the cries of the oppressed.

A Church of the People

Many radical movements protest the institutional monopoly over the means to grace. They seek to restore the church to the common people, believing that to be a church is to be a church of the poor.

Diverse movements, from the "Little Brothers" of the twelfth century to the early Irish Brethren of the nineteenth century, brought the reality of a shared Christian life to the sacrament of Christ's body. The Little Brothers experienced "the table of the Lord" when the people of Assisi shared their bread with them. The Irish Brethren believed that the essence of being a church could be found in the reality of breaking bread together.

In North Africa, the Donatists spoke for many when they asked what the emperor, as imperial ruler, had to do with the church. Radical movements are often been places in which the principle of a priesthood of all believers can be most fully realized.

Radical Ecumenicity

Although members of radical movements are often repressed minorities, their social vision is not sectarian. These movements' universality is expressed through an "apostolic succession" of faith and life, in contrast to official Roman Catholicism which claims to have a continuous line of bishops traceable to the apostles of the New Testament.

Early Anabaptists based their mission on Psalm 24:1, which states that "The earth is the Lord's and all that is in it, the world and all who live in it." This passage reflected the Anabaptists' universal vision of their role in God's purposes. Many radical movements see themselves as harbingers of an age to come, not as minority remnants of faithfulness. Seventeenth-century Quaker missionaries responded to "that of God in every one," speaking to that which was universal, not exclusive.

Radical movements give new meaning to the New Testament terms "sojourner" and "pilgrim." Many members of radical movements believe they have true citizenship in a kingdom which transcends the traditional boundaries of race, ethnicity, politics, culture, nationhood, and patriotism. In the eighteenth century, John Wesley saw the whole world as his parish. John Kline, the Church of the Brethren peacemaker during the American Civil War, was moved by a love for the human family which far surpassed any patriotic loyalties.

A Church of Mission

When the Christian church became an established institution much of its fundamental missionary identity was lost. Catholicism only partially recovered the original vision of mission by establishing missionary orders within the church, limited to clergy. Radical movements, looking to early Christianity for guidance, see themselves as communities of mission, in which every member is called to witness. (2)

(2) The Spirit of the Lord is upon me, because he has anointed me to bring good news to the poor. He has sent me to proclaim release to the captives and recovery of sight to the blind, to let the oppressed go free, to proclaim the year of the Lord's favor. (Luke 4:18-19)

Many radical movements seek to restore the early church's identity as a community of contrast. In order to remain faithful to this original vision of mission, radical movements resist conforming to prevailing social values. A modern example of this can be seen in the Basic Ecclesial Communities of Latin America, which have been recognized as being primary structures of evangelization.

Jesus' communitarian vision of mission as "a city set on a hill" has inspired radical movements throughout the centuries. (Matt. 5:14). These movements do not generally seek social survival, but rather faithfulness in mission. Therefore, their strategies of mission tend to be more holistic than have those of the established church.

A Transforming Community

Often persecuted as dissidents, many radical movements find the suffering witness of martyrdom to be a strategic alternative to the official exercise of coercive power. Like many other radicals who suffered official repression, the Anabaptists of sixteenth-century Europe believed that the gospel should not be protected by the sword. According to this vision, the church needs neither coercive power nor secular force to carry out its mission. Authentic Christian transformation is found in servanthood and vicarious suffering, epitomized in the cross, not in the sword.

The inner strength of these movements is made manifest in concrete social transformation. (3) Examples of this can be seen in each movement discussed here, in their concern for social justice and human well-being. All of these movements put their beliefs into practice, seeking spiritual resources for authentic transformation, and proving their social relevance despite their lack of political and economic clout.

> *(3) Here is my servant whom I uphold, ... I have put my spirit upon him; he will bring forth justice to the nations. ... [H]e will faithfully bring forth justice. He will not grow faint or be crushed until he has established justice in the earth. (Isa. 42:1, 3-4)*

Simply by daring to be radically non-conformist, many of these movements are agents of social transformation. In the fifteenth century, Peter Chelčický and the Czech Brethren based their protest of the prevailing social class system on the gospel. The Quakers protested social conventions of the period by using familiar pronouns to address all as equals, by wearing undyed homespun clothing to protest the slave labor on which the textile industry was based, and by basing retail prices on the costs of production. These protests made real contributions to social transformation.

A Paradigm of the Future

We sometimes imagine that movements of radical renewal are exclusively oriented by, and tied to, their roots in the past. However, these roots are the source of radical movements' essentially eschatological perspective.

The radical movements represented here all include Spirit-inspired visionaries, in the best sense of the term. The movements' steadfast perseverance in the face of persecution is often based on an eschatological vision of the future. Some movements see their intense suffering as the birth pains that will bring forth a new order.

Images of the new humanity and the new creation play a fundamental role in these movements' sense of identity and missionary purpose. These New Testament metaphors must have stirred their leaders' imaginations. For them, Christ's salvation offers dimensions of reconciliation and restoration which prevailing views in Christendom fail to appreciate fully. Francis of Assisi's extraordinary sensitivity to God's presence in all of the created order offers an example of this.

Conclusion

This is the story of a people inspired by the same biblical images which fed the identity of the early church. Humanly precarious images of pilgrimage have offered them great comfort. Their sense of restored communion has been nurtured by scriptural images of peoplehood. The living presence of the Spirit of Christ has offered the Christian people a source of constant renewal, and images of God's new order emerging have challenged them. Images of transformation have been continual sources of encouragement to this people in their ongoing witness under the sign of the cross.

Notes

[1] Ruth Duck, 1974. Used by permission in *Hymnal: A Worship Book* (Scottdale, PA: Mennonite Publishing House, 1992), 419.

About Pandora Press

Pandora Press is a small, independently owned press dedicated to making available modestly priced books that deal with Anabaptist, Mennonite, and Believers Church topics, both historical and theological. We welcome comments from our readers.

Visit our full-service online Bookstore:
www.pandorapress.com

Esther and Malcolm Wenger, poetry by Ann Wenger, *Healing the Wounds* (Kitchener: Pandora Press, 2001; co-published with Herald Press).
   Softcover, 210 pp. ISBN 1-894710-09-6.
   Prices not yet available.
[Experiences of Mennonite missionaries with the Cheyenne people]

Pedro A. Sandín-Fremaint, *Cuentos y Encuentros: Hacia una Educación Transformadora* (Kitchener: Pandora Press, 2001).
   Softcover 163 pp ISBN 1-894710-08-8.
   $12.00 US/ $16.00 Canadian. Postage $5.00 US/$7.00 Canadian.
[Spanish. Stories and discussion questions for Christian education]

A. James Reimer, *Mennonites and Classical Theology: Dogmatic Foundations for Christian Ethics* (Kitchener: Pandora Press, 2001; co-published with Herald Press)
   Softcover, 650pp. ISBN 0-9685543-7-7
   $52.00 U.S./$65.00 Canadian. Postage: $5.00 U.S./$7.00 Can.
[A theological interpretation of Mennonite experience in 20th C.]

Walter Klaassen, *Anabaptism: Neither Catholic nor Protestant*, 3rd ed (Kitchener: Pandora Press, 2001; co-pub. Herald Press)
   Softcover, 122pp. ISBN 1-894710-01-0
   $12.00 U.S./$15.00 Can. Postage: $3.00 U.S./$4.00 Can.
[A classic interpretation and study guide, now available again]

Dale Schrag & James Juhnke, eds., *Anabaptist Visions for the new Millennium: A search for identity* (Kitchener: Pandora Press, 2001; co-published with Herald Press)

    Softcover, 242 pp. ISBN 1-894710-00-2

    $18.00 U.S./$24.00 Canadian. Postage $4.00 U.S./$5.00 Can.

[Twenty-eight essays presented at Bethel College, June, 2000]

Harry Loewen, ed., *Road to Freedom: Mennonites Escape the Land of Suffering* (Kitchener: Pandora Press, 2000; co-published with Herald Press)

    Hardcover, large format, 302pp. ISBN 0-9685543-5-0

    $35.00 U.S./$39.50 Canadian. Postage: $7.00 U.S./$8.00 Can.

[Life experiences documented with personal stories and photos]

Alan Kreider and Stuart Murray, eds., *Coming Home: Stories of Anabaptists in Britain and Ireland* (Kitchener: Pandora Press, 2000; co-published with Herald Press)

    Softcover, 220pp. ISBN 0-9685543-6-9

    $22.00 U.S./$25.00 Canadian. Postage: $4.00 U.S./$5.00 Can.

[Anabaptist encounters in the U.K.; personal stories/articles]

Edna Schroeder Thiessen and Angela Showalter, *A Life Displaced: A Mennonite Woman's Flight from War-Torn Poland* (Kitchener: Pandora Press, 2000; co-published with Herald Press)

    Softcover, xii, 218pp. ISBN 0-9685543-2-6

    $20.00 U.S./$24.00 Canadian. Postage: $4.00 U.S./$5.00 Can.

[A true story: moving, richly-detailed, told with candor and courage]

Stuart Murray, *Biblical Interpretation in the Anabaptist Tradition* (Kitchener: Pandora Press, 2000; co-published with Herald Press)

    Softcover, 310pp. ISBN 0-9685543-3-4

    $28.00 U.S./$32.00 Canadian. Postage: $4.00 U.S./$5.00 Can.

[How Anabaptists read the Bible; considerations for today's church]

Apocalypticism and Millennialism, ed. by Loren L. Johns (Kitchener: Pandora Press, 2000; co-published with Herald Press)

    Softcover, 419pp; Scripture and name indeces

    ISBN 0-9683462-9-4

    $37.50 U.S./$44.00 Canadian. Postage: $5.00 U.S./$6.00 Can.

[A clear, careful, and balanced collection: pastoral and scholarly]

Later Writings by Pilgram Marpeck and his Circle. Volume 1: The Exposé, A Dialogue and Marpeck's Response to Caspar Schwenckfeld
Translated by Walter Klaassen, Werner Packull, and John Rempel
(Kitchener: Pandora Press, 1999; co-published with Herald Press)
　　Softcover, 157pp.　ISBN 0-9683462-6-X
　　$20.00 U.S./$23.00 Canadian. Postage: $4.00 U.S./$5.00 Can.
[Previously untranslated writings by Marpeck and his Circle]

John Driver, *Radical Faith. An Alternative History of the Christian Church*, edited by Carrie Snyder.
(Kitchener: Pandora Press, 1999; co-published with Herald Press)
　　Softcover, 334pp. ISBN 0-9683462-8-6
　　$32.00 U.S./$35.00 Canadian. Postage: $5.00 U.S./$6.00 Can.
[A history of the church as it is seldom told – from the margins]

C. Arnold Snyder, *From Anabaptist Seed. The Historical Core of Anabaptist-Related Identity*
(Kitchener: Pandora Press, 1999; co-published with Herald Press)
　　Softcover, 53pp.; discussion questions.　ISBN 0-9685543-0-X
　　$5.00 U.S./$6.25 Canadian. Postage: $2.00 U.S./$2.50 Can.
[Ideal for group study, commissioned by Mennonite World Conf.]
　　Also available in Spanish translation: *De Semilla Anabautista*,
　　from Pandora Press only.

John D. Thiesen, *Mennonite and Nazi? Attitudes Among Mennonite Colonists in Latin America, 1933-1945.*
(Kitchener: Pandora Press, 1999; co-published with Herald Press)
　　Softcover, 330pp., 2 maps, 24 b/w illustrations, bibliography,
index. ISBN 0-9683462-5-1
　　$25.00 U.S./$28.00 Canadian. Postage: $4.00 U.S./$5.00 Can.
[Careful and objective study of an explosive topic]

Lifting the Veil, a translation of *Aus meinem Leben: Erinnerungen von J.H. Janzen.* Ed. by Leonard Friesen; trans. by Walter Klaassen
(Kitchener: Pandora Press, 1998; co-pub. with Herald Press).
　　Softcover, 128pp.; 4pp. of illustrations.　ISBN 0-9683462-1-9
　　$12.50 U.S./$14.00 Canadian. Postage: $4.00 U.S. and Can.
[Memoir, confession, critical observation of Mennonite life in Russia]

Leonard Gross, *The Golden Years of the Hutterites*, rev. ed.
(Kitchener: Pandora Press, 1998; co-pub. with Herald Press).
  Softcover, 280pp., index. ISBN 0-9683462-3-5
  $22.00 U.S./$25.00 Canadian. Postage: $4.00 U.S./$5.00 Can.
[Classic study of early Hutterite movement, now available again]

The Believers Church: A Voluntary Church, ed. by William H. Brackney
(Kitchener: Pandora Press, 1998; co-published with Herald Press).
  Softcover, viii, 237pp., index. ISBN 0-9683462-0-0
  $25.00 U.S./$27.50 Canadian. Postage: $4.00 U.S./$5.00 Can.
[Papers from the 12th Believers Church Conference, Hamilton, ON]

An Annotated Hutterite Bibliography, compiled by Maria H.
Krisztinkovich, ed. by Peter C. Erb (Kitchener, Ont.: Pandora Press, 1998).
  (Ca. 2,700 entries) 312pp., cerlox bound, electronic, or both.
  ISBN (paper) 0-9698762-8-9/(disk) 0-9698762-9-7
  $15.00 each, U.S. and Canadian. Postage: $6.00 U.S. and Can.
[The most extensive bibliography on Hutterite literature available]

Jacobus ten Doornkaat Koolman, *Dirk Philips. Friend and Colleague of
Menno Simons*, trans. W. E. Keeney, ed. C. A. Snyder
(Kitchener: Pandora Press, 1998; co-pub. with Herald Press).
  Softcover, xviii, 236pp., index. ISBN: 0-9698762-3-8
  $23.50 U.S./$28.50 Canadian. Postage: $4.00 U.S./$5.00 Can.
[The definitive biography of Dirk Philips, now available in English]

Sarah Dyck, ed./tr., *The Silence Echoes: Memoirs of Trauma & Tears*
(Kitchener: Pandora Press, 1997; co-published with Herald Press).
  Softcover, xii, 236pp., 2 maps. ISBN: 0-9698762-7-0
  $17.50 U.S./$19.50 Canadian. Postage: $4.00 U.S./$5.00 Can.
[First person accounts of life in the Soviet Union, trans. from German]

Wes Harrison, *Andreas Ehrenpreis and Hutterite Faith and Practice*
(Kitchener: Pandora Press, 1997; co-published with Herald Press).
  Softcover, xxiv, 274pp., 2 maps, index. ISBN 0-9698762-6-2
  $26.50 U.S./$32.00 Canadian. Postage: $4.00 U.S./$5.00 Can.
[First biography of this important seventeenth century Hutterite leader]

C. Arnold Snyder, *Anabaptist History and Theology: Revised Student Edition* (Kitchener: Pandora Press, 1997; co-pub. Herald Press).

Softcover, xiv, 466pp., 7 maps, 28 illustrations, index, bibliography. ISBN 0-9698762-5-4

$35.00 U.S./$38.00 Canadian. Postage: $5.00 U.S./$6.00 Can.

[Abridged, rewritten edition for undergraduates and the non-specialist]

Nancey Murphy, *Reconciling Theology and Science: A Radical Reformation Perspective* (Kitchener, Ont.: Pandora Press, 1997; co-pub. Herald Press).

Softcover, x, 103pp., index. ISBN 0-9698762-4-6

$14.50 U.S./$17.50 Canadian. Postage: $3.50 U.S./$4.00 Can.

[Exploration of the supposed conflict between Christianity and Science]

C. Arnold Snyder and Linda A. Huebert Hecht, eds, *Profiles of Anabaptist Women: Sixteenth Century Reforming Pioneers* (Waterloo, Ont.: Wilfrid Laurier University Press, 1996).

Softcover, xxii, 442pp. ISBN: 0-88920-277-X

$28.95 U.S. or Canadian. Postage: $5.00 U.S./$6.00 Can.

[Biographical sketches of more than 50 Anabaptist women; a first]

The Limits of Perfection: A Conversation with J. Lawrence Burkholder 2nd ed., with a new epilogue by J. Lawrence Burkholder, Rodney Sawatsky and Scott Holland, eds.
(Kitchener: Pandora Press, 1996).

Softcover, x, 154pp. ISBN 0-9698762-2-X

$10.00 U.S./$13.00 Canadian. Postage: $2.00 U.S./$3.00 Can.

[J.L. Burkholder on his life experiences; eight Mennonites respond]

C. Arnold Snyder, *Anabaptist History and Theology: An Introduction* (Kitchener: Pandora Press, 1995).   ISBN 0-9698762-0-3

Softcover, x, 434pp., 6 maps, 29 illustrations, index, bibliography.

$35.00 U.S./$38.00 Canadian. Postage: $5.00 U.S./$6.00 Can.

[Comprehensive survey; unabridged version, fully documented]

C. Arnold Snyder, *The Life and Thought of Michael Sattler*
(Scottdale: Herald Press, 1984).

   Hardcover, viii, 260pp. ISBN 0-8361-1264-4

    $10.00 U.S./$12.00 Canadian. Postage: $4.00 U.S./$5.00 Can.

[First full-length biography of this Anabaptist leader and martyr]

Pandora Press
33 Kent Avenue
Kitchener, Ontario
Canada N2G 3R2
Tel./Fax: (519) 578-2381
E-mail:
info@pandorapress.com
Web site:
www.pandorapress.com

Herald Press
616 Walnut Avenue
Scottdale, PA
U.S.A. 15683
Orders: (800) 245-7894
E-mail:
hp@mph.org
Web site:
www.mph.org